Relation*shift*®

The
Right Words
for What
You Really
Want to Say

KRISTINE GRANT
Marriage & Family Therapist | Relationship Expert

Published by

Hasmark Publishing

www.hasmarkpublishing.com

Copyright © 2018 Kristine Rose Grant

First Edition

Permission should be addressed in writing to Kristine Grant at kristine@kristinegrant.com

Editor: Thornton Sully

Cover & Book Design: Anne Karklins

Photographer: Yelena Yahontova

ISBN 13: 978-1-989161-21-0

ISBN 10: 1989161219

Dedication

"When I want to hug you
I can hug you
And when I want to kiss you
I can
And when I kiss you
I can taste the breath of you
Like the wind in a kindly dream"

This book is dedicated
to my precious daughter, Alana Joy,
who at the age of five
whispered those very words into my ear.

Acknowledgments

I wish to thank all of those who entrusted me over the years to author these *Inspired Heart Letters*. Their willingness alone to be more open, to take emotional risks, and to love even more, is an amazing testimonial in and of itself. By sharing many of the stories behind the letters, their personal journeys have allowed this book to occur.

I wish to acknowledge Thornton Sully, a wonderfully insightful and caring editor whose prodigy for words keenly checked every nook and cranny in order to polish this book to a radiant shine.

Although I have had over twenty-two years experience serving others as a Marriage & Family Therapist, clearly, my ghostwriting letter service does not fall within the recognized scope of traditional psychotherapy. As a Certified Relationship Coach, however, I offer the *Inspired Heart Letters* method as a creative way to shift any sort of relationship dynamic toward more personal satisfaction and joy.

AUTHOR'S NOTE

While personal identities and certain details regarding the life stories revealed throughout the following pages are altered to one degree or another, the more salient messages, wrapped in universal or common human circumstances, stand on their own. The intention of this book is not biographical. Rather, it is written in a way to share the merits of letters, offer a philosophical approach to better cope and learn acceptance around relationship matters, and inspire more love to occur within our connections to others while staying in integrity. Therefore, the stories depicted throughout this book are not relevant other than to illustrate commonly shared life predicaments, mindsets, and emotional reactions while offering a way to move through the pain, learn the lesson, receive the gift, and find peace.

The letters shared throughout this book are valid. The names of all individuals mentioned in the stories surrounding the letters shared have been altered or changed in order to protect the identities and privacy of those involved. Certain changes have also been made regarding the setting and chronological events or circumstances including particular descriptions of those individuals. Any resemblance between fictional names and descriptions of real people is strictly coincidental.

Table of Contents

Introduction

Hello, Dear Reader,

Have you ever felt emotionally stuck or have struggled to find peace? If you can't seem to find the answer to resolve a particular conflict with a lover, spouse, parent or child, or if you wish to deepen or enhance your connection with another, this book can truly help. Through the right words delivered in a letter, you will experience a better sense of clarity. There is a real chance that your letter can bring about a change of heart for everyone it touches, as have the many letters I am sharing with you throughout this book.

Writing letters is a true art form that has largely disappeared. Letters are lost to easier, often cryptic, text messages or overwhelming email chats intended to expedite our "to do" lists before moving on to the next business at hand. In a world where emoticons are the fast-food substitute for genuine thought, receiving a letter composed just for you carries more meaning than ever. No matter how clever a digital greeting card may be, receiving an actual card with personalized thoughts is so much more interesting, considerate, and delightful. Receiving a heartfelt letter is priceless.

We are all Divine beings. I am blessed to be an instrument of peace, composing healing letters for others. I draw upon my years as a seasoned Marriage & Family Therapist, and Relationship Coach, braiding my professional experience and intuitions into the revelations my clients offer me about themselves and the conflicts that prompted them to seek my help.

I translate the language and the yearnings of the heart – your heart – into the written word. In this book I share intriguing stories that span a wide range of relationship matters, and I prescribe ways to prevent or deal with emotional pain. I offer an inspired way to create a new perspective or a new direction for deeper, more rewarding connections to others in your life. And here's a surprise: letters composed with the hope of changing someone else may actually succeed in changing you!

Throughout the many illustrative vignettes, philosophies, and lessons I share, you may recognize yourself or someone you know who has dealt with similar feelings or life circumstances. Letters I have composed on behalf of others featured here continue to bear fruit.

This form of helpful ghostwriting or creating *Inspired Heart Letters* is largely a non-traditional methodology. I wrote this book as a coaching tool to empower you with a greater appreciation for your own ability to write amazing letters by citing letters, I myself have authored, that have changed lives. What's more, I am guided to show you how to easily write your own heartfelt letters!

Ready to begin? Thanks so much for joining me!

With love,

Kristine

Chapter 1

HOW THE *INSPIRED HEART® LETTERS* EVOLVED

It is the tragic tale of a humble man.

Well over one hundred years ago Edmond Rostand wrote the famous play *Cyrano de Bergerac.* Cyrano had a burning desire to win the heart of the lovely Roxanne. However, Cyrano was intimidated by his own sense of inadequacy. Rather than reveal his desire openly, Cyrano assists Christian, her more handsome suitor, in capturing Roxanne's affections by writing exquisitely romantic, seductive letters for Christian to woo her with. They are the very words, the heartfelt letters alone that caused Roxanne to fall in love.

I have helped families, couples, and individuals to be more open, honest, and to face underlying truths in order to move forward with much more strength or resiliency. Over fifteen years ago, I began helping clients in a unique way, by actually writing letters to their significant others for them, when they felt too self-conscious or bewildered to do it themselves. As I began to compile results, this approach became validated, as I could see my clients gain more successful connections with others.

Similar to Cyrano de Bergerac, while I am easily and compassionately able to construct effective letters that enhance romance, romantic or love relationships are just one of the many realms for which I write. Letters can be written for any relationship situation. In my experience, many of these thoughtfully crafted *Inspired Heart Letters* are perfect for any relationship matter where there is a need to share and accept the truth, gain respect, mark a boundary, forgive and release a painful memory, or propose a solution.

My daughter is now a young adult. She still knows how to charm me by creating whimsical cards and writing her own heartfelt sentiments. Just like me, most parents have kept every card or letter their children have ever written. Teachers line their classrooms or offices with cards, and cherish every letter received from their students and their parents. Letters of appreciation from co-workers, clients, or bosses are never tossed out. Likewise, when we receive a letter from anyone we hold dear, we feel appreciated. Loving, romantic, thoughtful cards commemorate birthdays, special events, Valentine's Day, and other significant holidays. We feel honored by receiving special cards and their messages. Even "just thinking of you" cards are treasured as symbols of love or endearment.

Words are like magic wands; they can destroy or build, having the power to damage or heal. For those able to stay connected in another's heart, words can transform any disparaging emotion to a more blissful outcome. Therefore, we must take responsibility for the words we express.

Nevertheless, some of us have difficulty finding the right words to powerfully convey what is in our heart and on our mind. Although we may be sharp-tongued, witty, and have an abundance of expressive language skills, that's not enough to communicate the words that will be received effectively by someone else and help the relationship.

So, what is it that often gets in the way of this kind of true communication? We do. We get in our own way despite good intentions, knowledge, insight, and excellent language skills!

It is one thing to write from an analytical perspective with well-organized, clear-cut language to determine the current issue. There may even be a viable solution addressed. However, when there is no heart-based communication, the receiver feels the void and is not emotionally moved by the letter. Conversely, if a letter is filled with emotion, often the letter lacks enough logic or does not offer a practical way to approach and move beyond the pain or sentiments to find a meaningful solution. More importantly, when one tries to write a meaningful letter in order to alleviate an emotional issue with another, all too often the elements of ego, history, and raw emotional wounds conflict with the true intention, or what should be conveyed to obtain the best outcome.

Feeling emotionally stuck, not knowing just how to soften and repair a difficult problem, can feel pretty exhausting, aggravating, or overwhelming. Let me show you a way to deepen your connections, resolve emotional or situational conflicts, and feel satisfied – even relieved – that you took the time, with thoughtful consideration, and spoke from your heart.

THE PRAYER OR AFFIRMATION – AN ENERGETIC TRANSMISSION

Throughout this book, the intuitive letters I write for others will be referred to as *Inspired Heart Letters*. I have come to realize that the words expressed in these transformative messages are indeed channeled through spirit. These letters are in accordance with the power of manifestation.

In order to create a desired outcome, or allow something even better to occur, I prescribe the following recipe: First, see the inspiration to share your thoughts and feelings as an invocation of the purest of intentions. The action that is called for is when your intention or prayer is expressed in written form, or otherwise, what is referred to as the *letter*, is actually given to an intended recipient. Then, the emotions that are inspired by the letter itself are deeply felt and guided by the law of attraction. This seems to create a stirring, a newfound clarity, and a sense of peace.

Once the letter is given, often the communicator feels a sense of relief. More than that, an energetic shift occurs, and the situation at hand becomes more aligned. Although a particular outcome may seem different than what was originally intended or hoped for, surely a difference is made, and what is in Divine order does come to pass.

The beauty of the written word, or receiving a communication by letter, is that the recipient is so much more available to absorb or hear what is being said. The power of the written word simply cannot be underestimated. What is written and then read can be mused over and reconsidered. There are no interruptions as you may experience in a conversation. There are no emotional defenses that may shroud a personal exchange. The words can be re-read for better understanding and reflection. There is an opportunity for time to pass and allow for contemplation. Most importantly, the written letter is the closest instrument for sharing a clear, precise communication.

A compelling letter serves as a self-empowerment tool allowing you to gain more successful connections with others. The expansive repertoire of *Inspired Heart Letters* includes themes such as writing to a former spouse in order to create a better co-parenting relationship and/or heal the wounds from a separation or divorce, creating a more harmonious family life for the children, to children from parents, in order to explain a family circumstance, mark a boundary, or gain more respect, and/or from those who need to forgive and release a painful memory. Some of these letters allow for a closure to take place that retains dignity and grace, creating a space for each party to more easily move forward with less emotional trauma or pain. Other letters have been written to another after years of no communication due to a disconnection or severe rift.

Some inspired messages simply call attention to an emotional issue that may be too difficult to express in conversation. Among the repertoire of enlightened messages are heartfelt poems as well as a guided outline to follow for verbal conflict resolution. In sum, these letters can address any emotional challenge or convey the underlying truth of what might lie heavy in your heart.

There is often a magical transformation that occurs when your heart's desires are truly expressed. Although I have been the instrument for writing the letter, it is actually quite more than an intuitive process, and requires that I draw from my experience and training as a family therapist to apprehend the best solutions for my clients.

I try to get to know a bit about my clients beyond just their care or concerns which they hope I can address on their behalf. Our interviews are intimate, which allows me to absorb their essence so that I convey their thoughts and feelings authentically. How many times have you spoken to a good friend and they suddenly interrupt you as you are giving them your feedback, and they exclaim, "That's exactly what I mean!" The letters seem to align or vibrate taking on the personality of the individual sending the letter and his or her particular communication style. Graciously, I am able to empathize and actually feel the pain involved in any given circumstance. After witnessing the wonderful, often profound results of this process, I am convinced these *Inspired Heart Letters* are essentially downloaded through me from the Divine in order to touch the heart of others. Often, tears have rolled down my cheeks as I am writing. I feel the sweetness, the underlying sadness, and the unending feelings of remorse, the sense of rejection, and the hope and vision for solving a situation in the best possible way.

As I mentioned, a real sense of peace and deeper understanding develops once a letter has been written. There are times when that is all that was needed to have a better sense of clarity and a shift in perspective. If just reading the letter is enough to invoke a clear understanding followed by a new realization, I advise the client to keep the letter to re-read and support their new insights. Many times this releases anguish and causes the confusion to simply vanish.

My ever growing library of these ghostwritten letters is precious and exquisite to me. They are formidable as each seems to have a life of its own. They each hold keys for healing within their matrix. For the purpose of sharing these letters, I have assigned a catchy phrase to remind me of the story behind its creation.

For example, the following *Inspired Heart Letter* is Isabella's story. It is one representation that captures the flavor of how this beautiful process works to resolve relationship issues.

Isabella's Story

"PETERED-OUT ON PETER PAN"

Isabella, a very pretty, petite, middle-aged woman of Italian descent with beautiful blue eyes, dark wavy hair, who possessed an outgoing personality and an outrageous laugh, once asked me to write a letter to Danny, her first love (whom she'd had a crush on since high school). Although Isabella had been married twice, she was now divorced and raising two sons. She always carried this fantasy, or notion, of this former high school sweetheart and what "might have been." In fact, she ran into Danny at her thirtieth high school reunion. A mutual attraction was still there and they rekindled their romance. However, there was a snag. Danny was struggling with his long-term involvement with another woman.

Danny's relationship with this other woman was apparently quite sickly. Isabella described this woman as controlling and manipulative. Even though Danny already knew it was poisonous, he could not entirely extricate himself from their sordid romance. In spite of his emotional baggage, Isabella continued to see Danny, all the while hoping he would finally end his involvement with this other woman. During this time, Isabella became increasingly confused and anxious. In essence, she thought "If only he would leave that woman once and for all, then surely Danny and I could sail off into the sunset and live happily ever after!"

When I inquired about Danny's past regarding his experience with healthy bonding and his overall relationship track record, Isabella shared that Danny had been divorced for several years. His mother, a single parent, raised him after his father abandoned them when he was a very young child. He left home when he was a teenager and had made his way through life on his own.

The following is an *Inspired Heart Letter* to Danny from Isabella. Her intention was to try to reach him through this letter in such a way that would compel him to finally free himself from his other dysfunctional relationship and choose to devote himself only to her:

DANNY BOY, THE PIPES ARE BLOWING
OR
PETERED-OUT ON PETER PAN

Inspired Heart® Letter

Dear Danny,

I honestly wanted to write to you in order that we might gain a better perspective on what is and what might be possible between us. You must admit that it was pretty awesome and certainly unexpected that we would come together again after thirty years. As we already discussed, it is interesting that our lives after high school ran such a similar course. (We each married, had two kids at the same time, divorced, and just happen to reside in the same neighborhood). What are the chances of that? It does give one pause to consider certain notions regarding parallel lives, destiny, and such. More than that, I find myself wondering about the idea that love conquers all. No matter what the future holds for us, just know I loved you then and actually still do.

So, what gets in the way of us moving forward? You have led me to understand that you are focused upon providing for your kids and dealing with financial obligations. I am also unclear with whether you continue to struggle with an attachment to your past relationship with Monica.

You probably know by now that I am pretty sensitive and compassionate, especially toward those whom I care about. Life is about taking risks. That is why I have written to you in this way. If, by chance, you are interested in getting to know me on a deeper level and have a real desire to be with me, then I need to let you know that I am sincere as well. I am real. I would like to be there for you. I am not interested in your financial picture or your past issues. I feel there is a genuine connection between us that goes beyond all the superficial stuff.

While I believe we each deserve to be happy, if I am not to be with you, I am fully prepared to walk away. At this point in my life, I am definitely not interested in just casual connections. I must be true to my heart. I am hoping you will read this letter with an open mind. From my perspective, I truly believe we can create a beautiful relationship together. I believe in you despite any personal setbacks. All things are possible. I am hoping we can deepen our connection, or at least explore the possibility of looking at new beginnings for us together. Life is too short… can we consider what may be possible and beautiful between us?

Okay, Danny, there you have it. I have opened myself to you. While I certainly don't want my heart to be trampled upon, I hope you will honestly let me know where we stand when the time is right for you. Either way, thanks for taking the time to read this.

Sincerely,

Isabella

Interestingly, after reading this "Danny Boy" *Inspired Heart Letter*, Isabella's reaction was as follows:

The minute I read the letter, I burst into tears. It became crystal clear to me how emotionally immature Danny was. I also realized just how unhealthy it was for me to stand on the sidelines, "twisting in the wind", wishing things would change. I saw the situation through new eyes. I no longer felt stuck. I was able to easily walk away.

While most of us contend with personal issues or have emotional baggage that we bring into our relationships, it is important to recognize what those obstacles are, then work toward healing past conditions and traumas that are keeping us down. I advocate that, in considering a new relationship, we acknowledge the baggage. However, it is best to seek partners who have a lighter load, or as I put it, "Only have one carry-on bag. Beyond that, any additional baggage is just too costly."

As a side note, Isabella continued to forgive herself and have compassion for why she had created a tendency toward unhealthy relationship drama. This brought awareness for what type of love connection she wanted to attract. She telephoned me recently to share that she is quite happy; she's enjoying a healthy, exclusive relationship with a terrific guy. Actually, I attended their wedding last summer.

WHAT IS TO BE GAINED?

As you are learning about the true value of the written word, you will also learn how to better communicate in letter form, or come to understand the do's and don'ts of writing a meaningful, compelling letter. More importantly, through the many vignettes discussed in the following chapters, you'll discover the common, universal themes found in relationship challenges. And, you'll begin to realize how so many people experience the same issues over and over again. Circumscribed within these difficult experiences is an emerging wisdom that holds promise for new understanding. A cleansing takes place and the psychic wound begins to heal.

While a wonderful letter may open the opportunity to heal a broken heart or a painful emotional situation, there is also an immeasurable reward that surfaces once you have achieved a true sense of closure. Misunderstandings, old resentments, or any unfinished business around your relationship matter can be cleaned up and finally put to rest when you are able to convey a noble salute to honor the experience and leave the situation behind once and for all. Otherwise, there is a chance you may find it difficult to move forward. It is not about having the last word; instead it is about finalizing and letting go or gracefully releasing any further negative connections.

So, consider the merits of letter writing as you read the following stories. These matters of the heart, I discovered, are struggles common to the human condition. Follow the simple guidance I will share with you and you will see any situation from a more powerful perspective that creates a deeper understanding. Find the way to forgive someone who has hurt you. Become more compassionate toward yourself and others. Lighten the emotional burden that accompanies a particular relationship dilemma. Yes… discover a way to heal.

HOW I WAS GUIDED TO BE A LETTER COACH

Just who is this formidable scribe? As one dedicated to helping people achieve health in their relationships, friends and even acquaintances want to pick my brain. Often, they are compelled to share with me very private information, including their relationship concerns. I enjoy my life's path steeped in helping others find solutions and gather powerful insights. It started as a young child; I was strongly empathetic, even able to physically feel the pain of others. In elementary school, I recall standing up to bullies to protect fellow schoolmates who were being victimized. Growing up, my family often described me as overly sensitive and pretty spunky. It's simply my feeling nature that continues fueling my quest to better understand just how to resolve difficult matters of the heart.

Perhaps more so than most, I experienced an array of relationship conflicts throughout my lifetime. Although I never had a tendency to hold a grudge for long, I was deeply saddened or bothered by any rift in my relationships. Yet, at times it was best to simply walk away or disengage from counter-productive or toxic connections. Some situations called for clear, unabashed communication, while other relationship issues were better resolved through a more gentle and persuasive approach. My own personal development is a direct result of mastery over relationship hurdles.

Janie's Story

"INITIATION AS A SCRIBE"

I wrote the very first *Inspired Heart Letter* after a friend and neighbor, Janie, called me complaining about a lovely man she had recently met. Jim was an attorney who was obviously quite enamored with her. He had left cards, flowers, candy, even balloons and teddy bears at her doorstep. However, Janie was not the least bit interested in dating him. She did exclaim how generous, kind, and interesting a person Jim was. Moreover, she did not want to hurt his feelings and would enjoy having him become a platonic friend. Actually, she was struggling with a personal legal matter and hoped he could help her by providing free legal advice. First, I suggested she have a clear-cut conversation with him, since it was certainly detrimental to keep stringing him along under false pretenses. Surely, we must treat others as we want to be treated.

Leading anyone down a primrose path most likely leads to more drama and emotional dissatisfaction for all concerned. Janie listened to my advice, yet felt somewhat embarrassed and emotionally weak. She could not bring herself to discuss her true desires in a direct conversation. I suggested she simply send him an email, although that may seem cold, or better yet, write a short letter and mail it.

Janie attempted to write a letter to her suitor, Jim. When I read the letter; her words came across as whiny, pathetic, and groveling. I told Janie that her letter would probably be received with offense rather than as an opening for companionship, gratitude, and honor that showed her appreciation, or how she valued Jim as a person worthy of friendship. Janie was impressed with my response and lamented that she simply did not have the talent or wherewithal to compose such a dynamic letter. At that point, I agreed to ghostwrite her letter, and if she approved, she could sign the letter and send it off to Jim. Janie was thrilled at this prospect.

In creating this letter, I easily grasped the issues at hand, and empathized with the situation by considering Janie's motives and higher intention. I was able intuitively, and with practicality, to predict Jim's feeling response to this letter written on Janie's behalf. The results of the letter seemed to satisfy Janie's situation.

Although this letter was written many years ago, to this day, Jim and Janie enjoy a light-hearted friendship. Shortly after receiving the letter, Jim provided Janie with more than simple legal advice. He wrote the necessary legal letter and provided paperwork that resolved her legal predicament.

Janie, always the socialite, began speaking about her letter's spectacular results with her many friends. Not only did Janie ask me to write more letters on her behalf, but also her friends began calling for letters and advice. I cannot begin to say how much satisfaction I have derived from this intuitive letter-writing service. Many of these success stories that I am so excited to share with you will be revealed throughout this book. Each letter is a jewel, a magical way of connecting to the actual heart of the matter. They seemed to energetically send out a positive signal that proved over and over to transform the stress surrounding a relationship matter into wonderful, healing results!

Often, it's difficult to communicate what we need; yet doing so is necessary for our integrity, or at least, to release pent-up emotions. Sometimes deal breakers occur, and we need to prepare for that possibility. In that event, we must take stock of what is healthy and decide if a situation is sustainable under current conditions. The consequences of committing to decisive steps may be heartbreaking, but the choices made must be viewed as yielding to the ultimate best result in the long run. Ryan and Marsha's story illustrates some of these principles.

Ryan's Story

"FIFTY SHADES OF GREEN"

One of the most frustrating and disturbing issues that can occur within a loving, romantic relationship is when one partner suddenly turns into someone else. Imagine if the person you thought you knew unexpectedly morphed into another person with a less attractive personality.

Ryan thought he had found true love with his girlfriend Marsha. After six months of courting her, Ryan proposed, and the couple made plans to wed the following year. Ryan was a proud, ambitious man, who had built a thriving business as a prominent commercial real estate investor. He was a fun-loving, charismatic person who loved a variety of activities, such as traveling, golf, playing jazz tunes on his saxophone, and hanging out at the local country club with friends.

Ryan had met Marsha while playing in a mixed doubles tennis match. He was immediately quite taken with how Marsha carried herself in a social setting; she knew how to engage everyone present. And it didn't hurt, from Ryan's point of view, that Marsha had lovely legs along with a tanned and toned physique. Ryan considered Marsha to be both amazingly athletic and beautifully feminine. More than that, he was exceedingly drawn to her sweet, attentive, and cuddly nature, which he found irresistible. They seemed to make a really great combo connecting in the most natural, wonderful way.

According to Ryan, Marsha had worked on and off in retail sales. Her parents had left her a moderate trust fund several years earlier. Marsha enjoyed a more relaxed lifestyle and was not very inclined to build a career for herself. Ryan was not concerned in the least; he was well-established financially and simply looked forward to enjoying more quality time with his bride to be. Their first year together was especially fun. Ryan and Marsha sailed to romantic destinations such as Bali and Australia. They also attended many local social gatherings and hosted their own dinner parties. However, soon their relationship started to unravel.

For no apparent reason that Ryan could name, Marsha started calling or text messaging him on his cell phone more frequently, often waking him up by calling late at night, "just to make sure he was alright." Once, while they were dining at a local hangout, Marsha accused Ryan of ogling another woman. At first he thought it was funny and just shook it off. However, soon after, they attended a company Christmas party at his firm. When Marsha met his new secretary, Lauren, she acted quite rude and condescending toward her. On the way home, Marsha told Ryan to fire the secretary since she did not get a very good "vibe" from the woman. Ryan took offense to her comment, and they argued during the entire ride home.

Although they saw each other on a fairly regular basis, Ryan was often busy at night, dining with prospective clients or business investors. Unfortunately, Marsha began grilling him about these evenings. She wanted to know exactly who the clients were, where they ate dinner, why he was out so late, how many cocktails they had and so on. Ryan's secretary reported that once when she returned from lunch she found Marsha in the secretary's office, seated at her desk, checking messages on her computer. Another time, Ryan spied Marsha's car parked at the corner near his house. She quickly drove off when he opened his front door. When Ryan confronted Marsha and essentially told her to "back off," she retaliated in a fit of anger complaining that he must be cheating on her since he did not always answer her calls.

Ryan had originally considered Marsha to be a hot, sexy lover, and a delightful partner. Now he saw her as not only silly but rather annoying and even somewhat creepy. In essence, Ryan was beginning to feel trapped, finding himself on the defensive much of the time, and pretty stressed out, especially if he happened to miss one of her calls (as he did not want to experience Marsha's backlash for not picking up the phone in time).

From Ryan's perspective, Marsha's behaviors made no sense. He had spent so many years focused on building his business and fortune that he had waited to settle down. Marsha was the first woman he had really desired to make a life with. Ryan contacted me, hoping to turn their relationship around before it ended in disaster. And so... the letter *50 Shades of Green* was born. (I am not talking about an Irish golf course!)

Turning Fifty Shades of Green:
The Jealous Heart

Inspired Heart® Letter

Hi Honey,

You know me, I am not one to hold back, so I must come right out and say it… our relationship is in trouble. Truly, this breaks my heart, Marsha. I am the same guy you met over a year ago. I work hard, I play hard, and I love hard. I have had the utmost respect for our relationship.

Maybe I have not been putting as much time into "us" lately as I have some pretty important business deals on the table. But isn't part of being committed to one another, also about honoring that notion of "WE"? That includes everything, even the day-to-day responsibilities, trusting that I am doing my best for us.

Let me explain that thought a bit further. My success in business alone is not my primary focus for happiness. Oh, it contributes to a much-improved lifestyle, for sure, but it is not so satisfying, if the woman I love and plan to spend the rest of my life with does not have my back. If you believe in me, my motives, and my sincerity, you will have no cause to check on me or doubt me in any way.

You are adorable, amazingly sexy, and can be great fun to be with. However, unless you can let go of your obvious insecurities, I cannot move forward with our marriage. When I asked you to be my wife it was a huge step and a big statement, since I do not know how to live unless I live with the truth. So, truthfully, I have fallen deeply in love with you… at least the phenomenal woman I met on the tennis court. I am bewildered regarding how you've been acting lately and certainly apprehensive about where we are headed.

I thought it best to write my feelings in this letter. Hopefully, you can receive it as a wake-up call to our unstable relationship. I do like to win, but whatever is happening with us is making me feel very disappointed, let down, and as though I have been thrown a curve ball. Although, I really do think we have so much going for us, I am not feeling like I am part of a winning team. Before things get too far out of hand, I wanted to share my misgivings, more than that, my care and concern.

Marsha, hopefully you can reconcile with yourself and see how your ridiculous jealousy is pushing me away and suffocating my desire to be with you. Sadly, it is destroying our dream, or at least my dream… you know that "happily ever after" thing. Okay then, hopefully, I have made myself pretty clear. Please give this some earnest thought. I am open to listening, yet no longer willing to defend myself to you. Trust me. I am praying that somehow we do work out.

When it feels right for you, let's schedule a long walk on the beach. I am crossing my fingers that this is just a blip on the screen, something you can easily work through; and we can move forward hand in hand.

Sincerely with Love,

Ryan

Although this was a very difficult message, Ryan took responsibility for what he felt was quickly becoming a defeating situation and was out of sync with his heart. This couple did end up taking some time out, hoping they might *course-correct* and find their way back to a new, healthier beginning. The last I heard, Marsha was seeking counseling. Hopefully, she is learning to see the truth of her self-sabotaging insecure thoughts and behaviors, along with her inability to allow herself the luxury of simply trusting that life can work out and that she is worthy of true love.

Since this *Inspired Heart Letter* was written from Ryan's experience, let's consider Marsha's perspective. Perhaps she was feeling ignored or left out since Ryan's professional life had become more time consuming, especially within the first few months after their engagement. Maybe Marsha was disappointed because she continued to expect Ryan's nonstop attention after the initial courting phase. This may have triggered a sense of fear, separation anxiety, suspicion, or mistrust.

When one partner becomes too needy, the other partner often will begin to experience distress. This could be rooted in an inability to satisfy their mate's relentless drive to solve "What's wrong with this picture?" Possessive, jealous behavior is a symptom of a deeper, pervasive sense of fear and mistrust. This desperate neediness of one partner pushes the other partner away. It feels like a heavy anchor and, left unchecked, it eventually drowns out every ounce of joy.

In any case, Ryan and Marsha's relationship was beginning to fall apart. Sneaky or passive-aggressive acts such as snooping through private emails and phone messages, throwing a temper tantrum, making assumptions or accusations, or demanding anything from a partner is a quick route to the end of the road. However, by staying open while expressing how you are feeling without blame, and checking in with your significant other through inquiry instead of through paranoid accusations or beliefs is often effective for clearing the air.

Our romantic partners do not ever complete who we are. That is not their job. Yet, when we are enjoying a healthy love connection, our life is certainly, if not magically, enhanced.

A Family Matter

"HEALING LETTER STORY"

A very powerful and life altering letter-writing experience occurred many years ago, after I was contacted by Tina, a lovely, vivacious single mother. At the time, Tina was trying to help her elderly father, Henry, to finally enjoy a long-awaited sense of peace over his irrepressible resentment toward one of Tina's sisters, Karen. Without going into too much detail, let's just say Karen had financially duped their Dear Old Dad and absconded with most of his life savings, which was quite a sizable sum of money. Moreover, while their father was assigned to Karen's care, she managed to control him through terrible threats, neglect, caustic remarks and other types of manipulative subterfuge.

It was quite an ordeal for Tina to finally rescue Henry from this terrible and sad situation. Fortunately, Tina was able to relocate him out of state and closer to her home where she was able to provide a much healthier lifestyle. At any rate, her father struggled daily with the notion that Karen, one of his children, took advantage of him financially, and mistreated him. What Henry felt was even more distressing was the thought that this conniving daughter would get away with it, and there was nothing he could really do, (short of spending the few years he had left battling her in court). Nevertheless, Henry simply could not emotionally let it go.

For at least two years, nearly every day Henry worried and complained about Karen, for what she had done. Finally, after Tina spoke with her other siblings, she approached me for help. I suggested that they help their dad to write his own open, honest letter to Karen, their "mean sister." This way, he could not only air his feelings, but arrive at a better sense of closure. So, I interviewed Henry, took some notes, as well as gathered notes from Tina and her other siblings, and formulated the Dad's having the Last Word letter.

The results of this gesture were astounding. Once Henry mailed that letter, his whole demeanor seemed to instantly change. He never spoke of the disheartening situation ever again. It was as though Henry could finally move on enjoying his own sense of integrity. The letter was

Henry's gesture for telling the truth and for letting his daughter, Karen, know that she had not fooled anyone. What's more, for posterity's sake, the cruel daughter could not put a different spin on what had happened. She could not tell a different story.

The letter, signed by Henry was his last word to Karen and evidence of her elder abuse. After sending the letter, Henry never saw or heard from Karen ever again. Henry passed away in 2007. This sad story did not have a happy ending other than to say the letter proved to be a powerful elixir that helped Tina's father to recover from his grief and feel more at peace.

Dana's Story

"REMEMBER THAT SHOVEL? DIG THIS!"

Dana had been in a challenging relationship with John for over three years. As Dana described it, they had a steamy love/hate relationship. At times, John became argumentative and physically aggressive toward her. Yet, their sexual attraction and overwhelming sense of passion maintained or perhaps energized their otherwise unhealthy, disturbed connection.

Once, while they vacationed in Hawaii, John and Dana argued over something ridiculous. It was shortly after sunset on a remote beach in Kauai. John grabbed Dana and threw her down, pulled her hair, and pushed her face into the sand. Dana had never fought back before. However, this time a sense of rage and disgust washed over her. She spied a large, plastic shovel nearby, most likely abandoned by some child who had been making a sand castle earlier in the day. Without giving it a second thought, Dana grabbed the shovel and began whacking John across the face with it. John was stunned since Dana normally engaged only in verbal attacks when provoked. She had never responded before with physical force.

Although those shovel whacks certainly stung, John was not seriously injured. After this session of repeated blows, the fight finally ended. They decided to break off their relationship once and for all. Or so it seemed.

Like so many cycles of domestic violence, Dana and John eventually got back together. The typical cycle starts with a violent or tumultuous incident; then, one partner leaves. Next, the couple finds their way back to one another and begins a so-called honeymoon phase. Usually, the instigator manipulates the situation to get back in their partner's arms, pledging remorse and vowing never to commit another assault. However, most often, the honeymoon phase ends with yet another violent episode, causing the couple to disengage before returning back to start the cycle over again.

Eventually, Dana and John began seeing one another and their relationship appeared normal for several months. Since they both enjoyed romantic getaways, John invited Dana on a ten-day vacation at a beautiful ocean resort in Cabo San Lucas, Baja California. The first couple of days went well. Then, after dinner one night, they returned to their suite where John continued to drink copious amounts of tequila.

Suddenly, John started insulting Dana and complaining about their relationship. The situation escalated. He started punching her in the face and kicking her in the stomach. When he finished battering her, she was lying curled up on the floor in the corner of the room overwhelmed and scared for her life. She had a black eye, various bruises, and her lip was swollen and cut from his ring.

Because they were in Mexico, (at the time Mexico's law enforcement had a reputation for rather nefarious practices and unfair treatment of so-called *Gringos*), Dana felt too afraid and intimidated to call the local police. John's rage seemed to finally subside after this; the couple didn't speak of it again. However, about a week later, after Dana was finally home in Southern California, she decided she never wished to see John again.

Dana was very afraid since his violence escalated with each new attack. She was so fearful of being viciously attacked again that she not only resolved to end the relationship, but sought a legal restraining order. However, the local police department informed her she should have filed a complaint in Mexico, rather than to have waited a week to file for a restraining order once she was stateside. Nevertheless, they took her statement and photographs of her week-old injuries even though she couldn't proceed with seeking legal protection.

Approximately six weeks later, the local district attorney contacted Dana. Serendipitously, they had discovered that another woman had

previously filed a complaint accusing John of physical aggression and battering some time ago. Dana was told the DA was directly involved now and a formal complaint was in the works. John was arrested and held for a hefty $10,000 bail; a trial date was also set.

Dana became panicky at the thought of John's arrest. She worried he would accuse her of seeking revenge because nearly two months had passed since their encounter in Mexico and subsequent breakup. She strongly felt he might stalk her and punish her one way or another for putting him through this ordeal.

By the time I wrote Dana's letter to John, he had already left numerous phone messages. Dana had not responded. As soon as she read the *Inspired Heart Letter* I had composed for John on her behalf, Dana felt a deep sense of relief. She carried a copy in her purse, taking it out and reading it several times as she found the words to be a source of comfort that strengthened her resolve. Soon after, Dana packed up some personal belongings John had previously left at her home and placed them into a bag with the *Inspired Heart Letter* attached. She waited until she knew he was not at home to drop the package on his doorstep.

Remember That Shovel?
Dig This!

Inspired Heart® Letter

Dear John,

I realize that we haven't communicated in a while. I do hope this letter finds you in a state of peace and contentment. I am starting to feel uplifted about my life and the new choices I am making. It feels really wholesome, like a new beginning. Nevertheless, I have to admit, I am still unsettled by what occurred in the final stages of our relationship. The terrible incidents that occurred between us in Kauai and Cabo left me feeling quite unloved, unappreciated, and disrespected. Unfortunately, my love for you became a source of pain. As the boundaries in our relationship came crashing down, and our experiences grew worse, my disappointment and frustration toward you was then reflected back to me. I started to feel badly about myself. I knew that our relationship was way too toxic to survive.

At times, I felt I was lying to myself, making up stories about how things might be better, or at least okay. However, the last straw was Cabo. I felt so hurt in every way. I felt diminished and ashamed of my weakness for staying in such an unhealthy relationship. At that point, I could no longer blame you, John. I was already aware of your faults. I could only blame myself for my own unhealthy endurance.

As you know, when we returned from Cabo, I reported your abuse. This was not out of a sense of revenge. My intention was only to set a real boundary, obtain a restraining order, and sever our ties. I needed to take care of myself and make sure I was not putting myself in harm's way ever again. What occurred after that, regarding your arrest, is simply the consequence of your actions. Hopefully, you will recognize certain boundaries should never be crossed.

Because of the love we once shared, for the good times we had, and because I simply care enough, I want to clear up any misgivings. I want you to know the truth. While it is far healthier for us to be apart, and I am moving forward in my life, I am also moved to clean up any misunderstandings from the past. I do forgive you and myself as well. I guess I just needed to feel complete with this. Good luck, John. I truly mean that with all sincerity.

Later that day, Dana received a text message from John. In his message, he assured Dana that even though he felt genuine love for her, he knew in his heart that they were wrong for one another. He apologized for his horrible behavior and the physical and emotional pain he had inflicted. John promised that he would never bother or harm her again. John received his letter over ten years ago. He has kept his promise.

No matter the circumstance, break-ups are difficult. Despite how horrible the connection turned out, often the person in a relationship who feels "dumped" cannot handle their sense of rejection and their partner may have to pry them out of their life. Healthy boundaries are essential. In order to emotionally thrive, we must maintain a zero tolerance for any type of abuse.

Leslie's Story

"HIT THE ROAD, JAKE"

I also wrote another *Inspired Heart Letter* for a woman, Leslie, who had been seeing a man, Jake, who proved to be quite controlling, jealous, demeaning at times, and altogether difficult to be around. After Leslie finally broke off their relationship, and although she refused to answer his phone calls or other attempts to contact her, Jake continued to pursue her to the point of harassment. Here is Leslie's final response:

Hit The Road, Jake

Inspired Heart® Letter

Hi Jake,

I did receive your recent messages and understand that you are displeased I've not responded. You need to know that while I believe there is a reason we met, and I appreciate the insights I have gained in knowing you, I have determined with certainty that it is unhealthy for me to continue seeing you. There is no "blame" regarding my decision. It is very apparent to me that being together is quite toxic, at least for me.

Please know that you have many attributes that I respect and find attractive. However, I definitely need to move on in order to regain my self-respect. In fact, with sincerity, I do wish you to be happy. At the same time, I have an obligation to myself. I realize we are simply an unhealthy match. I do not wish to be contacted. I hope you will respect me enough to honor this decision.

Leslie

Once Jake received this simple, yet direct, *Inspired Heart* note, he finally quit bothering Leslie once and for all. Leslie was able to convey a direct message to Jake that did not involve any sort of power struggle. She did not play the so-called "Making You Wrong Game." Instead, she took a firm position, and in nearly a business-like or matter-of-fact style, let him know she was not going to participate in any further drama.

Most people who use my intuitive letter-writing service are individuals who feel overwhelmed or worn-out from a personal relationship that is frightening, terribly sad, remorseful, confusing, or emotionally draining. They might struggle to find the best way to approach a situation to try and resolve the matter. Their emotional triggers may have been pushed, or they may be afraid of facing their emotions. Often, they feel internally stuck or blocked and may have trouble accessing their feelings.

This book seeks to guide you in ways that considers various common relationship dynamics, suggestions for composing effective letters, and offers lessons on how to rise above whatever drama is occurring so it can be seen from a different perspective.

Chapter 2

GUIDANCE FOR WRITING YOUR POWERFUL HEALING LETTER

For those interested in writing their own letters, I have some sage advice. First, when I have attempted to write a letter to a significant other on my own behalf, it is usually more than a bit challenging. One of the main reasons I can write compelling messages for clients is that I do not possess the egos of those clients. I do not have their emotional triggers or whatever their personal and relationship history brings to the mix that often obstructs clear, impressive, positive communication. Therefore, it is imperative to exorcise or let go of any emotional wound that binds you.

GETTING OUT OF YOUR OWN WAY

Just as Alice in Wonderland peered through the looking glass, (only to see how quite surprisingly different everything seemed)... do we ever really see our true self? Is our life story or current circumstance accurate? Or, do we ultimately choose how we experience life and our relationship with others based upon what we have agreed is true?

It is important to look at the situation you are concerned about through a very broad lens. It might require a sufficient time-out from any emotional reactivity or your own power struggle. A common desire is to want the last word or to dominate the issue from a one-sided, self-centered perspective. When you are undergoing emotional stress, it can be difficult to discern what is real, or see the whole picture. More importantly, to know what you do and do not have influence over for changing the circumstance at hand is a key component for communicating effectively.

Under certain circumstances, the "die has been cast," and there is no hope for change. There is nothing more you can do. Accepting what is, or has happened, as being beyond your control is the first step toward developing a sense of calm. Hopefully, this is eventually followed by forgiveness and release.

Let's Get Started!

PERSPECTIVE

Begin your journey for writing your amazing letter by clearing your mind from all the emotional clutter and allow your heart to open. As you go within and connect more deeply with your true nature, you may see your situation somewhat differently and perhaps come to realize a new shift in your perspective.

Start by taking a few deep breaths. As you begin to relax, focus upon your heart center. You might envision a bright light swirling or illuminating from your heart. I suggest taking in slow, deep breaths. Hold your breath for a few seconds. Then, slowly release your breath. Repeat this several times until you begin to relax. Next, focus upon a simple, positive thought. For example, repeat a phrase such as "I am blessed" or "I am love" – just something simple that resonates with you. If you are open to chanting, you may wish to say any sort of sacred chant or prayer. For instance, repeat an ancient Hawaiian prayer, such as "I am sorry. Please forgive me. I love you. Thank you." As you surrender to this experience, you should begin to feel more clear and centered.

Once you are feeling a better sense of calm, imagine you are ascending onto a cloud or a mountaintop. It does not matter where your mind leads you; just have the sense of moving to a higher, more distant, and very safe place. At this point, or once you have mentally arrived, take a look as though looking down upon your life situation. Begin to see it through a more distant, broader, less entangled, or more objective perspective. While remaining less emotionally attached, in your imagination, stay open to new insights or information that may emerge.

This exercise will assist you toward arriving at a broader sense of the relationship dynamics. Perhaps it will offer a new realization such as a particular life lesson you may be encountering or other profound wisdom discovered through a more objective perspective.

FOCUS

When writing a letter, be clear on what your focus or intention actually is. Notice whether you truly want to have peace around the matter and heal the situation. Or, are you feeling so indignant, angry, or frustrated that you are compelled to only state your case? Getting out of your own way, blowing past your egocentric needs, and being willing to see the bigger picture is most important for resolving the matter to its ultimate end. After all, working through our relationship issues is one of the best ways for us to grow individually.

THE UNRECOGNIZED GIFT

No matter what you are going through, if you pay close attention and take a more objective view, the issue at hand always creates an opportunity to glean a better understanding. Try looking at your relationship dilemma as though you were watching it on film at the movie theater or reading it as a story in a book. Take notice of how you have been acting. What role are you playing… and what role is your significant other cast in? Then consider what area within you is not healthy or healed. I believe we create our own realities. With that, how can we blame anyone else for what we choose to experience?

You can certainly choose not to be a victim of any circumstance. When we are able to move our ego aside and take a closer look at the blessing behind the experience, we gain incredible insights. Often, similar situations keep reappearing although the character(s) in the story may be different, or the place and circumstances might be new.

It is wise to notice the dynamics or underlying theme that rears its ugly head or reappears again and again. This awareness puts you on the road to learning the lesson and completing the pattern once and for all. With that in mind, you can begin to realize the silver lining that is available to all our emotional challenges.

INTUITIVE COMMUNICATION

As a deeply intuitive communicator, I can write a letter that carries the universal frequency of love, hope, and forgiveness. I believe the letters I write are Divinely channeled through me. Being a *channel* simply means that I am the conduit between my client's soul's desire and his or her earthly expression of that by way of the written word. You can learn this skill if you are willing to let go of being in charge and are more open to spirit or God's grace.

These *Inspired Heart Letters* carry an energetic frequency that is particular to the person(s) for whom the letter is written. Although there are certain elements to consider when writing your letter, it is best not to attempt to compose a letter using any type of absolute step-by-step process. These letters allow a higher wisdom to come through when you are an open receiver. Therefore, refrain from needing to follow a recipe; instead, be open to the flow of creativity. However, just to get you started, I do offer a way to compose your magical *Inspired Heart Letter* by imparting practical knowledge and considerations, along with a great deal of wisdom, or do's and don'ts, and actual examples for composing the various parts of your letter.

In arriving at the bigger picture or theme of the letter, it is important to tap into what the true nature of the situation is. Through this awareness, you can write an effective letter. However, it is most important to be open and clear to the higher message, life lesson, or initiation that the relationship challenge offers. Once you can identify with the bigger picture, the opportunity for personal evolvement, despite the pain or heartache associated with the experience, can be received.

Therefore, in order to capture the best advice for writing a powerful influential letter, be mindful of the following:

- **Intention:** Consider what your true underlying goal is, or what you hope to actually achieve through this letter. Check in to make sure your intention is not ego-based or part of a power play. In other words, try to focus upon the best possible outcome, not just for yourself, but also for all parties concerned.

- **Ego Interference:** Find clarity regarding your perspective. Compassion and compromise are two ingredients that are often found in resolving a relational issue. Ask yourself, "Is it better to be right than loved?" Is the perceived power gained by having the last word more important than creating or repairing healthy connections?

- **Creative Writing versus using an identified process:** There is no step-by-step recipe for composing an *Inspired Heart Letter*. Open your heart to receive and your innate wisdom will guide you along the way.

- **Taking the Time:** An eloquent letter, instead of a text message, is important. It has been taught, "It is not what is said, rather, how it is said that makes a difference." The same is true for written communications; how the message is conveyed with the right language and stated in a meaningful context is the glue that holds the intention.

- **Keep It Real:** Heartfelt communications are just that: being honest, vulnerable, and hopeful, while forgiving ourselves and others and staying in a state of gratitude for the lesson learned. This is a key component to a winning letter. Focusing on these merits is a much healthier way for achieving higher knowledge and finding true relief. A clear outlook is often realized once the letter is completed.

- **Attached to Outcome:** Sometimes we focus on what we can fix right now. Do not fixate on a desired outcome. Instead, let go of trying to control anything. Let go of any worry, fear, or regret. Release any thoughts of how the issue at hand should be resolved. The more we are able to trust and surrender to our highest good, the more open we are to experiencing an even better outcome than was hoped for. Higher love is letting go of fear. So, take the plunge; mail or give that letter. Then let go, and allow your highest good and the good of all concerned to manifest.

- **Creating the Sacred Space:** Make sure you are rested, relaxed, and have a quiet, undisturbed, appropriately lit, and otherwise comfortable space that is suitable for writing or keyboarding. (Some people prepare themselves by taking a soothing sea salt bath or walking in nature before settling down to write.) Then create your own inspired writing space in the atmosphere that feels good for you. You may consider placing scented candles, flowers, art, or crystals nearby. Make this a place for gathering your thoughts in a serene environment that sings to you or invites your heart to open.

- **Ritual:** This is optional, yet I suggest that a ritual may not only empower your mental or emotional outlook regarding the matter, but it may energetically enrich the communication process altogether. Some engaged in the process of healing through letter writing are drawn to ritualize the letter's invocation as a type of mantra. This may include the use of guided visualizations, such as seeing the letter in a shimmering white, peaceful blue, or golden light, while feeling an essence of love as it heals any negative emotions. You may find satisfaction with lighting candles, or reading the letter aloud as a prayer. In certain instances, you might consider burning the letter, burying the letter under a full moon, or sleeping with the letter under your pillow. Any ritual you are drawn to may be a rewarding element that captures and marks the essence or intention of the message as a sacred invocation. Simply saying a prayer or positive thought aloud, such as, "More peace, harmony, and love is given and received through this letter," may further enhance and empower the results.

- **Intuition:** In my experience, trust and allowance are the keys to opening your intuitive channel. Tapping into your innate intuitive process may be different for you than for someone else. In order to allow Divine information to come forth, it is imperative to be relaxed and to focus upon opening your heart while disengaging from obsessive, intrusive thoughts or relying solely upon your mental analysis. This may be guided by your breath and simple trust that a higher wisdom or guidance will surely emerge.

- **Trust:** It is a fine blending of knowledge, awareness, asking for the highest or best outcome for all involved; and believing you will safely arrive at your destination, or rather, at the most appropriate written expression for the situation at hand.

Like anything else, the more confident that you become, the more pleasure you will derive from this form of letter writing. In time, writing these *Inspired Heart Letters* may become as joyful an experience for you as it is for me.

ORGANIZING YOUR THOUGHTS FOR LETTER WRITING

Typically, before I ghostwrite a healing letter, I usually ask the following questions, or ponder the following considerations that better equip me for organizing and writing an *Inspired Heart Letter*:

1. What is your true heart's desire? In other words, if the ultimate wish could be granted, what is it that you hope for that would create the absolute best results? Holding a space for your heart's desire, or for what you believe is the ultimate results of your letter, is a starting point for dialing in on your true intention.

2. What perceived fears or obstacles are there? Consider what most likely, or may possibly obstruct the best or desired results to occur. The first thoughts that come to mind are usually the most obvious fears, yet by delving a bit deeper, often there is an even bigger fear or perceived obstacle that is underlying and usually more difficult to readily access. (More discussion on this is to follow later in this chapter.)

3. What background or history between you and the person receiving your letter may influence how your letter is received? Consider not only the presenting problem or issue, but look at the background and history of the relationship. Further, explore your personal history and the personal development and history of your significant other. Notice possible emotional scars or imprints, including family history, cultural expectations, rules, roles, or persistent relationship patterns both positive and unhealthy. Think about anything that may have influenced your relationship dynamics or may have contributed to the current situation. Look at any possible blame, shame, or self-hatred patterns or tendencies toward chronic victimization. Power struggles, whether overt or covert bullying tactics, or any patterns of manipulation should also be acknowledged. Instead of playing the "blame game," work toward creating a radical shift for taking responsibility, or for admitting your own contribution to the issue at hand. Be willing to pause. Take time out for a deeper sense of self-reflection.

4. What is your gut telling you? Check in with your own intuition. What feels out of alignment? Sometimes, there are silent messages that surface. During those times, you may experience bouts of confusion, since you may be hanging on to something that is what you expected, but is just not realistic. When you stop, and really delve into your feeling state, then you can come to terms with the answer that you actually know however unreal or out of step it may be with what you originally considered as true. This is when the intuition kicks in. Once you arrive at that still-point, or align with your heart center, and when you are able to trust your own gut feelings despite social, cultural, family, or self-imposed expectations, then the written word begins to take on a life of its own.

THE MECHANICS FOR WRITING AN EFFECTIVE LETTER

Knowing just how to formulate your letter onto the page is an important feature for writing a powerful letter. Unlike email notes or text messages, personal letters are in a class by themselves. The notion of the letter, or what you are striving to convey, is the most salient part or the meat and potatoes of your message. How the letter is written projects a certain tone, cadence, and sentiment. Writing from the heart with access to logic and wisdom is the key component. For actually putting your letter together or weaving your thoughts and words in the most compelling way, the following points are noteworthy:

CHOOSE THE RIGHT WORDS

Most importantly, when writing your letter, remember the language, or specificity of words, must be carefully considered. This is where the magic of "reframing your thoughts" can perform wonders. Your expressed language should invite your recipient to be open, to allow forgiveness, gratitude, and appreciation to occur. It is only with compassionate communication that the healing can take place, or at least, an opening for resolving the conflict can be inspired. The letter is not aimed at being right, or proving a point. Letters that heal do not shame or chastise anyone. They are not guilt-laden, nor do they seek ego-gratifying revenge in any way. Letters that carry a negative agenda even on a subliminal level will not be very effective and may even backfire, creating more confusion or upset. Just how your words and phrases are strung together or how your letter is formatted is immensely important. Just like a song, letters carry a certain melody that can be either pleasing or out of tune.

One of the best ways to capture the interest of your letter's recipient is to begin your letter on a positive note. Even simply stating how often you think of the other person or how you hope the letter finds them in a state of peace starts a more inviting flow. Perhaps you may consider painting a beautiful scene with your words as the backdrop to your letter. For example, "*On this cold winter night, while snuggled under a comforter next to a roaring fire, my thoughts turn to you...*" This creates a sort of image or visual that calls for a more open, warmhearted feeling for the reader.

NO NEED TO COMPLAIN

Next, while it is important to state the direction or concern regarding your letter, make sure you do not use depreciating phrases or words that make the recipient out to be wrong or inadequate, such as, *"You just do not know how much I really care."* Instead, a phrase such as *"I would love the opportunity to show you just how much I really care."* is much more compelling. Letters that allude to griping, sniveling, or groveling, are real turn-offs. For example, *"You do not really understand how I feel.";* *"You never had to endure what I went through.";* *"I felt so devastated after you left.";* *"Why can't you understand how this feels for me?"* or *"I don't think I can make it without you"* are definite DO NOT approaches to effective letter writing.

Rather, a more positive, open, and confident style or a way whereby you are not fixated on your personal pain but focused on just how the situation may be resolved is really powerful. The focus of your words or message should create a deeper compassionate understanding around the conflict. Ideally, your letter should convey a true intention for finding a way to rectify or begin to heal a situation.

These *Inspired Heart Letters* often serve to provide an improved sense of clarity. Moreover, upon writing the letter, you may be surprised at how your original feelings shift from initially seeking some type of power, control, or even revenge, to recognizing the actual reason for why the problem has occurred, while, at the same time, compassionately forgiving yourself and anyone else. It is a deeper process and quite powerful when you take the time to earnestly consider how you have contributed to the situation at hand. Perhaps you reacted indifferently or offensively; poorly communicated your grievances before things got out of hand; or simply turned a blind eye and remained in such denial, the conflict was allowed to persist or grow.

Once you have achieved a newfound personal awareness regarding your possible underlying motive and degree of contribution to the issue at hand, the next step is to find a way to truly forgive yourself. This raises your personal awareness. You have now evolved and broadened your capacity to face the dynamics for your concerns, perhaps through new eyes. Then, there is an opportunity to accept the current reality or let go of what you may not be able to influence, change, or control. If you are able to surrender and hope for the best, the healing begins.

SHEDDING LIGHT ON THE PROBLEM

Be patient. Be kind. Again, please understand that there is nothing positive to be gained just by proving you are, or were, right and the other person is somehow wrong. Recognize, own, and accept your and their human fallibilities, yet, be empathetic. We all only do what we know or feel is right at the time whatever path was taken; whatever we said or did in the moment, it seemed to be the best course of action.

This is not to say your message skirts around the perceived problem. However, expressing your concerns or dismay in a softer, gentler or even healthier way usually helps to keep your reader open to better hear or understand what you wish to express. Otherwise, your reader may become defensive or shut down. For example, *"I know our children could not have a better mother than you. Although we are separated, I hope we will somehow help them feel like we are a whole family with two loving parents."* Or, another example: *"You have been my best friend for all these years. I can't imagine losing our friendship over something said out of turn. I would never want to deny ourselves the opportunity to play Bingo together when we are in our eighties."*

A powerful letter can include many elements such as charm, wit, humor, sentimentality, sensuality, acknowledgment of the situation at hand, the role played, the lesson learned, and always with absolute honesty and sincerity. Most importantly, it can offer a way to resolve the issue. For example, *"I hope you will grasp the true meaning of this letter, what I hold dear, and just how much I adore you."* Or, *"If you are open, I would love to meet with you over coffee or a walk on the beach."* Or, *"It would mean so much to me to look in your eyes and share my heart. I know we can find a way... together."*

Refer to a time when the relationship was in a more loving, compatible, or healthier place. Include certain terms of endearment that recall when your relationship was in a more positive mode. You may find some humor despite the current challenge at hand. Offer support through nurturance, sympathy or compassion, acceptance, gratitude or forgiveness. You may also, with sincerity, ask for their support in these ways.

This is part of the beauty, tapestry, and ultimate mystery of life. Every opportunity that awakens our emotions and our mental awareness allows the possibility for personal renewal and growth. Therefore, try to let go of any doubt, fear, or worry regarding what your heart guides you to say. By putting forth effort in order to connect with another for the purpose of healing, to more deeply understand, or even love more dearly, allows your heart and the heart of another the opportunity to expand and create an opening for receiving new blessings, some of which may be entirely unexpected.

Another word of advice is to stay in the present. While considering ongoing emotional patterns that keep us stuck, truly successful letters require the ability to remain focused and stay on track with what is currently out of balance, stagnant, or problematic. This encourages you to be more solution-oriented as opposed to lending a sense of helplessness or drowning in a never-ending litany of history or complaints. Consider the more salient concern(s), or highlight the desired resolution, rather than primarily focusing upon what has previously gone wrong.

US VERSUS ME

Creating a "we" identity generates a more collaborative conversation that invites your letter recipient to be part of the solution instead of the problem. Clarifying your underlying emotions, (i.e. instead of feeling "pissed off," acknowledge the deeper truth, which may be an overwhelming sense of sadness, loss, or rejection etc.). Strive for clarity and be hopeful.

GOOD LETTER VIBES

Thoughts translated into words contain a certain energetic frequency. Some may think the term energetic frequency is metaphorical, but during my years of practice, by allowing my intuitive skills equal billing with logic and reason, I honestly do feel these frequencies in the material world. As you yourself surrender to your intuitions, I believe you will experience the same phenomenon.

The underlying subtle energy of thoughts and words are felt by the person who wrote the letter as well as by the person reading the letter. Letters that aspire toward taking the high road are creative and can influence a sense of love, care, or other positive emotions. Words or expressions that are unkind, judgmental, or accusatory are of a lower, denser, resonance. They most likely will cause increased anxiety and friction. The person reading the letter may feel angry or upset and put-off or reject the letter. Therefore, it is very important to keep the overall tone of your letter at a higher, lighter vibration. Avoid dwelling on negative emotions, such as shame, blame, guilt, conveying any feelings of rejection, or abandonment. On the contrary, offer more open, loving, higher states of emotion, such as gratitude, acceptance, appreciation, respect, etc. Raise the emotional frequency so your letter will be more positively received. Remember love, especially unconditional love, vibrates at a much higher frequency.

ACKNOWLEDGE WHAT IS REAL AND CONSIDER WHAT IS TO CHANGE

While the opening of your letter should encourage whoever receives the letter to read further, the main content of the letter's purpose offers a platform for describing your concerns or how you view the current problem. It discusses or explains your vision for healing the matter. You should be able to illustrate what that looks like. It is also the part of the letter where you can state what you truly appreciate about your significant other. Therefore, this section of your letter reveals your perspective and the insights you have gained from the experience. Your words may also convey other realizations or commitments such as setting new boundaries or being open to a new way of dealing with the matter. You can also openly share just what it is you are willing to contribute or do. It is the part in your message that allows the reader to discover just how you see the issue and what your thoughts are for working through it toward a realistic solution. Through the many vignettes and letters provided throughout this book, you will find a great deal of content that may lend various ideas for resolving conflicts.

CLOSING YOUR LETTER

The closing part of your letter, regardless of the letter's intention or goal, often ends with expressing gratitude to the other person for accepting and reading through your message. Unless it is a "Dear John" type of letter, or a letter for which you wish to gracefully disconnect from the letter recipient, the closing message most often will pose a way to invite the other person to consider a new possibility to reconnect as well as to join you in seeking a way to heal or improve the situation.

Truly inspired letters are like artwork; each has its own flavor, style, and color. When the blank canvas invites you to begin your letter, remember the best art reveals the light as well as the shadows.

Sharon's Story

"FEELING SHUT OUT"

To further illustrate the aforementioned points, I once wrote an *Inspired Heart Letter* for a middle-aged lady, Sharon, who was going through the final stages of a messy divorce after over thirty years of marriage. Sharon's husband had an affair and wanted out of the marriage. Several months later, Sharon decided to start a fresh life and relocate out of state.

Unfortunately, her thirty-year-old daughter Sandy, who was married and expecting her second child, took offense that her mother moved so far away. In retaliation, she wrote a rather scathing and demoralizing letter to her mother. In her letter, Sandy complained about her childhood, in particular, growing up in a home where her parents commonly argued. She reminisced about her mother's former bouts with alcohol, and essentially accused Sharon of being selfish and uncaring. Needless to say, Sharon was very hurt and upset. She felt quite stuck, not knowing just how to respond to her daughter's angry letter. After three months, she contacted me to write the following *Inspired Heart Letter*.

Mommy Issues

Inspired Heart® Letter

Hello Sandy,

How are you, my daughter? After giving it considerable thought, I am responding to your revealing letter from last December. I thought it best to allow some time to let the emotional dust settle before sending this message in reply. Frankly, my first impression was "Whoa"... I was struck with such sadness that you seem to be carrying so much anger. It has to be a burden.

Sandy, I have known you your whole life... my heart truly goes out to you. I do hear what you are saying, and, sadly, there is some truth to what you have expressed. While I always wished to be the best mother to you, and although it was never my intention, I see there were times I let you down. Although I cannot turn back the clock, I hope we can move forward. I do think of you all the time.

With real compassion, I feel that you certainly must be facing incredible challenges by having to give so much to others as a wife, a mother, and an expectant mother, and, at the same time, working so hard at your job. It must still be painful, no matter the history or circumstance, to have your parents end up divorced... and then, have me, your mom, relocate to Florida.

Please understand I have not abandoned you, My Love. There is nothing I want more than to heal our relationship and step into the light of love and caring. If you will allow, I would deeply appreciate the opportunity to visit you and help you in any way before and/or after your new baby son arrives.

My eyes fill with tears just thinking about you, and how much I miss you. You are beautiful and intelligent. It warms my heart to hear you laugh. I do want to find some peace between us and cherish the good parts, continue sharing what is in our hearts and on our mind, and build a closer, more trusting relationship. I hope you want the same.

Although it was certainly painful, I am grateful that you felt safe enough to share your feelings and the truth of what lies heavy in your heart. It has been said that forgiveness is a precious gift we give to ourselves. I hope you will consider taking me up on my offer to visit you and allow me to care for you in any way I can. Either way, just know I am holding you in my heart and only want the very best for you.

Love always,

Mom

To illuminate this point even further, notice that instead of joining her daughter in a power struggle, Sharon honestly and lovingly acknowledged Sandy's feelings and experience. The following excerpt demonstrates this point:

I was struck with such sadness that you seem to be carrying so much anger. It has to be a burden. Sandy, I have known you your whole life... my heart truly goes out to you. I do hear what you are saying, and sadly, there is some truth to what you have expressed. While I always wished to be the best mother to you, and although it was never my intention, I see there were times I let you down. Although I cannot turn back the clock, I hope we can move forward. I do think of you all the time...

- The words conveyed in this excerpt place a different spin on things. Instead of being either defensive or offensive toward her daughter's bold, chastising letter, she acknowledges Sandy's assertions to a certain degree. Sharon agrees and admits to her own ineptitude, or frailties, as well as admitting there was some truth to her daughter's claims from the past. Toward the end of this letter, the following excerpt appears:

Although it was certainly painful, I am grateful that you felt safe enough to share your feelings and the truth of what lies heavy in your heart...

- Again, this takes the element of indignation or ego out of Sharon's response and replaces it with a kind and nurturing quality that reinforces the notion of a more ideal mother-daughter bond. In the final stage of this letter, Sharon offers to visit her daughter, Sandy, in order to care for her before or after the birth of her second child. This is an invitation that allows Sandy a chance to reply and accept an opportunity to receive a loving kindness and care from her mother and strive to heal their relationship.

A compelling influence is not achieved through force. Instead, real power comes through rising above the slings and arrows. With compassion, love, and caring, we can raise the frequency of the relationship to a new level.

I surmised there was a more prevalent underlying truth conveyed in Sandy's resentful letter. Perhaps this related more to her feelings of being overwhelmed by her current life circumstance and a sense of abandonment. Since Sandy, the daughter, was dealing with so much personal responsibility, maybe what arose from her perception was the notion that while she felt stuck, her mother had the freedom to leave her burdens behind and start a fresh new beginning. Sharon reports that this *Inspired Heart Letter* has resulted in a much closer connection with her daughter. Sandy did take her up on her offer and Sharon was able to witness the birth of her grandson.

There is a certain frequency that we carry depending on our emotional reactivity to any given situation. Emotions such as shame, guilt, grief, deception, and jealousy vibrate at a very low frequency. When people are aware and dissatisfied with the frequency they are operating on, they can adjust the dial. Most people know their negative thinking perpetuates their funk. When you are experiencing anxiety or despair, remind yourself of more positive notions such as your finer attributes or even what you are grateful for.

Anger also radiates at a lower vibration, yet somewhat higher as there is a type of energy behind the rage or resentment that provokes an outward expression and moves the otherwise stagnant energy. Yet the ability to forgive and accept yourself or another starts to raise the vibration considerably. When we can move beyond that, to the point of feeling a sense of absolute love with a focus on gratitude and a willingness to be in a more loving, gentle, and thriving emotional state, then the vibration shifts and rises tremendously.

It is in this higher vibrational frequency, or moving beyond the ego with absolute love, where we create a more loving, peaceful reality. This aligns with Dr. Norman Vincent Peale's concept of the *Power of Positive Thinking*. Furthermore, when our thoughts move from thinking to believing in positive ways, we begin to shift our perceptions altogether. These perceptual shifts are then followed by more positive, loving feelings, which results in attracting more joyful, satisfying experiences.

SELF-SABOTAGE & EMOTIONAL ALCHEMY

Awareness of unconscious, self-sabotaging patterns in relationships is the key that unlocks the door for finding more love and relationship success. Often, a client will ask me to write a letter in order to cause the letter recipient to feel shame, guilt, or sadness. However, the *Inspired Heart Letters* are not a means for that sort of power play or manipulation. At times, it is quite evident to me that a client is stuck in his or her patterns or mired in their unconscious negative programming, with limited ability to participate in truly healthy, loving, or connected relationships. This is the biggest hurdle to cross as far as writing a personal, healing letter for conflict resolution.

More often, we do not see our own limiting or self-destructive emotional and/or behavior patterns, and we certainly cannot easily access our subconscious drives. Therefore, before composing a letter, I suggest you organize your thoughts and consider your patterns and the role you played in shaping the relationship you are trying to improve.

Review your inherited legacy, the long-standing family beliefs or judgmental views that were passed on to you. For example, you may have grown up in a home in which your family considered: *Men who cry are weak; Women are too needy and never satisfied; Children are meant to be seen, not heard;* or *You can only achieve success through hard work.* Consider these and other cultural prejudices that may have limited your worldview, and may interfere with your ability to be open to another's perspective. I have named some of the more obvious ones, and you may search your own history to uncover others that may be more subtle and personal, but every bit as pervasive. Be aware of this as you compose your letter.

Write down a list of any previous relationships that were unsuccessful and therein try to locate common threads or similar dynamics that continue to plague your attempt for finding healthier connections. You may seek the professional feedback and advice from a psychotherapist or relationship coach. Journaling, meditating, and even viewing your relationships over your lifetime as a scripted movie or story, may evoke some "aha" moments of clarity and more objective perceptions. By discovering these unhealthy patterns, and accepting the notion that you and no one else are actually responsible for your current happiness, you can begin to transform.

With a newfound awareness, you have an opportunity to reconsider which elements in your life are wholesome and which have been destructive. This may include people, career choices, your work or home environment, or whether there is an unhealthy sense of obligation toward certain emotionally draining family members or a significant other, and, most importantly, what stories along the way regarding how you perceive yourself and the world around you have you come to believe. Being responsible for your life experiences, especially within the realm of relationship matters, is a pivotal step toward reclaiming yourself.

As we become emotionally and/or psychologically healthier, undoubtedly our relationships with others will change. Like the saying, *Water seeks its own level,* we draw to us relationships that mirror back just where we are at regarding what we feel we deserve and what we feel is possible.

DADDY ISSUES

Once upon a time, a client, I will refer to as "Stacey," (a pretty lady in her late forties who had never married nor had any children), asked me to write a letter from her to her father. What she revealed to me was that she grew up an only child. Her parents were childhood sweethearts and maintained a loving relationship throughout their marriage. However, her father developed a drinking problem. When he had too much alcohol, he would often experience blackouts and become delusional.

During these blackout periods, there were times when he would begin accusing his young daughter, Stacey, of outrageous behaviors and would not only insult her, but occasionally become physically abusive. Stacey described certain frightening events between herself and her father in the presence of her mother, including once, at a family friend's party, whereby her father screamed, hit, and even kicked her under the table! Stacey recalled these episodes as having occurred when she was around the age of seven or eight, or even younger.

Once he recovered from the blackout, her father had no recollection whatsoever regarding the horrible incidents. For whatever reason, her mother never came to her rescue or confronted her father about these terrible attacks (at least, not to Stacey's knowledge). While her father was never held accountable, she never once blamed her mother for failing to protect her. Actually, she described her mother as being very fragile, innocent, and angelic. Stacey believed that her own soul came to earth to watch over her mother.

Stacey claimed that while growing up, her mother always treated her in a loving, kind manner. On the other hand, Stacey described her father's usual behavior toward her as distant and aloof. She had no recollection of her father ever being affectionate or nurturing toward her. However, as she was growing up, she did appreciate his efforts for attending every one of her sporting events without fail. Over time, it seems her father did seek help for his alcoholism, and his blackout episodes finally stopped.

Unfortunately, her mother passed away from a malignant brain tumor when Stacey was about thirty years old. Shortly afterwards, her father married a woman with adult-aged children. He seemed to start a new life without really including Stacey. Moreover, she had come to believe that her father had maligned her to his new wife, who in turn shared his misgivings with her own children. As a result, Stacey felt her dad had both abandoned and betrayed her. What was even more painful was that Stacey never understood why their relationship was so difficult.

Although she visited on occasion, Stacey never quite felt welcome in her dad's home. Ironically, and yet not surprising, she earned a living as a practicing alternative healing-arts therapist who specialized in women's intimacy issues. Her heart seemed to be in the right place, and she had made strides toward her own spiritual and emotional evolvement, yet she could not recognize or accept her own underlying resistance to being able to face the truth and change her outlook. Instead, she placed much of her focus and energy upon others, especially her father and his need to change or transform.

When Stacey contacted me to write an *Inspired Heart Letter* to her dad, she happened to share that her now elderly father had previously promised to leave her some valuable real estate as her inheritance. However, when she pressed him, he refused to produce a copy of the will. It seemed that she never really knew where she stood with her dad. However, more recently, with her encouragement, her father started checking in with her via cell phone on a regular basis. Despite this, she did not trust that he actually cared enough or would carry through with his promise to leave her the home. It seemed as though Stacey believed that if only her dad would produce the evidence of that promise, she could finally feel validated by him. In other words, Stacey needed a more visible, tangible confirmation of his love.

At first, Stacey led me to believe that she only desired to enjoy a more honest, open rapport, have a more authentic bond with her dad, lay all grudges aside, and feel that she was a welcomed part of his family. However, in my experience with her, it did not take long to see that Stacey continued to resist coming to terms with the past and was not truly ready to forgive her father. She seemed almost obsessed with a need to have her father openly acknowledge his awful behavior and cold indifference and ask for her forgiveness.

I cautioned Stacey that it would be unwise and ineffective to come right out and ask or demand an apology from someone. It was even less appropriate to bring up a possible inheritance matter, at least at this stage, whereby the focus of the letter is better served not through condemnation or other power plays, but rather, by sharing a higher intention and allowing the door to open for a better sense of emotional integrity.

When we stand in our power and live in grace, we can encourage a purging of outworn patterns in our relationships with others. We may even inspire that long-awaited apology or admission to be said. After all, what is a victim and what is a bully? They are only people with a sense of limited power, or a misguided need for more power.

Although Stacey claimed to have worked on her own healing over the years, it was evident to me that she was unable to lay down her sword and be at peace. Often, in dysfunctional families who are struggling with alcoholism or other addictions, while the elephant is in the room, the family places its focus on other more benign or acceptable things to complain about. I surmise that it was simply too painful for this woman to realize that her dear mother failed to protect her and that her father was never called out for his terrible drunken behavior during her formative years.

Stacey kept returning to the issues surrounding her possible inheritance rather than coming to terms with her own deeper wounding from her father's egregious acts and lack of emotional support, including her mother's failure to stand up for her. Sadly, she seemed to lack a sense of feeling connected, not only to her father, but to anyone else for that matter. Perhaps this caused her to inherit some rather unhealthy perceptions about life in general along with certain outworn misguided coping skills.

Her beliefs about her family dynamics, most likely, carried over into her personal life experiences. As a result of remaining stuck in an old pattern of emotional lack and limitation, and other negative beliefs, she continued to live her life quite alone, usually feeling as though she was on the outside looking in. At the time of our encounter, Stacey had been unable to find a lasting romantic relationship that she could really trust or rely upon.

Referring to the old Buddhist saying: *To judge someone is like drinking a glass of poison and expecting the other person to die.* We must first claim ourselves, which then transpires into an emotional healing for the situation at hand. Again, while feeling accepted by others is a universal need, we must accept ourselves first. Although, our relationships can definitely serve to enhance our life experiences, they cannot and *do not complete us.*

There is no redeeming value in either being vindictive or scratching old wounds. Sometimes, there is a secondary gain for hanging on to old emotional pain such as gaining sympathy and attention from others. However, it can also deprive us from maintaining a better focus for moving forward and taking the right action. Wouldn't you rather have the issue resolved?

Inspired Heart Letters often create an even bigger healing for the person sending the letter as it can serve to be a type of bridge that allows us to transition while letting go of the past without further bitterness. Ideally, before composing a compelling letter, the possibility of self-sabotaging tendencies or other emotional obstacles should be contemplated, realized, and released. That course-corrects the intention for a healing to take place. In my experience as an intuitive letter writer, often it is not until the letter is written that the client sees the obvious truth and finds relief.

Letters are not a panacea, but an element that can contribute to the wellbeing of the letter writer. In Stacey's case, writing the letter may have opened her up to the possibility of seeking professional therapy for issues the letter itself helped uncover. Based on her agenda, I realized Stacey was not ready for an *Inspired Heart Letter.* Her relationship with her father remains a work in progress, and the proposed letter was a first step toward healing, certainly not the last.

MORE ON THE TONE AND FLAVOR OF THE LETTER

While several letters and letter excerpts are contained in the following chapters of this book, it is most important to take note of each letter's style and intention. Some of the letters discussed are written in a rather bold, straightforward, unabashed style, which intuitively ignites a more radical shift. Other letters are written with more neutrality or offer a compromise, or even to humbly call forth and recognize what faulty judgment or previous mistakes have been made by the one issuing the letter. Certain letters focus on what is to be gained by finally putting the grievance to rest. Such letters may invite the recipient to meet the other halfway in order to resolve a conflict, pointing out that no one really "wins" while illuminating how much more there is to lose by continuing to battle over old, outworn issues. Still, other letters serve to rekindle or inspire more love to occur simply through acknowledging the merits, beauty, and gifts that are received through a loving connection. There are letters that are a long, overdue plea for forgiveness and convey a deep sadness and regret for one's emotional ineptitude. Yet, some letters serve to allow the person issuing the letter to intrepidly move on with integrity. This type of message is a powerful way to clean up the past, and acknowledge the gift, whether it is finding healthier boundaries or other initiations of self-awareness. It is also a way to recognize and finally put an end to unhealthy emotional and/or behavior patterns.

If you consider that the written word is powerful and carries an energetic resonance, then the letters are formidable written communications that require careful thought and purity of mind and heart. In short, the best advice for composing a truly heartfelt letter is to be aware, stay open, trust, and come from your heart.

STORIES AND LESSONS SHARED

In the following chapters, I share some of the more dominant dynamic relationship themes. You may recognize some, or many, of these common issues for the familiar thread running through them, which you may relate to as pertinent to your own life or the lives of other people you know. Again, this allows us to become more tolerant, and compassionate, and glean a deeper understanding when we feel disappointed or frustrated with others or ourselves. These stories and letters may teach us to recognize that we are not alone.

Simply know that these are universal heartfelt challenges, and there is a delightful vibrational shift that occurs when we rise above the ego and let go of fear in order to reach for the truth. Life is theater in the sense that while scenes, roles, costumes, and dialogues are different, the language of the heart remains unchanged.

MAINTAINING A SUCCESSFUL OUTCOME

These *Inspired Heart Letters* can unlock a relationship that has been stuck or resistant to heal and move forward. However, it is very important to understand that although this may be a huge step toward relationship recovery, it is only the beginning. There are plenty of helpful tips and solid information discussed and outlined throughout this book that, if followed, will guide the reader on learning ways to build, nourish, and maintain healthier, deeply meaningful, and more loving connections.

Chapter 3

Letter Theme – Dating

DATING DILEMMAS: SINGLES LOOKING FOR LOVE

For those of you fortunate enough to be enjoying a solid, committed relationship, you may bypass this chapter. Most likely, you have excellent relationship karma when it comes to romantic partnerships and are considered lucky in love. On the other hand, others of you may not be romantically inclined, or simply have no desire to date. However, for those readers who are fervently negotiating their way through the unpredictable, often frustrating, and certainly challenging realm of modern day dating, you may wish to read on.

They say the world was created in seven days. For most singles, finding true love, experiencing – you know, that long wished-for type of pure-hearted, sexy, and enduring romance – well, that would mean the world to them. However, some singles looking for love argue the notion, *The good ones are all taken! I am too old. No one will want me. I always fall for the bad boys… and they all cheat! Relationships are a hassle… you get used, abused, and spit out!* Or, *There are things about me that no one knows, and they are just unlovable.* Sometimes, when you feel so completely disillusioned by the love you seek; let down, put down, and heartbroken, it is difficult to consider new possibilities or a brand-new reality. Yet, what if you could experience a loving partnership that is based upon trust, forgiveness, acceptance, sharing, respect, and a deeper passion? Fortunately, as I see it, our world is changing. We are embarking upon a time where relationships are deeper, richer, and so much more satisfying. In these transformational times, if you believe real love is possible, you can now be awakened to call forth a more sacred union that is blissfully enjoyed within a much deeper dimension.

The following *Inspired Heart Letters* and their stories I am about to share with you hopefully will help you to see the struggles and the triumphs of others seeking to create a devoted, passionate partnership that is no less than magical!

Julia's Story

"STEVIE WONDER"

Julia contacted me to write a letter after she found herself in a very puzzling predicament with a man she had recently begun dating. She could not help but question his motives. Her suitor, Stephan, was an accomplished businessman who enjoyed a wide circle of friends, and was divorced for several years with grown or nearly grown children. Stephan had a very happy-go-lucky attitude, was a good father, and deeply cared about others. Julia and Stephan met at a Sunday football party he hosted at his lovely home near the ocean. Julia enjoyed his foppish ways and sense of fun and felt immediately comfortable in his company. Stephan entertained her over dinners, dancing, and going to the movies.

They had only been dating for a few weeks when Stephan invited her to a local charity event for Halloween. Perhaps it was his Dracula costume that foreshadowed their evening and, interestingly enough, Julia dressed as a fetching Little Red Riding Hood. What was quite unpredictable, though, was how their evening unfolded.

Shortly after they arrived at the party, Julia, (feeling a bit conspicuous since she did not know any of his friends), felt more than slighted when Stephan went on his own to mingle about the room, merrily engaging in various conversations and even dancing with other women. All the while, *Little Red Riding Hood* was left feeling completely ignored by this *Dracula* named Stephan. She felt utterly abandoned and left alone to awkwardly roam about the ballroom disguised in a costume and not knowing a soul! Julia felt ridiculous and rather indignant. Yes, despite her beauty and charming personality, her ego took a real nosedive and her disenchantment with Stephan only increased. After well over an hour had passed, Julia called a cab and left the event without saying goodbye.

In the following days, she became consumed with bewilderment. After all, she initially was very impressed with Stephan and felt hopeful that he would make a great boyfriend. He had treated her with so much respect and given her ample attention when they were on previous dates. All Julia kept asking herself was, *I wonder why he ever asked me out to begin with... I wonder why he took me to that charity ball... I wonder why he left me all by myself... I wonder why he was dancing and talking to other women... I wonder what I did to obviously turn him off? I wonder, I wonder, I wonder...*

Julia did not enjoy feeling in the dark about Stephan and felt she deserved an answer. Because they had only known each other a short time, and since she had never before experienced anything similar on a date, Julia did not have the confidence to confront Stephan either in person or over the phone. She knew she might run into him in the community, and she wanted to leave him with the thought that he had, infact, blown a wonderful opportunity with her. Julia also wanted Stephan to know she had not overlooked his shabby treatment. She felt she outclassed him, despite his social standing, and she would not be victimized by that *bloodsucking Dracula.*

When I spoke with Julia, her ego was seriously bruised. Regarding past relationship patterns, she showed a tendency to put all her eggs in one basket. Julia fantasized, hoping and investing emotionally, before she devoted the time to get to know a man. She skipped interviewing and observing him first, which would have allowed her to discover his core values and see if they matched up with hers.

We discussed Julia's history with relationships further. She had been a teenaged mother and married three times previously. Her father had been unfaithful in his marriage to her mother. Her mother had married no less than five times. When she was a very little girl, she remembers her parents frequently argued. Her father had left them by the time Julia was five. While she agreed that her underlying abandonment issues repeatedly surfaced in other relationships, she also became aware of her tendency to wish for peace whatever the cost. The price she paid was a constant struggle to communicate her needs effectively rather than defensively.

Stephan tried calling Julia several times leaving messages regarding how he admired her, and how he would enjoy seeing her again. More importantly, Stephan wondered why Julia had left the party without him.

In response to Stephan's attempts to reconnect via phone, Julia sent him her "Stevie Wonder" letter I wrote on her behalf. Although the *Inspired Heart Letters* are meaningful, they are not remarkably long. To date, the longest letter I have written has been no more than two pages in length; Stephan's letter was no exception.

Stevie Wonder

Inspired Heart® Letter

Hi Stephan,

Thanks for your message, although I still feel somewhat confused. Perhaps that is because you are... (confused that is). I do find you attractive as well, and I also know you can be quite charming. More important, I think your heart is in the right place, (at least as far as being concerned with your lady friends). However, it is quite apparent to me that our dating styles are very different. If I am not mistaken, you clearly asked me to the Broomstick Ball, although... as you say, you were preoccupied.

Again, I appreciate your phone calls and the voice message. I accept your gestures as an attempt to make amends. I do wish you all the best, but as far as "dating" goes, we may be better friends than lovers.

Perhaps we will see one another again at one of these local social venues. Best of luck. I hope you find what you really want.

Take care,

Julia

Stephan replied with a rather lengthy three-page letter of apology. He explained why he had fraternized with the other women: One lady was a friend who had recently lost her father, who knew Stephan; another lady friend was a business associate he needed to talk with about an important business matter, and so it went. Stephan acknowledged his rather boorish behavior and admitted to being self-absorbed and remiss in attending to Julia. He pleaded with her for a chance to redeem himself.

Julia appreciated Stephan's detailed written response. She considered his open, if not humble, plea to give him the opportunity to try to make up for his social ineptitude rather compelling. To further assuage her sense of wonder, and to see if their initial attraction could be salvaged, she agreed to see him again.

At Stephan's persistence, they finally tried to date for a short time thereafter. However, Julia could not bring herself to trust Stephan fully. Eventually, they both agreed to shift from a romantic focus to just being friends. Nevertheless, Julia did locate a degree of personal power, since she was able to consider and acknowledge some of her internal blocks for obtaining deep emotional connections with others.

To this day, she still tends, at times, to question her lovability, or whether she can have and keep a loving relationship without settling for less than complete respect and unconditional love. I will say, she is definitely finding her way though. Julia is better able to find the humor in life, to perhaps not take herself quite so seriously while waiting for the other shoe to drop, relationship-wise. Instead, her newfound confidence seems to be reflected in her personal aspirations such as a rewarding career in sales and marketing, a valuable increase in very supportive friendships, and her growing belief that she can find and keep true love.

Allan's Story

"REHEATING THE SOUFFLÉ"

Some time ago, I received a letter request from a repeat client, Allan, who claimed full responsibility for allowing a romantic relationship with Cynthia to dissipate and eventually fall apart altogether. Allan had met Cynthia during a local Salsa dance class. He found her to not only be very attractive and a great dancer, but he truly enjoyed her vivacious personality. Their relationship lasted approximately eight months before it crumbled. Allan lamented that he had become distracted with work and health related concerns and simply did not take the time to invest in their relationship. Then, before he knew it… poof! Cynthia was gone.

Looking back, the couple had been sexually involved and Allan considered their sex life to be quite satisfying. However, Allan believed he came to take Cynthia for granted and thereby had failed to fuel the relationship by giving less time and energy or enthusiasm to it. *Old habits die young.* Likewise, eventually, their relationship just withered away.

I contend that a relationship is a separate and vulnerable entity. If it is not cared for and given regular doses of love and encouragement, over time, it will not grow or thrive. So, while Allan was looking the other way and not focusing on what he and Cynthia were creating, months later, he found himself to be quite alone and filled with regret.

Before contacting me, Allan had bumped into Cynthia in the community. She let him know she was dating someone else. A few months later, he happened to see her again. This time, she reported that she was no longer dating the other gentleman. However, Allan did not sense that Cynthia was open to rekindling their relationship. Soon after that encounter, I received Allan's call.

Allan revealed his sentiments by saying he could not stop thinking about Cynthia, what they could have been, and how he had failed miserably by being unavailable. We really looked at that. I shared one of my analogies about new relationships with Allan. I told him that the way I see it, most relationships are similar to a pregnancy. *A relationship is an actual entity created by the two individuals together.*

The first two to three months, the seed for creating a new relationship, (again *the entity*) is planted. The prospective couple initially is hopeful and anticipates the joy and wonder of bringing in a new relationship. During this initial stage, or the *first trimester*, much can occur. For instance, the seed may not take hold; there can be a sort of "miscarriage" if the relationship is unsatisfactory, despite the idea of wanting a healthy relationship. The relationship may be aborted altogether, in which case there are obvious toxic or inappropriate values or behaviors that kill off any hope for a relationship to occur. Or, the seed that is planted may take root and begin to grow. No matter how much individuals desire to have relationships, sometimes a "false pregnancy" is experienced, whereby there was only an illusion of a relationship with no substance to begin with. Either way, the relationship is terminated early on.

Getting past this initial stage, or during the *second trimester*, (approximately six months into the relationship), the two are now considered an actual couple; they are officially "pregnant!" They are showing up as a couple. However, the reality of the situation begins to set in. The new couple must consider the established commitment of exclusivity and the growing responsibility toward one another. Most of all, the relationship must be seriously desired and well-nourished emotionally on a regular basis.

I don't pass judgment on the shape or parameters of a relationship; some from the beginning are agreed upon, to be open, meaning there is not the intent of sexual exclusivity. Most of those who come to me for help, however, believe in monogamy, and a committed relationship that is one-on-one. Letters are written with this value of fidelity at the core.

By the eighth, ninth, or even tenth month, or the *third trimester*, the courtship itself may not be as whimsical or flavored by the newness of the attraction. The couple often relaxes and may not put as much effort or energy toward maintaining the initial beauty and hope once recognized. They find themselves, on one level or another, taking a step back, reconsidering the viability of sharing more time. At this point, they may even look at a possible marriage or living together through more analytical, less romantic eyes.

Enough time has elapsed by this trimester stage whereby the less charming aspects of each partner's personality may arise. Each of them may feel secure enough to let their guard down and be less careful about how they are interacting. Pause may be given, as they consider, *Just what are we giving birth to anyway?*

I have, so often, seen that at or near the close of the first year invested in a relationship, there is a certain *quid pro quo*, or unsaid contract that is being formed. Sometimes, the emotions formed are not altogether healthy or stable and do not hold promise for true love and longevity. This can be a difficult time filled with painful contractions and agonizing labor. Unfortunately, it seems that many couples do not have the stomach for it. All too often, they cut their losses and simply move on.

Unlike our parents and other generations before, it seems that we are among a generation that seeks instant gratification and has superficial notions of what a relationship is. Too many people seem to have an unwillingness to focus on the value of investing, building, and maintaining a truly deep and fulfilling love for one another. On the other hand, I also see that the superficial views are becoming worn-out or outdated.

More people are beginning to seek deeper, more meaningful relationships and wish to know themselves better. They want to "step up to the plate and hit a home run" while finding and experiencing the rewards of their efforts in the realm of love.

Back to Allan's dilemma; I was able to write an honest, humble, and quite compelling letter for him to give to Cynthia:

An Invitation to Love –Reheating the Souffle

Inspired Heart® Letter

Dear Cynthia,

I just want to take this opportunity to touch in with you and share some deeper thoughts. To be honest, I still care about you, although I may not have given you that impression, since I faded in and out of your life – at least toward the end of our time spent together. To set the record straight, and even if we never see each other again, I am compelled to let you know what I absolutely admire about you and what I find so beautiful about you both inside and out.

For starters, Cynthia, I adore your sense of fun, your amazing wit, charm, uncommon beauty and especially that unique, wonderful laugh of yours. I admire the way you approach life with such grace and the close loving connection you have with your daughter, Chloe.

It is not often that anyone meets someone they connect with in so many ways. I loved the way you made me feel, both physically and emotionally, and how we easily communicated with each other. I felt an undeniable passion between us, both in and out of the bedroom.

You were such a joy to be with, so spontaneous at times. I smile remembering that night you ran like a teenager into the bedroom to turn up the music... speaking of which, how much we enjoyed a wide variety of music together was also special to me.

So, yes, I had to let you in on my thoughts and feelings. I stand here with a heavy heart, wondering how I could ever have let you get away, at least without knowing the truth of just how I do miss you. I wonder how things might have turned out differently, if I had been more open and fearless.

Cynthia, I am hoping you will give "us" some thought. If there is a chance you'd like to see me again, I would like nothing other than to recalibrate and take some time to become even closer than before... without any walls up, to be more open with one another. I acknowledge and am sincerely invested in the thought of what a waste it would be if we did not take this chance.

You are so lovely. I own the fact that, yes, it is my real heart's desire to find love... truly, deeply, and with real partnership. Thanks for allowing me to share where I am coming from. Whatever happens, know that I care.

Yours,

Allan

Cynthia wrote back to Allan immediately after receiving his letter. Her response: "*Very few men can make me cry. Thank you for this letter. When can we have dinner together?*"

Allan called me later on to report that since the letter was received, over six months prior, he and Cynthia were able to regain their relationship with a brand-new vision and a continued sense of delight. Actually, in Allan's words: "*It has been amazing getting back with Cynthia. All she wants to do now is jump my bones... and she is still talking about that letter (lol).*"

When Love Is Not Returned

Nick's Story

"HEAD OVER HEELS: TAKING A STAND"

One client, Nick, shared his unfortunate circumstance with the woman of his dreams, Lulu. They met through their shared social circle. Lulu was a very close friend of Sasha, the paramour of one of Nick's closest friends, Carl. Therefore, Lulu was often included at many of the social functions they all attended. Nick was instantly love-struck upon meeting Lulu. He was more than pleased to share time, meals, dancing, and conversation with her whenever he could. Lulu had been divorced for several years. She was raised in the Middle East, and her previous husband was described as *über* controlling and altogether mean.

Lulu's demeanor was alluring, yet somewhat aloof. While the rather detached Lulu graciously accepted Nick's dinner invitations, the paid ski trips, tickets to concerts, and other social outings, she remained flirtatious toward him, but never actually responded, even in the slightest way, to his numerous romantic overtures. It seemed apparent that this lady enjoyed being in the power seat. While Lulu enjoyed the social camaraderie and paid entertainment perks, she certainly did not seem very interested in Nick's company otherwise.

Lulu's elusive nature continued to wreak havoc on Nick's emotional wellbeing. There was an obvious inner challenge that pressed upon his increasing desire to win her over. At one point, Nick was able to see just how unhealthy this situation was. He began to resent Lulu for being so charming, alluring, and encouraging, as he always felt in the end that he was being used, or manipulated, before he was simply dismissed over and over again.

When Nick contacted me to write his letter to Lulu, he was depleted. His sense of total rejection and shameful feelings over being taken advantage of were quite overwhelming. Nick knew that he had allowed himself to experience quite enough of this "weird game-playing." He no longer desired to place himself in harm's way emotionally with Lulu. However, he realized that he could not write her off without running into her at the many community social events they both attended unless he voluntarily went into social seclusion himself.

While Nick initially implored me to write a letter on his behalf to discourage Lulu from showing up at these shared social venues, I readily saw that Nick needed to gain a renewed sense of his personal power. There is nothing as unattractive as when someone appears overly invested and far too interested in the reactions of another. When the outcome of your communication with a particular love interest is demanded rather than simply allowed, it just seems to create more emotional unrest.

It was apparent to me that Nick could yield more attention and respect from Lulu if he replaced his anxious, doting pattern with a more polite, yet independent demeanor. At the same time, he could exercise integrity and sophistication with a proper message to Lulu informing her of his preference for new, healthier, and, from his standpoint, honest social boundaries.

To give you an idea of how this was best conveyed, I have included one of the most salient parts of the "Head over Heels – Taking a Stand" letter from Nick:

Head Over Heels

Inspired Heart® Letter

EXCERPT

Lulu,

Now that I have had a chance to draw back and understand that there could never be anything beyond a platonic, social friendship between us, I have to thank you for the experience anyhow. I feel that my awareness meter has gone way up and now I realize more fully that I cannot afford to live on assumptions or false hope. And, if I am going to experience the kind of intimacy that is real or be in a truly romantic, satisfying relationship including passion and adventure, (key components that I need to share with a lady), I must be more consciously focused on the truth.

Take care,

Nick

Lulu never acknowledged receiving Nick's letter. However, soon after, she discontinued attending the same parties and other social events. After Lulu moved on, Nick met someone else and has been enjoying a relationship with this other lady for nearly three years. Nick described his new girlfriend as physically beautiful, considerate, attentive, appreciative, very romantic, and altogether a real sweetheart.

Taking responsibility for understanding that when we continue to give to others with an underlying agenda of expecting to receive something back can backfire. We may not be able to demand respect, yet we can command respect from others and from ourselves just by staying truthful and standing in our own power despite life's disappointments. A mantra suggested herein may simply be: *I am no longer attached to outcomes.* Believe in yourself, in life's beautiful opportunities, and chances are excellent that you will begin to reap the benefits of what you believe in.

Testing the Waters… Friendship or Love?

George's Story

"MORE THAN FRIENDS"

George was quite enamored by a woman, Sheila; he romantically had dated her in the past. However, back then, the timing seemed to be wrong and their paths went in different directions. A few years later, George and Sheila ran into one another at a local social event and by the end of the evening, they decided to try casually dating one another again. When I was asked to write this letter, although they had been steadily seeing one another for over three months, their association remained platonic.

This time around, George was ultimately seeking a committed relationship. He was not interested in having a fling, and he was hoping to rekindle their romance. He enjoyed their time together so much that he was afraid of blowing it by coming on too strong, or worse, finding out that his romantic overtures would be rejected. More importantly, George did not want to risk losing their friendship as he cherished their time together, so he struggled with his ability to communicate in a more direct way. The following is an excerpt from George's letter:

More Than Friends

Inspired Heart® Letter

EXCERPT

Sheila,

With all that I have just shared with you, again, I find our connection in friendship to be priceless. Therefore, I do not want to overstep any bounds by confessing to you how much I wish we could become more than friends. With a great deal of soul searching, I find myself wanting to be in a committed partnership with a special woman. In fact, I hope to have a life partner or be married again. If you are at all interested in exploring our relationship to see what new romantic adventures await us, please let me know.

Again, preserving our friendship and our quality time together is deeply important to me no matter where your feelings are at. I also understand that timing is everything, yet life is too short for me not to express what is in my heart. Whew! I said it! Well, I do look forward to our time together on Saturday and to hear your thoughts on where we stand."

Yours,

George

With a true sense of style and valor, George had the letter delivered to Sheila's workplace along with an amazing bouquet of flowers. When he picked her up for their outing the following Saturday, Sheila also had a letter prepared for George, which she read to him in the car. As it turns out, they both shared similar sentiments such as a mutual physical attraction, and a desire to find lasting love and partnership. Likewise, they both cherished their time together as friends agreeing upon George's terminology that their connection in friendship was "priceless"

Interestingly, Sheila's real concern prior to becoming romantically involved with George was she worried about their different political views. Sheila is a staunch Republican and George is a Democrat. Incredible! The thought of denying true love for the sake of politics seemed ludicrous to me, although George's lady friend obviously held a deep concern for political agendas. Sheila was finally able to share what she considered to be a possible deal-breaker, as well as what she valued as important.

Nevertheless, through this conversation initiated through letters, these two were finally able to shed some light upon their mutual attraction for one another, their romantic aspirations, and George was able to calm Sheila's fears over their political differences. Open, honest communication may seem daunting at times, but, as was conveyed in George's letter, "Life is too short not to express what is in one's heart."

Cheryl's Story

"BEFORE YOU BLOW OUT THE CANDLES"

Cheryl, a drop-dead gorgeous *femme-fatal* redhead, who turned heads wherever she went, seemed to end up with men who definitely desired her, yet also felt they had to compete for power when they were with her. Underneath her sultry good looks, she was actually a very soft, gentle soul who craved to be cared for and had difficulty trusting that a man would ever be true to her.

While the men she became involved with were not necessarily physically attractive, they usually were good providers and seemed to offer Cheryl the caring and stability she craved. There was one man, Kevin, in particular, whom she knew over many years. From time to time, they tried to make a go of their relationship. However, it seemed that Kevin resented the attention Cheryl received when they were out together. Too often, he felt compelled to put her down verbally, and otherwise "put her in her place."

Cheryl described Kevin's pattern of behavior as the "rubber-band effect." He was at times exceptionally romantic, attentive, considerate, and nurturing, while other times, he gave mixed messages that seemed self-centered and controlling. For instance, he wanted her to be available for him at his convenience, yet he also wanted her to be independent and get a higher paying job, so she could pay her way.

Finally, Cheryl had her fill of the crazy-making drama, and took a time-out by moving about two hours away. She found a high paying position in executive sales for an elegant fashion and lifestyle magazine, and was moving forward with her life. She wished to prove to Kevin that she was intelligent, capable, and self-sufficient.

There is an inherent need to have completion for matters of the heart. And when it is not achieved, it may become confusing and remain troubling. Despite her relocation and new start in life, Cheryl and Kevin did remain in touch. They even visited one another on certain weekends. However, Cheryl's feelings for Kevin waxed and waned in synchronicity with his apparent mood swings.

Although she was trying to re-establish herself in a new community, at times, it seemed, Kevin could not keep from antagonizing her, even from a distance. I saw that Cheryl had a tendency to cave in and try to fix their broken relationship. However, when she dishonored herself, by placating Kevin's ego and denying her own worth, their rapport became exceedingly difficult. It was clear she also needed to have a boosted sense of personal power.

Once, after Kevin had insulted her on the telephone, he alluded that he had been seeing other women. Moreover, Kevin had not been in contact with Cheryl for a couple weeks. It was nearing his birthday, when Kevin sent a simple, contrived *Mother's Day* greeting to Cheryl via text message. Cheryl received it as a limp excuse for keeping her on the hook and called upon me to write an *Inspired Heart Letter* to Kevin. The letter was Cheryl's response and, actually, a clear indicator that she was on the road to success:

Before You Blow Out The Candles

Inspired Heart® Letter

Dear Kevin,

Thanks for the Mother's Day wish. I guess this means you still like me after all, (lol). I have been quite busy, as you might imagine… re-establishing myself. The desert is so gorgeous, but definitely warming up!

It is so funny how life works out. It seems that change is one thing we can all count on. Moving away was the best thing for me. I am definitely becoming more fearless and trusting since each day brings a new experience; and it feels so good. In spite of those heartfelt disappointments surrounding our time together, all the new blessings and opportunities that are coming in continue to amaze me. I guess that's just life's process; by letting go and trusting, we are able to grow despite the little setbacks along the way.

Well, Kevin, while I am busy re-inventing myself, I truly wish you all the best. As I already have, I hope you can see the goodness and the gift that was there by sharing our time together. Again, thanks for the thoughtful message, as it feels so good to know we have actually cleared up the past. By the way, have a Happy Birthday, Kevin. I will definitely raise my glass to you then.

Yours truly,

Cheryl

Through this exhausting and demeaning experience with Kevin, Cheryl received a huge wake-up call. She claimed that just reading this short, yet significant letter fueled her sense for resolving any emotional loose ends and moving on. She concluded that along with the *Kevin experience*, her previous choices for potential partners were oddly based in illusion. Cheryl had to learn the lesson of self-reliance and the ability to trust her own wisdom to make sound decisions that supported her personal evolvement.

Cheryl learned also to appreciate her innate strength and has definitely developed the determination to find a deeper, healthier, more loving relationship. It seems that Cheryl had difficulty locating her own true core values and subjugated her needs for the sake of being in a relationship, no matter the price. When we have journeyed so deeply into the abyss, yet find our way back to ourselves, the lesson is so profound and so encouraging that it will never be repeated.

Cheryl saw Kevin a year later. In their conversation, he mentioned that receiving this significant letter was devastating. In his words, "It just killed me…" I believe this suggests that his power to exert control through his back and forth or "rubber-band" maneuvers had finally been squelched. Or should we say, he finally got it that Cheryl ultimately *just blew him off.* Furthermore, soon after, Kevin attempted to re-establish their relationship with a vow to marry Cheryl.

Apparently, when it seemed that Cheryl no longer needed Kevin to feel whole and complete, suddenly she appeared more desirable to him. Or, perhaps, Kevin actually recognized her value. An interesting human phenomenon is that we more often hold increased value for that which is earned.

Cheryl admitted that her ability to detach without further remorse energetically created an opening. This resulted in a new dynamic between Cheryl and Kevin. I call it *the gift of the chase.* When someone acts too needy, is too accommodating, or functions in a co-dependent mode, they fail to honor themselves first; they sell themselves way too short and lose their worth in the eyes of the other.

Cheryl gave up pursuing her romantic dream by placing so much of her energy into pleasing Kevin at her own emotional expense. Some-times, it takes getting really clear, and a well written communication can provide that support. After delivery of this letter, Cheryl actually was able to walk away with her head held high and her personal integrity intact.

What's more, Kevin's attitude toward Cheryl shifted. He understood that he no longer held any real power over her. In that instant, his cocky attitude felt depleted and he began to look at Cheryl with renewed interest.

Most likely, Kevin's ego was challenged by the sense of rejection that surfaced with Cheryl's newfound independence. As a result, this served to ignite a renewed desire to pursue her once again. Unfortunately, the energy that could have been positively focused upon building a healthy foundation for love, instead, was spent in a power play.

For some, real intimacy seems unreachable. They have difficulty trusting that someone will just love them as they are. For them, the quest for love goes hand in hand with pain. The pain they knew as a child growing up is familiar, feels natural, and therefore is within their comfort zone of what they have come to know and expect. It is the underlying wounded heart that gets in the way of enjoying love on a deeper level or in a healthier way.

Although Cheryl and Kevin finally parted company, Cheryl learned a profound lesson by recognizing her own self-worth. That lesson was understanding that being vindictive is not only counter-productive, but contradicts the advice of our better angels.

Choosing to End an Unfulfilling Relationship

THE DEARLY DEPARTED

Not enough may be said regarding the importance of having defined, clear-cut, personal boundaries. Knowing what your own deal breakers are. I call it the *Must Be* list. If you are in a relationship that you find dishonoring or lacking in integrity, or if your value system is violated, the wisest choice may be to walk away. We do not have the power to change someone else. However, we can inspire others in our life to change by communicating our needs, preferences, and relationship goals.

Getting clear on what exactly that looks like is your responsibility. By developing your own personal guidelines, you are taking the first step toward self-reliance. When we can trust our judgment, decisions around relationship concerns are so much easier. This also means that we too can be inspired by others. Staying open to change is positive, but staying focused on what we will and will not tolerate increases our relationship success with ourselves and anyone else.

When we choose to leave a dysfunctional, toxic, or dissatisfying relationship, there certainly can be a grieving process that takes place. We may hold onto feelings of denial and anger or emotionally shut down before finally accepting that it is really over. The order of these emotional states may fluctuate. Once we have concluded that there is nothing else to be done then we can surrender. At that moment, we are ready to finally take that flight into a healthier way of being. Then we can consider new prospects for happiness, and are able to forgive and move forward. There is something to be said, however, for leaving a relationship in style.

There is another type of healing that is felt when we have regained our personal integrity; when we no longer feel confused, victimized, or resentful, and can hold our head up with real thankfulness for the experience. Moreover, I find it very satisfying to leave a relationship in such a way that denies the former partner the opportunity to redeem themselves at the other person's expense.

When someone breaks off the relationship and moves on, the person who was left behind may try to justify the situation by claiming their former partner turned out to be an awful person in some way. This is face-saving ego gratification and a common reaction or coping mechanism for failed romance and relationships. However, if the person who breaks off the relationship presents themself in such a way that is beautiful or elegant and offers kindness, compassion, and well wishes, the other partner being left behind may ponder just how he or she could let a fabulous person like that get away. At the very least, there is less opportunity for negativity to follow.

On the other hand, if we let our emotions get the best of us and leave in a vengeful rage, or with some type of negative drama, the person being left actually may have a sense of relief, since the person leaving acted like such a terrible person. Moreover, it serves to justify the idea that the failed relationship was the fault of that *bitch* or that *bastard*, and lets the other person off the hook for sharing in the responsibility for what took place.

I advise that when a relationship is over, try to put some pep in your step, some glide in your stride; and while it is best to make a clean break, burning emotional bridges along the way can often backfire. This should be considered if you frequent the same local spots or have common friendships or other associations. Should you happen to encounter your previous partner, act graciously, kindly, and even joyfully and discover how self-empowering that can be.

Jennifer's Story

"BOY IN THE HOOD"

Jennifer knew Greg since she was only four and he was ten. Jennifer always looked up to Greg with deep admiration. Not only were they neighbors, but their mothers were best friends until Greg's mother passed away some years ago. Their worlds remained connected through this close family friendship.

At one point, long after each had divorced, they found a type of tender comfort with one another. Over time, they acknowledged their long-time underlying attraction and eventually became romantically involved. Since they each had born witness to one another's former marriage disasters, knew each other's children, and otherwise had followed each other's lives, they had an unusual, yet relaxed, connection.

Jennifer yearned to be in a committed, caring relationship. She felt uneasy being alone without a man in her life. Her marriage had been rocky, to say the least, before she and her former husband called it quits.

She considered Greg to be the "Steady-Eddy" rock; someone she could trust; someone she felt she knew. She rationalized that they would be a great match. However, it seemed that Jennifer's destiny to find true love was not to simply slip into a cushy-comfy relationship, at least, not yet. You see, wherever we go, we take ourselves with us. Unless we can truly face our emotional pain head on and transform it, chances are that sacred wound, that dysfunctional pattern, will continue to wreak havoc in future relationships. And so it was for Jennifer.

Before you knew it, Jennifer dove right into Greg's arms. Oops! Unfortunately though, despite their long-standing neighborhood affiliation etc., Jennifer soon discovered that Greg was a womanizer. Instead of enjoying the peace and security she so longed for, she found herself snooping in his emails, checking his phone messages, and yes, discovering his two-timing ways with another woman.

Jennifer was quite distraught when she asked me to write her letter to Greg. She was terribly hurt and felt betrayed on many levels. Although their romance was short-lived and Greg was surely a disappointment, she felt even more upset that he did not take her seriously, that he still considered her to be the little kid down the street. Actually, Jennifer felt ashamed that she had thrown herself into this situation without first considering what their mutual aim would be beyond the physical intimacy and her need for connection. Jennifer wished to redeem herself and move on in the best way.

Boy in the Hood

Inspired Heart® Letter

Greg,

I just want to share with you where I am at in looking at how we fit into one another's experience. You have been a part of my life for most of my life, and that is pretty amazing in itself. I think I fell in love with you the first time that I saw you while riding my tricycle. Ever since then, to one degree or another, we have been involved, either as friends or lovers. Just knowing you, whether we see each other or not, has truly been a source of comfort. Actually, when I think about it, we have known each other for about 38 years!

I have had the privilege of seeing your life evolve through its own twists and turns, and I am very proud of all of your accomplishments. I see you as a loving father to your gorgeous daughters and as a great contributor through your work. And, my life has also been an adventure, mostly within the realm of relationships. With my birthday approaching, bringing in this New Year and with my dad's passing last year, I am taking some time to reflect on what I have learned with regards to physical and emotional connections. I am beginning to realize what I hold dear for my future. I fully realize that I need to make some real shifts in how I live and approach life.

Although, we certainly have a long history, Greg, our relationship has never felt quite defined for me. I am certain that I need more *stability in my life on all levels. Not only am I making strides with my career, but also I can no longer settle for anything less than true love with a committed romantic partner. My wish is that you receive this letter in the light of respect for our very long-term friendship.*

As you know, real friendship is based on trust and honesty. In short, with all honesty, I must draw a line on any further physical relationship with you. Please know that although our romantic connection has proven to be a disappointment, I acknowledge our family-like bond. I do care and will remain your dear friend forever."

Always,

Jennifer

I have followed Jennifer's story over the years. She and Greg touch in with one another from time to time, although their rapport is quite different now. Based on the feedback from Jennifer, Greg seems to have a growing admiration for her. In fact, he has alluded that he considers himself to be more than a notch below her regarding class and integrity.

Greg made the analogy once by drawing a comparison to Jennifer, considering her as being like a fine steak while he believes he is only a hamburger. Pass the pickles!

Mark's Story

"BLACK BIRD BYE-BYE"

Mark, a handsome, young man in his late twenties who worked in the computer industry, had been living with his girlfriend, Georgina, until she lost her job and decided to take a break from life by backpacking through Europe with another girlfriend before returning back home to look for a new job. Mark graciously supported her sense of adventure, and thought to himself, upon her return home, he would propose marriage.

As it turned out, once she embarked upon her European travels, Georgina seemed to disappear off the radar altogether. While he worried about her safety and whereabouts, occasionally, Mark would receive a short phone call or text message. Then, weeks would go by without returning Mark's numerous phone calls. When they did speak on the phone, Georgina seemed evasive, emotionally cut off, and farther away than ever.

When her money ran out and she returned to America, (some months later), she not only broke off her relationship with Mark, but decided to move back with her parents. Perhaps because she felt unsuccessful in life, trapped, too needy... (God only knows), for some reason, Georgina seemed depressed, despondent, and unable to talk about her change of heart, or why she distanced herself from Mark. Georgina walked out of the relationship altogether through a rather cryptic email, simply saying she had a lot to figure out, needed to be with her family on the East Coast, was starting to see a therapist, and must move on.

As a result, Mark experienced a profound sense of confusion and betrayal. Moreover, he loved Georgina and was quite worried about her wellbeing. Shortly after this, he contacted me. The following is an excerpt from Mark's letter.

Black Bird, Bye-Bye

Inspired Heart® Letter

EXCERPT

Georgina,

The end of our relationship, and eventually, the end of my belief that we would finally be together for the rest of our lives, has been a very sad and disappointing experience for me. It is probably one of the most difficult emotional experiences that I have endured to this point in my life.

Over the last several months, I have learned the hard way, that some lessons in life can be overwhelmingly difficult and painful. Ironically, those tend to be the important ones. Right now, I am trying not only to focus on a positive future that includes healthy relationships and, hopefully, building a life with the right person, but now I realize that I need to honor myself in the process, (regardless of what impact that may have). I am solely responsible for my own happiness, including surrounding myself with positive, sincere, supportive people, who I can rely on and who share similar values.

Although I experienced a great deal of heartache during our relationship, and in the weeks and months following our breakup, instead of trying to assign blame and holding onto any negative emotions, I am trying to take responsibility for my life and my happiness by looking forward instead of looking back.

At this point, after listening to your messages over the last couple weeks and trying to understand your perspective and the situation you found yourself in, I do believe that you are sincerely sorry; and I appreciate your apology. Thank you for that. There are still things that I cannot, and probably will never understand. But, I think we can both benefit from being hopeful for the future and learning from the past.

I appreciate that you want me to be happy. I really do wish that for you as well. I could never wish you anything less

Take care,

Mark

Mark did receive a heartfelt reply from Georgina. She telephoned him to explain her disappearance and need to end their relationship. She actually became involved with another man she met while she was in France and was dealing with some drama surrounding that relationship.

Being honest with the facts, even if your partner is not, speaks well of you and helps you stand tall as you walk the road of relationship breakup and recovery.

Grace's Story

"THE VIRTUE OF FORGIVENESS"

Another client, Grace, who struggled over time with the fantasy of having a solid, romantic relationship with a long-distance lover, Blake, whom she thought was an ideal partner, was finally forced to see her situation for what it really was. Grace tried to deal with her uncertainty and bewilderment for a while. Eventually, she discovered during a telephone conversation, Blake was not really committed, or for that matter, faithful. She found out he was seeing another woman on the side. The following letter was written.

Sympathy for the Devil

Inspired Heart® Letter

Dear Blake,

After our brief conversation last week, I had to catch my breath before sharing my final thoughts regarding our experience together. I now realize that we must each take responsibility for how we live, how we allow others to treat us, and, more importantly, how we treat ourselves. I appreciate your honesty by coming clean with me and sharing your duplicity. I actually felt a certain sense of relief knowing that this is the end of any further game-playing, which often left me feeling unsure or confused. More than that, Blake, I can and do forgive you.

It feels like I am off the hook in a weird, but wonderful, way. I finally realize the truth of us. Whenever there was a real sense of closeness, it somehow was disrupted. I have gained so much insight through knowing you. I now clearly understand that you and I could never have a genuine, loving intimacy, or true commitment to one another. Between your complexities and my willingness to only hope for the best, our relationship was inevitably doomed.

Having said all of that, I am now even more committed to finding real love and being in an amazing partnership with the right man. So, I guess, on that note, I forgive myself as well. I forgive myself for entertaining the notion, or putting any undue energy toward the possibility of finding true love with you. Nevertheless, as a final result, thankfully, a lesson for having a deeper sense of self-respect was well learned. Please take care, may your future be truly blessed.

Sincerely,

Grace

Fortunately, Grace was able to see that she had placed all her eggs in one basket before she and Blake had arrived at a mutual commitment regarding their connection. She was certainly hurt, yet considered this experience to sharpen her awareness and diminish her tendency to follow her heart based upon assumptions. Discovering each other's values or notions for what sort of connection you both are seeking is paramount before deciding to invest your hopes or dreams or fantasizing about a particular outcome which may be unrealistic.

HOW TO *BE* IN ORDER TO *HAVE* A HEALTHY RELATIONSHIP

Among the sample letters, excerpts from letters written, and the scenarios that brought forth these *Inspired Heart Letters*, for all of those who are seeking the fulfillment of love and healthy partnership with another, the common ground surrounding each situation previously described, is discovered with the following pearls of wisdom:

- Develop a healthy relationship with yourself before you look to find happiness with someone else. Relationships do not complete who you are. They can, however, be an enhancement to your life and to a sense of wellbeing.

- Treat others as you wish to be treated.

- Treat yourself as you wished to be treated by others.

- Take time to compare and contrast your core values with a prospective romantic partner.

- A definition of a healthy relationship is when each person in that coupling is allowed the freedom to be who they are, (as long as there is mutual honoring and respect), without fear of any negative retribution from their significant other.

- Be mindful that healthy, loving relationships naturally complement one another. They do not detract or diminish either partner. I believe this is wonderfully coined in the expression, *Why do I have to give up me to be loved by you?*

- Consider what type of relationships you tend to attract. Often, there are common themes or a particular life lesson offered through the challenge, or the satisfaction, experienced when you open your heart to another.

- Clean up any unresolved negative feelings about yourself or other(s). The need to forgive may go even farther back than you can remember. Infants and children are born with emotions and experience life at face value. Feeling unsafe, unlovable, guilty, ashamed, abandoned, inadequate, angry, or rejected, etc. may be the result of early negative experiences that influenced your sense of self. When we are out of alignment with our true nature and disconnected from our souls, we may create foul, hurtful patterns that continue to show up in our relationships with others. There may be an unconscious negative emotional programming that sets one up for failure.

- Trust that underneath it all, we each create our own life experiences. We alone are responsible for our happiness and wellbeing. As it has been said before, *Negativity is unrealized good.* Perceived failures can contribute to a deeper wisdom about ourselves.

- Rather than casting aspersions or blaming anyone else, decide to be more aware and personally accountable. Take stock of what does and does not work for you or your relationship.

- Be open and available to receive more positive loving experiences. Finally, be thankful for the newfound wisdom received.

Open for Love

DESPERADOS

When our hopes are dashed or we feel disappointed, and when our heart breaks, often there are one of two mindsets that develop. The first reaction may be an overwhelming sense of need. *I need to feel loved, I need to find love, I need to be in a relationship, I need to finally get married,* or (especially for women), *my clock is ticking… I need to have children and a sense of family…* or *I just don't want to grow old alone.* These beliefs are usually followed by an ever growing, (although perhaps unrealized), desperation. The notion that somehow you may never find true love or the opportunity has passed you by sends a radical message to your brain, or to your ego and identity. This instills an underlying yet intense sense of fear. It is almost as though some sort of sink or swim survival mechanism kicks in. Often, this propels the *single person looking for love* to effort and strive even more in order to find their soul mate. It's as though they are on a mission and their very sense of ever finding true happiness depends upon finding their own special someone.

Unfortunately, what we chase after more often eludes us. All those single bars or *meat markets* are crammed full of single people waiting and hoping to find their perfect match. Finding the *Happy Hour* crowd, as you mix and mingle, you may notice that sometimes they are hooking up or meeting someone and sometimes ending up as just part of the "two o'clock shuffle." While it's entirely possible you serendipitously meet your perfect partner, you might become vaguely aware that you have lowered your standards, if not your expectations. For some, this might be leaving with someone or even just anyone. Or for others, after another night of disappointment, just shuffling out the door and shuffling home to face yet another day… alone.

When people are afraid, they may become aggressive or act overly seductive trying anything to win at finding love. With all this social bravado, they may wear themselves out trying to impress and actually end up losing their confidence. Fear is like radar. It can fill up the room and be felt with every encounter. When anyone comes across as too needy or desperate, their prospect for finding someone fabulous to love is greatly diminished.

So, rather than sitting at the edge of your bar stool, leaning forward, with eyes glazed, craning your neck and leering at someone from across the bar, you might want to consider just how very unappealing you may appear. Love is letting go of fear. Stop searching for love. Instead, allow love to arrive because you *know* it will. You can manifest love only when you are truly available for it and not afraid to receive it nor afraid of losing it. Confidence is a great substitute for alcohol, and without the hangover!

SHUT-DOWNS

The other mindset that may result after enough emotional wounding around hurtful or disappointing relationships is to simply become closed off emotionally. There are plenty of jaded cynics out there. It truly saddens me when I encounter so many single people who are suspicious, untrusting, and actually predict that love is painful, or just not worth the hassle. These single types are so completely wounded that they may decide they are through with love and the sense of being used or taken advantage of, or being lied or cheated on, or strung along for years without a real commitment etc.. I see them as hardened, unapproachable, and to a certain degree living in a self-imposed prison of lonely regret or resentment. Given enough time, unfortunately with a negative attitude, the heart closes and the individual may become apathetic, numb or what is referred to as *shut-down.*

The *shut-down* single usually does not want to hear about their friends who are "in love." In fact, after hearing that a friend has found someone or is newly engaged for example, the news is likely met with a negative reaction such as "*So what's wrong with him or her?... Have you done a background check yet?... Why did she get divorced anyway?... Why hasn't he ever married before?*" The list goes on. Since misery does love company, it may be unnerving for the shut-down friend to consider that one of their own may actually be leaving the herd.

Our experiences especially within the realm of dating and relation-ships are opportunities in which to grow. For the *single looking for love,* one can contemplate what works and does not work. A deeper personal awareness can then become heightened for finding the right attributes in another that meshes with whom the individuals involved really are. The key is to take the time to get to know someone. Instead of quickly dismissing a potential partner based purely on a superficial list of social status or physical traits, there might actually be an opportunity missed for discovering an emotionally substantial, positive connection.

Why do we take everything so personally? If you meet someone who turns out to be a jerk, then why would you either somehow make it your fault or draw the conclusion that all men or all women are jerks? Personally, I cannot fathom giving anyone that type of power. After the bad experience with someone is over, that unfortunate creep goes on his or her merry or not so merry way. So what?

Too often the soon-to-be *shut down* single wallows in the drama, the pain, and cannot seem to rise above the post-traumatic stress. Take the time to grieve and work through the pain, but not too much time. Life is too short; you are too precious. Avoid judgment, condemnation, or giving up on love. Instead, feel happy that you have managed to extricate yourself from a difficult or unhappy situation and now have an opportunity to move on.

Remember, keep your heart open. That is the key. Living in fear of rejection or desperation surrounding matters of your heart is painful and emotionally draining. Shutting down, throwing your hands up and walking away from all hope of finding love is worse. Affirm your own lovability without trying but by being in your true nature, just as you are. Thank God or the universe for bringing your perfect loving partner to you at the right time and in the right way. And be all that you wish to attract. When you are open, clear, and know you are lovable, chances are you will not attract a jaded cynic and you will easily notice and not be so attracted to *Desperados* or others that simply come on too strong or try too hard. Instead, you might just meet someone who resonates where you do, in a positive, loving space. So relax, trust in the universal law of attraction. Believe.

Chapter 4

Letter Theme – Marriage

TANGLED KNOTS: MARITAL CONFLICTS
LETTERS TO A SPOUSE

When love leads to marriage, the challenge is staying in love throughout the various stages of life. I often thought that the symbolism of the bride's veil is such that after the initial courtship is over, or once the knot is tied and the veil has been lifted, the new Mister and Misses must face life's challenges together. For some, losing the zest for the notion of "happily ever after" can be rather devastating.

I contend that as humans, our relationships are our best teachers, since we have unique opportunities to learn deeply about ourselves from matters of the heart. This is quite true within the logistics of marriage. The binding marital commitment, or the promise to love and to hold… no matter what, creates the opportunity to cherish the marriage as a unique entity. What the couple builds together is fundamental, or even more important than individual, separate desires.

I can consider no better analogy than a garden. Marriages that flourish must be planted with loving intentions that can only take root, grow, and blossom with plenty of care and attention. Trust is the compost, the enriched soil, from which all else grows. When the trust is broken for whatever reason, it weakens the allegiance toward one another. Guilt, shame, and resentment are emotional states that disguise the underlying fear that may tarnish the sanctity of the relationship.

If you are single and looking to find true love, and perhaps marriage, you can attract your soul mate for a healthy relationship by showing up with integrity, honor, and consideration. More than that, you magnetize love from another by being authentic, taking good care of yourself physically, emotionally, and spiritually, and speaking your truth with kindness, while living in gratitude and appreciation. These elements must also be enlivened and contained in the ongoing marital experience. Moreover, couples who support one another during times of stress actually strengthen their bond.

Sometimes, we can lose sight of ourselves and of the bigger picture, which is the marriage itself. When this occurs, we may not be as attractive to one another. The marriage may become more fragile, undernourished, or starved for love and affection. And, one spouse alone cannot maintain a marriage, as this is definitely a joint effort.

There is something to be said for those who take the plunge with all the ideal enthusiasm of a romantic and for those who maintain the honor and diligence attributed to sound partnerships. More often, those individuals or couples who do "the work" lovingly and consciously, evolve over time. Couples are in the unique situation to mirror back to one another that which is loving and wholesome or that which is in need of emotional/psychic repair.

Our personal foundation, of course, is heavily influenced by our parents and early childhood experiences. Our ability to give and receive love is in direct alignment with how open we are to being in our true nature without learned negative coping skills, or other self-preserving defense mechanisms. For example, a child who experiences emotional rejection from parent(s) or caretakers may emotionally shut down or insulate him or herself from feeling safe enough to be open and vulnerable. This individual may develop a personality style that may be manipulative, self-centered, or inevitably pushes love away.

When someone is emotionally armored, then the possibility for intimacy is greatly diminished. And, whereas, *water seeks its own level*, there tends to be a magnetic force attracting another who also struggles with intimacy, although usually expressed in a different way. For example, narcissistic personality types often find themselves in a relationship with a co-dependent personality. Ostensibly, it seems that they may each be getting their needs met. The narcissist may act in self-absorbed, self-gratifying ways that attract the co-dependent who minimizes his or her own innate need for love through feelings of unworthiness and focuses on catering to the whims of the narcissist. However, these personality types never truly feel safe to be in an authentic loving relationship. They are unwilling to let their emotional defenses down. Moreover, they do not enjoy the sense of personal freedom that comes with having a loving relationship toward their own self, let alone with another.

Suzanne's Story

"WAKE-UP CALL"

The following letter proved to be no less than an act of Divine intervention for Suzanne, a lovely and stunningly beautiful woman, with a gentle spirit. Suzanne had given up so many of life's opportunities while trapped in a dysfunctional marriage bereft of the type of love and supportive caring that her soul craved. Suzanne described her husband, David, as being an unyielding perfectionist. No matter how much she tried to be the most perfect wife in every way, David somehow always made her feel wrong and as though she was just not good enough. He was often critical, belittling and seemed indifferent to her need to feel accepted and cherished.

Whenever Suzanne tried to talk to her husband, they usually ended up arguing and David would take off, sometimes for days. Moreover, as their connection grew more distant, Suzanne suspected that David was seeing another woman on the side. Despite six months of couple's therapy including a marital retreat, their marriage remained bitterly painful.

Suzanne could not bear the loneliness and frustration she felt and finally gathered the strength to leave her marriage. She initially called upon me to write an *Inspired Heart Letter* to David as a final gesture to possibly salvage their relationship. However, as she and I discussed their long-standing and depleted situation, and, more importantly, how she must take responsibility for her own happiness, Suzanne began to see the light.

She soon realized that she was in a dead-end marriage and a self-imposed prison. While she was married to the wrong guy, ultimately she created her own reality. The following is her letter to David. This *Inspired Heart Letter* issued David his walking papers and Suzanne's passage to freedom:

Sleeping Beauty

Inspired Heart® Letter

Dear David,

This is just a note of appreciation. I trust you will receive it in that light. I simply must give you my genuine, heartfelt thanks for being there for me throughout the years. Yes, it is true. Although perhaps I did not always consciously want all those painful, draining experiences with you, it seems that actually in an odd way, I discovered in the process of <u>forgiveness</u>, that I surely needed to learn some very important truths about myself.

I would like to share with you that our relationship, the good, the bad, and certainly the ugly, has turned out to be a real gift for me. It has been said, the "most meaningful gifts in life are often wrapped in sandpaper." Our trials and tribulations were indeed painful for me. It was despairing, at times, to realize that my dream of enjoying a fulfilling life with you, (including true love, passion, intimacy, commitment, honoring one another, growing through life's challenges, just knowing that, no matter what, we could weather any storm and keep growing together in a loving partnership), would simply never ever happen. However, despite those awful, hideous rocks in the road, this whole experience has finally changed me forever!

If you care to know, keeping reading…

I am also so very grateful to you for allowing me the time and space to heal. This has been an inward journey, David. I have come to learn that I do create my own reality. Now I am seeing and starting to experience and know who I really am. I find the more honest I can be with my life or the more I honor my feelings, stay in complete integrity regarding how I am treated by others and more importantly, how I regard and treat myself, the happier my life is. As a result, all new possibilities are manifesting... and that is undeniably rewarding!

Yes, this whole Suzanne-David episode does seem to have a happier ending after all. It feels as though I have emerged from a weird trance. Just like Sleeping Beauty, if you can imagine, who could only be awakened by true love.

You are not, and never were my Prince Charming. But that does not mean, you cannot be the Prince Charming for someone else. I am now awakened to a newfound sense of myself, discovering my innate beauty. My absolute self-worth is far more powerful than anything.

If it was not for our tempestuous journey together, I fear I may have never realized, and on such a deep level, my own strength and fortitude. Because of you, our difficulties... or rather challenges, I am no longer able to ever give my power away to another, not for the sake of "peace" or to appease anyone else. When I forfeit my own values and when I forsake my own need to express myself or deny what I need, or what I know to be true, and tolerate others' cruelty, manipulations, drama, and overall disrespect, then I am out of integrity with life, and with myself.

Thankfully, I am quite clear that I can now more fully be in a loving, healthy relationship where I can freely surrender myself and my heart while feeling safe. I now only surround myself with others who are open, kind, and actually respect and appreciate me for who I am.

Again, this has, in fact, been such a difficult lesson. While you may not believe it, I am sincere when I say Thank You! It was you, David, that through it all, helped me to finally fly free... to have my "butterfly moment." In saying goodbye to you, I do hold you in the light of peace.

I hope you too can find the silver lining in our experience. You know, relationships have often been a challenge for me. Matters of the heart haven't previously been an area that came easily or that I ever felt strong or courageous in. Just as the song goes, "I was looking for love in all the wrong places." The way I feel now, I no longer have to search for love, I am whole. I am enough. And I am very lovable just as I am. Good luck in your journey, David.

Have a good life. Thanks again,"

Suzanne

You see, often our most meaningful lessons in life are discovered through emotional trauma or setbacks. Our teachers may show up in the most unexpected ways. In Suzanne's case, while her husband continued to demoralize her, she spent years trying to fix their marriage. Yet, no matter what, she could never measure up to his ideals. I believe our soul agrees to or invites us into certain painful situations that creates an opportunity to evolve and remember who we truly are: someone who is simply Divine, loving, and lovable.

Suzanne had a dramatic awakening as a result of this letter. Truly, she awoke to her own personal power, and moved forward with a renewed sense of purpose and passion. This letter is a gift to so many who feel stuck while trying to swim against the tide.

That old saying, *When life hands you a lemon, make lemonade,* defines the sweetness that is available when we move to a higher ground.

Valery's Story

"RAGGEDY ANDY"

Once, there was a woman, Valery, who held a very important job in a major international import company. She was very bright, with an astute business sense, quite attractive, sophisticated, and rather gentle in nature. She enjoyed her high-profile position in the financial world and took the demands of her job in stride.

Valery married a gentleman from the British Isles, Andre, who was approximately fifteen years her senior. He was an accomplished artist who relocated to her well-appointed luxury home in North Carolina. However, during their six years of marriage, Andre had not worked, nor had he financially contributed to their wellbeing. Instead, this lady often complained to her close friends that she felt resentful for his lack of responsibility toward shared living expenses.

Not only was he dead weight financially, but he continued to make unreasonable demands of her time and energy. For example, after she had worked a twelve-hour day, Andre would call his wife and demand she stop for groceries at the store on her way home. (After all, she was already in the car, why should he have to make the extra effort?) Valery and Andre's arguments and marital dissatisfaction continued to increase, until Valery ran out of steam, and tried to pacify the situation.

One night, Valery recalled opening the refrigerator and a bottle of water flew out and smashed on the floor. Andre immediately growled at her to *"Clean up the 'bloody mess' before I could possibly cut my foot!"* Well, instead of chasing him around the house with the biggest shard of broken glass, Valery succumbed to his wishes and quickly cleaned up the mess without the least snivel. This refined, capable woman was experiencing acute health challenges, such as migraine headaches, debilitating back pain, and insomnia.

Her friends implored her to leave this parasite, but she held steadfast hoping her marriage would somehow be successful. Perhaps it was just that, an overwhelming fear of failure, since she was such an accomplished winner in other aspects of her life. At any rate, despite Valery's attempts to communicate her angst, the marriage continued to be a source of frustration and depletion. Finally, she called upon me to intervene and write an *Inspired Heart Letter*. It went like this:

Raggedy Andy

Inspired Heart® Letter

Dear Andre,

After today's awful argument, I felt quite upset and frustrated with you, with myself, and with how we behave as a couple. I managed to somehow take pause, seize the opportunity to earnestly reflect back upon how we live, and take a reality check on just how far we have fallen from being the passionately in-love and dynamic couple we once were.

With the understanding that one's mental outlook, emotions, and physical body are interrelated, I am convinced that my overwhelming disappointment and sadness have a direct consequence upon my health. I made a firm decision today, Andre. That decision is to choose "life and the pursuit of happiness" even if that means I must be liberated from our marriage.

While we began our marriage with the best of intentions, somehow it has gotten way out of balance. We have been cast in the unfavorable roles of me, the provider, and you, the dependent. Moreover, we have been acting our parts like an ongoing broken record. I get to be seen as domineering and you get to be seen as oppositional-defiant. All the while, this has taken a very toxic toll on our relationship.

When we first started out as a couple, it was my clear understanding that you and I would build an amazing life together while we each pursued our own careers and talents. I believed in you then, and actually, I still do believe that you are immensely creative and knowledgeable. However, as your career path has veered, somehow, one way or another, I've received the brunt of your misguided decisions, whereupon your feeling displaced is then my fault. Evidently, you are feeling stuck, your outlook is limited, and I am paying a huge price for that in so many ways.

I do realize that I am not responsible for your happiness. However, I am fully aware that I am responsible for my own happiness. Being co-dependent is a luxury I am no longer willing or able to afford. Therefore, quite simply, Andre, I am putting you on notice. First, know that it is my utmost desire for us to thrive as a couple within a beautiful relationship steeped with kindness, compassion, respect, and honor. I must feel like I am in a true partnership in every sense of the word. I am no longer invested in continued feelings of resentment and disillusion. With that in mind, I invite you to meet me halfway, as my husband, life partner, and lover, in order to salvage the love we still share; and create an opportunity for birthing a new relationship based upon integrity, mutual sharing, trust, and emotional support.

I am henceforth issuing my resignation as bread winner, indentured servant, and the identified-patient in this marriage. I am no longer willing to live my life as a "human doing" instead as a "human being." In order to be healthy and vibrant in all ways, I need to both give and receive love and support. We must come together and discuss all possibilities for creating peace, joy, and satisfaction. Otherwise, I will reconsider my own options for happiness.

I love you, but I am not willing to endure this stagnate marriage. Either we both admit that our marriage is failing and we choose a brighter path, or we give it a proper burial and each goes our own way. Again, I choose to be happy and embrace life.

I am most interested in having a heart-to-heart talk and hope that we can work toward some sort of resolution. If you are willing, let's schedule a dinner date to discuss our marriage.

Yours truly,

Valery

This letter seemed to have quite an impact on this lady. After reading the letter, Valery called me to mention that her initial reaction was to break down in tears. Then, she enjoyed the first full night of sleep in six years. Shortly after issuing this letter to Andre, she decided to move forward and file for divorce. Andre was aghast. He actually dropped to his knees and begged her to participate in couples counseling. I believe they gave that a whirl.

STAY IN YOUR HEART

The heart's intelligence is said to far outweigh any cognitive, brain-based understanding. The heart inspires us to honor our feelings, be creative, and find the silver lining in any predicament. Often, people tend to rely on their brainpower to solve situations that may not speak to the heart's inner compass. When we ignore the stirrings of the heart, that still voice within, we are essentially cut off from the neck and thereby emotionally cut off. As mentioned earlier, the care and nurturing of relationships is an ongoing investment, negotiation, and responsibility that can offer immense payoffs for lasting, joyful love.

Jessica's Story

"MARRIED TO A MOB"

One woman, Jessica, contacted me, after being married for only six months to Keith, complaining that she and her new husband were getting off track and feeling increasingly disconnected, since they often bickered over interfering in-laws, a difficult former spouse, and issues regarding the step children from her husband's first marriage. At one point, Keith had slammed the front door in a fit of anger and a crystal ornament shattered in the process. Keith understood the negative extended family dynamics. Out of sheer frustration, he proposed that they pull up stakes, leave the stress behind, and relocate from the West Coast to New York. This was her letter to her beloved:

When the Door Slams Shut, Open a Window

Inspired Heart® Letter

My Dearest Keith,

I have been struggling with how to put this into words that you will understand, so please bear with me... the bottom line is that I need to feel like I am on my honeymoon, instead of just spending so much energy trying to salvage our marriage.

I love you so much and I am committed to having a beautiful marriage with you, however, being a married couple involves two willing partners who are genuinely devoted to invest in their marriage with honor, love, respect, and commitment. If our marriage is not a priority for both of us, then it may be doomed.

This does not mean we pack up and move to the East Coast or some other distant land in order to escape the blended-family circumstances. Honestly, we must be able to enjoy our lives together anywhere on this entire planet, including here in Los Angeles. If we cannot live here because of the pressures doled out by others, then we must reconsider to see if we are in a truly powerful, loving relationship or have we allowed others to zap our power from us.

I must admit, I am short on patience at times, trying to cope with the demands and nuances of the family I married into. What compounds my frustration and leaves me feeling so sad is seeing our communication start to dwindle when what I really need is for us to be able to openly discuss our feelings without the other going off the deep end or running away.

I know you can make me very happy, my love. It is your kind and passionate heart that I fell in love with. We are newlyweds. This can be both the most wonderful and difficult stage of our marriage. It is so important to handle our marriage with TLC. Otherwise, resentment may set in, communication will shut down, and the door to happiness will close.

Of course, I know there are issues surrounding your children and dealing with your ex-wife that remain challenging. However, apart from supporting you in an attempt to gain their respect and cooperation, I feel that I am becoming the target for all your stress. If you would kindly take a moment to consider what this experience has been for me, perhaps you will stop and think before you lash out at me again.

It is not so easy to step into someone's life and gain acceptance from in-laws and stepchildren. This is not to mention your ex-spouse's resistance to the new wife as well. Despite these obstacles, I am really striving to maintain my composure and see a brighter future ahead. I know that if we put our marriage first and support one another in staying strong, we can see our way through anything. I believe it is important to set a healthy foundation for our marriage. With that in mind, we must agree to always act respectfully to one another.

When you asked me to marry you, you asked me just what I was planning for the rest of my life. Well, Keith, I answered that my plan is to spend my life with you. My plan, which I hope is still yours as *well, is to spend our life being in love. We need to creatively come up with solid measures that will help us to always claim, and forever maintain, our love together.*

If there are stressful issues, then let's try to figure out healthy ways to alleviate the stress together. If there is a lack of feeling respected, then, likewise, let's make a plan around healing that. Respect, trust, and love are the essential ingredients for any relationship to thrive. However, we each must care enough to claim this.

Finally, in the business of marriage, let's hope we can be abundantly successful. I propose we schedule an appointment, ideally in a calm romantic setting, where we can share our hearts and what is on our mind. I do appreciate that I married a man who is open to looking at situations, take stock of the matter, and formulate a new game plan. As your wife, I am willing to support us in staying strong with our convictions... without caving into emotional pressure from others.

Just know that I am actually pretty easy to live with. As long as I feel I can trust my heart in your hands, you can lean on me, and I will always be there for you.

I love you,

Jessica

This letter had a profound effect on turning their marriage back to its original form – actually, to an even better, stronger union. With determination, Keith and Jessica were able to set healthier boundaries regarding other family members and made certain proactive "rules of engagement" regarding possible future conflicts. This couple grew increasingly secure in their love and support for one another. They now share regular time-out occasions to communicate from the heart including romantic dates for which they enjoy themselves immensely.

The approach taken for writing this letter was from a position of being a truly supportive partner. The letter was not to air complaints, but rather, to offer several problem-solving suggestions and proposals for dealing with the family dynamics at play in constructive ways that only encourage more cohesive love to form. There was no blaming, whining, or threats issued. However, gentle reminders, observations, and wisdom were offered.

Loretta's Story

"THE DOMINO EFFECT"

The following letter from a frustrated wife, Loretta, to her difficult husband, Neil, is another example of airing your concerns constructively. In this case, after several years of a fairly consistent and reliably satisfactory marriage, Loretta complained that over the last year or so, Neil seemed to be going through some type of mid-life change or emotional upheaval. Loretta shared that she could never really count on Neil to be consistent whereby he often displayed behaviors or reactions that did not align with the man she thought she married. For example, if they were dining out and the service was slow, or the entree not cooked the way he liked, Neil may politely discuss the matter with the waiter or *maître de*. At other times, under a similar circumstance, Neil may become overtly demanding, argumentative, and wreak havoc to the point of public annoyance and Loretta's embarrassment. What's more, when he was in this kind of mood, he usually blamed Loretta, making his dissatisfaction her fault somehow. Well, Loretta figured an *Inspired Heart Letter* to Neil was long overdue. Here's the honest truth, from Loretta to her hubby:

Stop in the Name of Love!

Inspired Heart® Letter

Neil,

You tell me you love me, you say you want us to be a couple, but perhaps you don't realize just how fragile relationships are. On that note, Neil, we know that life can turn on a dime. So, if you really love me, then you must bend. For the sake of our marriage, and our family, you cannot afford to suddenly go sideways on me with temper flares, acting snide, or being disrespectful. Maybe this is becoming a pattern for you, but it is not a healthy one.

Try this on for size: I am married to an incredibly kind, loving, overall great guy who enjoys being a family and is a wonderful father and so forth. Then, out of the blue, I get blasted by this same man who wakes up with a pompous, domineering, and belittling attitude throwing F-bombs around. How do you think that makes me feel?

We have acknowledged that neither of us is perfect, but that does not justify flaunting your bad mood or taking your stress out on me. I am not such a rock, Neil... I am your wife. I thought we had agreed our home is our sanctuary for peace. I need to be able to depend on you emotionally. Trying to second guess whether you are upset with me; if you are just overworked; depressed; or feeling guilty over something is too draining. I try to treat you with respect, be considerate, and let you know that I do appreciate your goodness.

I know we are on the same page as far as wanting our marriage to work. I also know myself though. If I am mistreated then I feel emotionally unsafe. It is hurtful and just creates more stress between us. Yes, it is such a turn-off, Neil. So, I am hoping we can nip this in the bud. The way you spoke to me this morning is not the first time I have seen this side of you.

Please just be clear with me. Let's figure out healthier ways for you to let go of the stress or to just be emotionally honest. I am here to listen, but I am definitely not here to be walked on. Maybe we should seek professional advice. Let me know how I can help.

Again, I do not know how to cope with your mood swings and it is something I will not ever learn to live with. I love you so very much. I value all the good parts and hope we can work through this together. We have a beautiful family and I know we are worth it. Thanks for reading through this letter.

With Love,

Loretta

Once Neil received this letter, he grew silent and seemed to avoid any discussion with Loretta. However, about a week went by, when he came home, hugged and kissed her. Then Neil apologized for ever treating her like such a jerk. Neil informed Loretta that he had just returned from his first private counseling session and felt quite hopeful that he can overcome the stress he had been feeling at his job, which had nothing to do with Loretta.

When we are free to be who we are while feeling trusted, supported, and seen for whom we truly are, inspired blessings surely will follow. Forgiving ourselves and others, embracing new possibilities, surrendering to the rhythm and flow, cleanses the soul. The inimitable energy of love is what we strive for, what heals us, and what is essential to our sense of purpose, joy, and wellbeing.

Whether you are in a marriage or committed partnership, it is quite important to understand one another's needs. Knowing just how to express love to your partner in a way they will actually acknowledge and feel adored, appreciated, and cherished can be tricky if either person relies only upon their own experience or how they, alone, tend to feel loved.

Gary Chapman writes in his book, *The Five Love Languages*, about the importance of recognizing how to convey our love to our significant other in a way that feels good to them. While some people respond mostly to physical touch, others need to hear verbal expressions of love. Or, one person may start feeling giddy when their husband or wife cooks a favorite meal for them or takes out the trash. Yet, quality time spent together or receiving special, thoughtful gifts may curl another's toes. No matter what the preferred "love language" may be, it is important to understand one another's turn-ons. Likewise, it is just as important to know and share with your partner what makes your heart flutter.

Theresa's Story

"THE LOVE LANGUAGE THAT CHANGES EVERYTHING"

The following *Inspired Heart Letter* was written as a gesture from a lovely woman, Theresa, to her husband, Jack, in order to rekindle the spark, the magic, and passionate desire there once was between them. Yes, Theresa and Jack were a devoted couple. However, their devotion over the last few years was primarily aimed toward providing a supportive, loving family life for their three children with a limited capacity to tend to one another's emotional and sensual needs.

Theresa considered Jack to be solid, reliable, and a really good father to their kids. However, their lives seemed forever consumed by routines and responsibilities with not much time together spent as a couple. Theresa found herself more often looking in the mirror, noticing a few grey hairs, an extra ten pounds, and seeing herself more and more as becoming a frumpy housewife, while she reflected upon the notion, *Is this all there is?* Theresa began to realize that she had nearly forgotten how to be sexy or even flirtatious toward her husband. With that, Theresa started to really take stock of her marriage. She became more conscious of her rapport with Jack. She even realized that with so much rushing around and being a responsible mom, she was often too tired to even kiss Jack good night, much less respond to his sexual overtures. What's more, although there was a time when Jack could not do enough for her, she couldn't recall the last time he had given her flowers or even brought her coffee in bed.

Before her relationship with Jack slipped entirely away, ending up in a real boring rut, Theresa decided to re-evaluate herself, her contribution, and basically do a *marriage makeover*. Well… with a newfound commitment to reboot their marriage, Theresa sent this letter to Jack:

Cupid's Aim

Inspired Heart® Letter

Jack,

With Valentine's Day approaching, I find myself considering what that actually means. In my mind, I feel so grateful for having you and our wonderful children in my life. Honestly though, my heart aches to once again experience that sense of joy, romance, and deep passion that brought us together in the first place. I fell in love with your kind heart, your caring nature, and your sense of fun which is truly like a breath of fresh air. It may not always seem like it, but I need to let you know how much I really do want our relationship to be special and more loving.

Love is a precious gift, and is uniquely special with any two people who are lucky enough to find it. Although our love language seems different... or the way we express our love may not be exactly the same, I now realize that I am not always a willing receiver when you act lovingly toward me. Likewise, it feels that my gestures of love have often gone unnoticed by you. Instead of feeling hurt or turned off, I see a bigger picture. I believe we both have been feeling somewhat misunderstood. Sadly, our original sense of feeling so "in love" has faded.

My Valentine's gift to you, Jack, is to make good on our marriage vows. That is simply to love and honor you without conditions other than being completely responsible for taking charge of my own happiness. You see, I am starting to realize how much I need to love myself first. That way, there is so much more to give you and our family.

Jack, I am now taking a stand for us... for our marriage... for our family. Obviously, we still do have a great deal to learn from one another. I hope you will agree that beyond being there for the kids, we need to be there for each other. Let's go back to the beginning, when we first met and we were so in tune with one another. Let's be really romantic. I'd like to start dating you again. Will you be my Valentine?

Your Loving Better-Half,

Theresa

Jack responded well to Theresa's letter. They started making their alone time together a priority, and were both deeply committed to being passionately "in love." The following summer, Jack surprised Theresa by taking her on a romantic vacation to Italy.

I once had a client call me requesting that I write a love poem, a message from her heart to her husband. This was not only in honor of Valentine's Day, but to express just how proud she was for how far they had grown during their marriage. She enjoyed this poem so much that she had it engraved as a gift. And here it is:

Valentine

(Poem)

Of all the ways that I have known you
From the wide eyes of a young girl
To being held in your loving arms so true
As a woman, now as your wife
A deeper knowing does unfurl.
With you, my love, I share my life

Our book is still a mystery
How in this love we came to be
I sing your praise, as we step into the light
Shedding what did not fit
Together, creating a real home
All to my hearts' sheer delight

Now when I see you, your eyes do smile
Climbing the peak, I can see only blue skies
The journey of this heart is worth the while
The true blue love of you
Radiant in your eyes

Yes, we have weathered some stormy time
Where I felt my heart disappear
Now, the sun shines bright
"We" feels so right
And the "Why" of us much more clear

Thank you, My Darling, for being so brave
The emotional risks indeed
Show me how much there is to save
Staying safe in your heart is all I need.

Be my Valentine forever

Inspired Heart Letters are an absolute delight for me not only to write, but also to witness the amazing results, or remarkable shifts that take place in the lives of my clients. That is why I was compelled to write this book, as I truly wish to share and inspire others through the healing gifts of the written word. What I have noted over the many years of assisting others with relational conflicts is there seems to be four main, or absolute, ingredients necessary for a healthy and lasting, loving relationship.

These key ingredients include: *communication, physical intimacy, respect, and emotional support.* If any one of these elements is missing or out of alignment, the relationship is in jeopardy and unless it begins to repair itself, it will not thrive. That is not to say that these attributes are expected to be fully in place from the beginning. However, with a conscious intention, these essential elements will illuminate, and the tarnished relationship will become polished and shine brightly once again.

If I were to capture all of these positive qualities of effective communication, physical intimacy and affection, continued respect, and emotional support under all circumstances for a loving relationship into a single concept, it would be trust. Trust is the key that feeds and allows all of the aforementioned conditions to exist. Trusting one another in the bedroom, in our communication, trusting that we are respected, understood, or emotionally accepted and supported is essential for inspiring a true *everlasting love* reality.

Just how this sense of complete and utter trust is conveyed within the relationship is developed and agreed upon only between the partners themselves. What works for one couple, may not be true for another and their relationship. Life is a potpourri of flavor and style. However, in the words of William Shakespeare, *"To thine own self be true."*

It cannot be said enough: The gift we give to our partners and ourselves when we are allowed to freely be who we truly are is absolutely the best gift for true love and contentment. As an intuitive writer of these very healing letters, I refrain from my own edification or judgment about how another's relationship should be. Instead, I tune into the individual's soul and help to provide words, or the lyrics, to their heart's song.

Powerful Conversations
(AN ALTERNATIVE CHOICE TO A WRITTEN LETTER)

On one occasion, rather than ghostwrite an *Inspired Heart Letter* for Amy, a woman who was having dire marital issues, I offered to draw up an outline similar to a *Power-Point* presentation highlighting her various areas of concern to her husband, Brad. This was in preparation for a face-to-face showdown, with full eye contact, sporting a straight spine, and calm, unwavering voice. She needed to take command of her own happiness and direction in life.

This scripted dialogue was a supportive way for Amy to maintain composure, and instead of becoming tongue-tied or derailed, she could remain on track with what she needed to express to her obtuse domineering husband. Amy apparently chose a difficult path. Unfortunately, it seemed, she chose a husband who needed to feel in control over her. There was a huge disconnect between them, and instead of building a solid, loving relationship, their energy was consumed by a *never-ending*, tumultuous power struggle.

Often, couples find themselves seriously dumbstruck, and wondering just how they ended up with Mister or Missus Wrong, living out a horrifying nightmare in their unfulfilled, frustrated rut. Well, it does take two to tango. Somehow, they each signed up for this journey, no matter how awful the consequences. It is only when at least one of the partners wishes to step off the merry-go-round that the predictable, exhausting, or even painful, negative pattern comes to a screeching halt. But this is also the moment when the valuable gift of positive self-regard and real self-honoring can be born.

Sadly, this particular couple's marriage, (at least from Amy's perspective), seemed to be failing across all of the aforementioned essential values. There was not much in the way of communication, physical affection/intimacy, respect, or support. However, before Amy threw in the towel, she was compelled to tell Brad, once and for all, just how she felt.

Amy usually responded to stressful communications with more of a soft, giggly demeanor. She would turn disappointments into jokes, or make light of inappropriate situations and behaviors from others. In reference to the *Inspired Heart Letter* approach, whereby the words are carefully designed in such a way as to lend an energetic resonance, with a spoken communication, it is not simply what is said, or the actual words used, more importantly; it is how it is expressed including tone, cadence, timing, breath and body language. That includes posture, good eye contact, and whether you cross your legs or arms. Moreover, personally, I find that if I know I am well groomed, rested, relaxed, and looking my best, my confidence is better sustained.

Brace yourself. The following is the *no holds barred* outlined written personal *Power-Point* (hand-held) presentation for this lady's verbal discourse:

Personal Power Points
(STRAIGHT TALK FROM A NOT-SO-WIMPY WIFE)

- **Communication**:

Brad, I need to express my feelings and my experience of what is going on. I may be wrong or may have a misperception, but if I cannot share my feelings without having my head bitten off or being cussed out, or you running out the door, or hanging up, how are we ever to clear things up and move forward? It seems that I am being made "wrong" before there is a chance to really talk it over. So, flying off the handle, trying to shut me down, and slamming doors, or running away does not "fix" anything. It does TURN ME OFF though, and I can't help but feel resentful when that happens. By the way, I have had my fill of F-bombs from you. If you cannot control yourself and speak respectfully, keep it to yourself. Verbal abuse is not what I am interested in."

- **Sex Life/Physical Intimacy**:

Having a sex life is mandatory for me. Just cuddling every night with the usual head on your chest loses its charm over time. Brad, I am craving a romantic, sensual, sexual experience. I can't help but feel sad and confused, since we are not even married one year, and our sex life is so sparse. This translates to one of three things: I married someone who no longer has a strong libido; I married someone who is passive aggressive and takes it out on me by withholding sex; or I am just simply being rejected. Please enlighten me, Brad. What is up (or not up) with this? This lack of physical intimacy is hurtful. I need to know why we have such a crappy sex life!

Moreover, I must also share that when we are being intimate, your bedroom conversation is demeaning and altogether not needed as it is not much of a turn on. I should not be placated by my husband constantly remarking in bed with "Is this what you want?" Don't you even know me by now? It feels like you are channel-surfing while trying to dial in to me with your "remote-control." And, why do you avoid eye contact when we are in bed together? There was a time when you couldn't keep your hands off of me. Where did our original passion go? I have asked you to get a complete physical to rule out a physical or psychological issue.

- **Being Supportive:** (Emotional Investment)

I find that you have not <u>really</u> invested in this relationship emotionally. Last summer, for about two weeks, I pinched myself, since Brad, you seemed to have turned over a new leaf and were acting kind, loving, nurturing, and like you really care or love me. However, that encouraging experience came to a screaming halt over my innocent inquiry regarding your relationship with your daughter. EGG-WALKING is not appealing to me either.

Tonight, I found myself alone in our marital therapy class! Isn't that telling? It seems that you expect me to tiptoe around your emotional states, (which seem to change with the wind), and whatever my feelings are... they are usually discounted. After this recent mood-swinging event or "good husband, bad husband," I see that you are actually quite a manipulator. Brad, you are entitled to your feelings as I am to mine. Our relationship cannot grow, or improve if you are only invested in how you are feeling and not considering my position.

- **Respect:** (Maintaining Healthy Boundaries)

I see that much of our conversation involves a lack of healthy boundaries, where you have given yourself license to practice a double standard and shirk any responsibilities for caring for the emotional wellbeing of your wife. In my experience, I see that you do not always respect me to my face. (Your foul language, sarcasm, shoving; the list goes on . . .) and only when we are alone, not in the presence of others. I am really trying to find the light at the end of the tunnel.

• **Summary/Conclusion:**

In short, Brad, our communication sucks; we have no good sex life to speak of; you seem to lack enough energy and commitment to create and maintain a healthy marriage; and overall the boundaries are crippled. At this point, I do not see any reason to continue this charade. I plan on re-establishing myself. You have put me through so much pain.

There is no more illusion that we will ever be a match made in Heaven. Just so you understand, I intend to create my own life and I am seeking a way that we can part company, so I can move on.

Note: While this Personal *Power-Point* oral conversation is a dramatic departure from an *Inspired Heart Letter* in many respects, the actual intention was for this lady to stop sitting on her deeply felt and unhealthy resentment and anguish. Rather, this was her opportunity to rise to the occasion, take action, stand up to a bully, and begin to move through her anger and discontent. It was imperative for her to begin to openly express herself at a level that may not be the optimum, but encompassed a much better sense of self-respect and self-care. Her outrage and anger verbally expressed in this more forceful style, was a way for Amy to get in touch with reality. As a result, she was better able to claim herself, denounce the icky relationship patterns, and find the strength to move on and move past her unhealthy ways. This verbally supported intervention profoundly impacted Amy's self-confidence. She dared herself to be real… and she won.

The results of this scripted Personal *Power-Point* conversation turned out to be a worthwhile way for Amy to finally stand up for herself. While she required additional coaching in order to build and maintain her inner resiliency and self-trust, her husband, Brad, not only listened attentively, but actually complimented her on how organized, important, and forthright their conversation was. Brad also mentioned that he thought it was the most meaningful conversation they had ever had. As Amy's confidence seemed to grow, I am informed that their marriage took a turn for the better.

FINDING YOUR VOICE

I always say that if you feel you cannot do something, just act as though you can. Get out of your own way and grow some backbone! A Personal *Power-Point* presentation can be quite a supportive strategy for clearing the air and really giving voice to your experience. It is an excellent way to begin to let go of unrealistic fears, resentment, and lighten the emotional load.

It is important to maintain composure though, so practice, practice, and, well… practice. Although being this verbally direct, without much finesse, surely can be rather overwhelming, prepare emotionally for the conversation. In this particular case, Amy had been clearly intimidated and had taken on a mouse-like character for so long that we had to consider a strategy that would empower her to directly communicate her grievances with conviction.

Returning to the idea that life is theater and we are all actors upon the stage, perhaps some folks need to try out for a different role. In this case, I suggested to Amy that she begin to consider herself as queen of her own castle, and actually envision an imaginary crown upon her head. After all, she certainly seemed to be living with a royal pain in the ass! Perhaps it was about time she stopped and considered her bottom line. Is it worth all of the pain and humiliation she had succumbed to in this marriage?

Decide what your own deal-breaker is. Relationships serve as mirrors that reflect our innermost feelings regarding how much we value ourselves.

I maintain that our teachers often come onto our path at times disguised as mean, demoralizing, controlling, *chi vampires* who can suck out our very life force if allowed. The gift in this type of encounter proves that once someone stands up to a bully, no longer is he or she interested or fearful of the bully's reaction, and thereby the dynamic changes and the negativity subsides or disappears altogether. Often, this causes a new paradigm shift whereby the relationship may dramatically improve or morph into a more empowered marital bond. Other times, it causes a loss of the unhealthy connection altogether resulting in each person taking a separate path. *Que sera, sera!* Either way, there is a real opportunity for increased self-awareness and personal growth.

To further illustrate the four attributes of love that are the fundamental building blocks for a more solid foundation of trust in any partnership, here is a brief overview:

THE FOUR AGREEMENTS FOR A LOVING RELATIONSHIP

Communication: Paying attention and listening from the heart are some of the most important features for effectively communicating. There is a real art to listening. This is a talent that does not always come naturally. There is a genuine gift in allowing our significant others to feel truly heard. While some people may be more focused on being right rather than being loved, so much more is to be gained by honoring one another both in giving and receiving heartfelt communications.

Instead of feeling as though you are egg-walking or dancing around a sensitive, difficult topic, stuffing your feelings, or even worse, blurting out your thoughts, creating regular occasions for verbal exchange before little snags or issues become big deals is simply wise. Realistically, talking it out is not always an even, or balanced, give-and-take communication especially when emotions are high or the ego is engaged.

Sometimes, there is strength in taking a time-out, or giving oneself time and physical distance to consider all aspects of the problem at hand and mentally and/or emotionally being able to process the situation before expounding on your position. Typically, at any given moment, the balance of your conversation may be uneven. However, by being compassionate and open to your partner, the conversations will, most likely, become more balanced. Then the notion of controlling the conversation becomes outmoded and is replaced by a mutual engagement instead of a power play.

One couple I admire comes to mind. Kimberly and Ron have been happily married for over twenty-five years. At the start of their marriage, they made a commitment to have a weekly bubble-bath date. The bubble-bath setting was a private, relaxing space. The purpose of this was simply to listen and express how they were feeling, to air what concerns they may have, and to comment upon what they appreciate about one another or about life in general. They also made a pact that they would always refrain from using foul language or derogatory name-calling. You see, they deliberately marked certain boundaries and invested energy toward growing and maintaining the business of their marriage. Together, they continue to focus on their main priority, which is their life together.

Physical Intimacy and/or Affection: When resentment sets in, one of the first places to find this is in the bedroom. Withholding affection or sex, or in certain instances, forcing a partner to engage in sexual acts against their will, is a prelude to doom. You already knew that!

Power plays in the bedroom may be an easy way to assert control, but is this really what you want to do? This manner of control can actually backfire. Hesitation to share sex may be an expression of fear, to work through with your partner, but to intentionally withhold sex and affection can be a harsh tool, or weapon, that unfortunately can be used at whim. It expresses resistance to being vulnerable. The essence of love is a willingness to freely expose your heart, your body, and all your senses. Sexual, or intimate, encounters involve surrender or trust at the deepest, most private, personal level.

When you feel absolutely safe in the arms of your partner, this naturally opens the door to a deeper experience of sensuality and exploration. Lovemaking, in every sense of the word, is joyous and wonderfully fulfilling when we not only desire our partner, but likewise feel desired by them. After all, this is a physical communion. With healthy physical intimacy, we are allowed to share a part of ourselves that is expressed and received with a type of freedom and exclusivity that feels completely accepted, enjoyed, and turns us on to desire.

Conversely, withholding or rationing sex is a passive-aggressive symptom often based upon hostility and anger. Direct acts of cruelty, humiliation, or acting out in spiteful ways in the bedroom such as sharing your sexual fantasies regarding lusting after someone else, or criticizing your lover's physicality or sexual performance, surely squelches any sense of real intimacy and can inhibit your partner's willingness to fully enjoy your sexual experience. Everyone has the right to discover and live in a comfortable, sharing, and private zone. At times, navigating through the twilight, or middle zone, may be somewhat awkward, yet together the couple eventually determines their own comfort level, or the atmosphere for lovemaking and physical affection that allows each to feel safe and free.

Talk fearlessly about your desires and limitations, and encourage your partner to do the same. Sexual expression has a life of its own. It flows and fluctuates into continuous cycles and changes to various states over time; otherwise it becomes too predictable, stagnate, and uninspired. Like a menu, you may want to try various selections, depending upon what piques your interest at the time. The soup de jour may be worth trying as long as you trust the chef and when you already know that the service is fabulous.

Naturally, good communication is foreplay to good sex. The seduction, the foreplay itself, is what seasons the intimacy, or the nature of your lovemaking. What's more, the aftermath, or dessert, whether it is conversation, holding one another, falling asleep in each other's arms, or sharing a bowl of ice cream, sweetens the whole encounter.

I contend that physical attraction, or having chemistry with another, is actually a barometer for our soul's alignment with one another. If couples evolve together over time, then they remain more aligned. That is quite promising for everlasting partnership. However, there are times when one partner simply outgrows his or her connection to their significant other and the relationship, or at least the relationship's dynamic, shifts or ends. These changes in course or final endings can be quite devastating, especially when there is time invested or children involved.

Emotional Support: One of the best reasons for getting married or remaining in a committed, exclusive relationship is that sense of being part of a partnership or team. Creating and striving for common goals includes sharing your resources for the common good of the couple or family, and emotionally relaxing, since you know you are no longer out there howling at the moon, trying to figure life out on your own. So, yes, that ultimate sense of security, social identity, and inner sense of connection is what can make the commitment of marriage so attractive. As part of the human experience, we naturally desire and search for or attract our soul mate or that special person with whom we will find a true sense of belonging.

Creating your life together may involve making important decisions or going through certain experiences such as buying a house, planning vacations, having children, inheriting stepchildren and in-laws, or building careers. You'll enjoy growing a social circle that may very well include other couples, sharing hobbies or fun activities, celebrating holidays and special occasions together, all the while creating sweet memories and your own family legacy.

Underlying this idealistic notion for being a couple is the reliance upon one another in times when we feel vulnerable through life's challenges, or when we are hit with a whammy, such as when unexpected sadness, devastation, or misery occurs. For instance, life's passages may, at times, be fraught by challenges, including health issues, death of loved ones, accidents, job losses, financial distress, worry, doubt, or even natural disasters. Working through stormy times together, no matter what, is one of the supportive pillars to the marital foundation.

In the business of marriage, include one another in all decisions instead of trying to protect the other by withholding the truth or your feelings. Keep the window open and resolve to maintain honesty above all else. This fuels deeper intimacy and emotional growth and maintains your heartfelt connection to one another. When we are clear about each of our intentions and we are compassionate to our partner's individual process, for example, their experience of becoming a parent, career challenges, health issues, aging, etc., then we are able to offer the sense of acceptance, encouragement, and understanding, or the emotional support that is a true measure of love.

Respect: Feeling allowed to express who you are without feeling that your partner is going to condemn you or run away allows you to be or live in your own true nature. This encourages each partner to avoid hiding behind the truth with certain game-playing tactics, such as manipulation by acts of deception, pretending, or denial. Each relationship subscribes to its particular set of emotional and physical boundaries.

Certain couples may seem to have stricter or looser boundaries than the expected norm. Nevertheless, the deal-breaker behaviors must be established and agreed upon from the start. It is wise to establish and secure the rules for acceptable behaviors on the marital playground. Demonstrate respect for one another and agree upon how each partner will honor their mutual values. Just as the couple previously discussed, Kimberly and Ron, made a verbal commitment and acted upon their agreement to always address each other respectfully.

Maintain those bubble-bath meetings or your *very own special, exclusive time together* to air any thoughts and feelings with safety. Each couple should create a pact for rendering a clear understanding of what feels respectful and what does not. This promise for maintaining mutual respect and honoring is what keeps our hearts feeling open and secure. It is up to each couple and their agreement for acceptable social decorum and what is considered an indiscretion, or foul play.

Respectful behaviors may, at times, call for denying a particular urge, such as flirting with someone at the office, unilaterally making plans without informing your partner, or complaining about your partner to others outside of the marriage. Further, the couple must decide for themselves regarding matters of privacy, such as email, internet access, personal privacy for bathing, grooming, toiletry, opposite-sex friendships, standing up for one another, and being mutually supportive as a couple socially. This may include: encounters with in-laws or extended family members, business or professional gatherings, social events, taking separate vacations, and enjoying separate hobbies or activities. Just as noted in Chapter 2 regarding the "Stevie Wonder" letter, attending a social engagement together only to find your partner conversing and dancing with other strange women or men while you are left alone, for many individuals, is quite unacceptable.

Family matters, including issues regarding child rearing, are more successful when the parents are working as a united front and not undermining one another. Otherwise, this only causes confusion, resentment, and gives the child opportunities for possible manipulation, or worse, feeling emotionally unsafe. Remember, it is very important to maintain mutual respect while focusing on ways to compromise and solve problems. Money matters – how the couple saves, spends, and shares their income – is another area that must be mutually agreed upon and followed.

To expect that each partner is going to want to do everything together, to always enjoy the same activities, and otherwise need to always be together may be quite unrealistic. Therefore, respecting each other's time, need for space, and individual interests should be part of a working agreement.

Avoid other ingredients for failure like using foul language, engaging in name-calling and other forms of verbal intimidation, such as threatening or issuing ultimatums, being too bossy or acting like a dictator. Conversely, manipulating through tears, locking oneself in the bathroom, or driving off in a huff only creates more drama and disconnection.

Do not indulge in undermining your partner or taking the path of least resistance by ignoring or placating your partner. Refuse to tolerate bad behavior and other ways of disrespecting yourself in the partnership. These types of unhealthy dynamics are always power struggles. For example, if one partner is a "control freak" and the other partner is a "mouse", or if one partner stands by and allows the other to act in inappropriate ways, this is a true indicator that the marriage, or partnership, is deeply troubled by a sense of insecurity or lack of trust. Moreover, any type of verbal or physical abuse is a definite deal-breaker and should never be tolerated under any circumstance.

Healthy communication, gratifying sexual or physical affection, emotional support, and respect are essential elements in any union. When put in place correctly, they take root for securing a solid foundation.

Most important, couples should never stop courting one another. Love is kept alive when couples are flirtatious, complimentary, genuinely interested in each other, playful, romantic, sensual, and seductive. Investing in the quality of the relationship, including: sharing ample time for being together, just relating, (or the process of giving and receiving without any agenda beyond that compelling urge to simply enjoy time spent together), honors their union and blesses their marriage or partnership.

What we do not effort toward or earn, we more often do not give as much value to. Couples who are mindful and conscientious without demoralizing or minimizing one another, without forsaking one another, and without neglecting the emotional responsibility for nurturing the relationship, find success. Making their marriage the ultimate priority supports the sanctity of their vows to always love, honor, and cherish one another under all circumstances.

LIKE FINE WINE

The beauty of realizing the importance and sacredness of marriage is realized over time. Emotionally stable individuals do change. It is healthy to grow and evolve as we turn the pages and complete each chapter of our lives. Being in love in our twenties may be experienced somewhat differently than being in love in our thirties, forties, fifties and beyond. While the essence of who we are remains somewhat constant, the experiences of life, over time, influence our outlook and what we consider valuable, or precious, as well as what we find ourselves accepting, if not cherishing, regarding the idiosyncrasies discovered in one another.

One elderly gentleman, who was quite devoted to his wife and reveled in the happiness and satisfaction of their long-term marriage, commented upon how endearing his wife's profuse verbal remarks were. Although other family members found her constant chattering to be somewhat annoying, her husband held a different opinion. Instead, this elderly husband acknowledged the positive aspects of his wife's *gift of gab*. He elaborated on how enjoyable it was to allow his wife to take over the conversation. He could then sit back and quietly admire her commentary as he basked in her delightful presence. Instead of irritation, he chose a different perspective. He saw his wife's verbal tendency as a delightful attribute to their relationship.

KEEPING IT LIGHT AND FLUFFY

The recipe for a light and fluffy, deliciously satisfying marriage calls for a fine blend of compassion, forgiveness, and self-respect spread over a thick layer of integrity and openness while being willing to change one's habits or perspective. This is followed by a sweet, tender, thoughtful caring, and flavored with enough spice to make one's romantic taste buds do tangos!

Vivian's Story

"BAND OF GOLD"

I once wrote a very meaningful letter for a wise young newlywed wife, Vivian, who sensed her relationship with her new husband, Tom, had suddenly shifted right after their wedding. She began wondering if his immediate change in behavior and attitude signaled that her new hubby was actually regretting their marriage. So, before moving forward on an emotional slippery slope and possibly ending up in divorce, Vivian asked me to write an endearing letter that would reset the template of their marriage. And here it is:

Band of Gold

Inspired Heart® Letter

My Dear Husband,

Now that we have finally tied the knot, I'd like to celebrate the close of our first week together as Mr. and Mrs. by sharing my thoughts, my intention, and my heart with you.

Sometimes, it is easier for me to collect my thoughts and express them on paper instead of speaking them to you directly. So, I hope you receive this knowing how very happy I am to be with you, to be facing the rest of our lives together as a couple, and to finally say, "You are my love, my hero, and my family."

Perhaps it is true, good things are worth waiting for. And, perhaps, it is also true that love does conquer all. I know it took so much from each of us to be flexible, forgiving, and to believe in our destiny through the bond of marriage. Although the road that was taken to get to this point was not always the most pleasant and did not always feel very safe. Nevertheless, Tom, we did take the plunge, and with that in mind, I pray that together we are much wiser and, therefore, able to create an amazing life together.

Our marriage will be what we create in the true sense of partnership. It will thrive and sustain only through our tender loving care. Compassionate communication, faithfulness, respect, and appreciation are mutual key components and necessary in order to grow a joyful life together. While our souls are definitely connected, and you are the love of my life, I need to convey to you my apprehension that we might forget to honor one another and fall into a comfort zone that does not glow with love, romance, and real intimacy.

A friend once told me that the sign of a healthy relationship is when both husband and wife are allowed the freedom to be who they truly are without receiving a negative reaction from one another. Therefore, our values must mesh. On that note, please let me express the following: Feelings that involve control, intimidation, jealousy, or unresolved anger are simply not permitted in our marriage. With healthy communication, I know that any negativity or insecurities can be resolved between us. So, again, I vow to always be honest, be true, and I will try to be as open as I can to work through any stumbling blocks along the way.

Tom, I am so proud of who you are and how you contribute to others in your work. My hope, Sweetheart, is that you will share your feelings with me. Know that our home is a safe haven, and apart from any stress that your workday brings. I am here for you, Tom. I do want the most perfect marriage we can manage. I want our children to be proud of us. I see myself as the jewel in your crown. Thanks for opening your big, beautiful heart to me. Just as Carl

Sandberg was quoted in our nuptials, "I love you for who you are… I love you more for who we will become."

Your loving wife, (I do like the sound of that!)

Vivian

As you might imagine, Tom appreciated this letter and was actually impressed that Vivian was able to call his attention to what she perceived as being out of touch with the business of everlasting love.

Chapter 5

Letter Theme – Divorce

DIVORCED & STILL FIGHTING: WHAT ABOUT THE KIDS? FRACTURED FAMILIES/CO-PARENTING

The shattered dream surrounding divorce often holds feelings of betrayal, or shame, and regret. Perhaps a sense of being lied to, duped, or somehow *ripped off* is ultimately experienced. Other feelings including resentment, guilt, or even a sense of relief may arise. A profound sense of loss or abandonment from a shattered marriage can shred your self-esteem.

Yes, the reality of the split is experienced no matter the circumstance that led up to the dissolution. Unless there is a well thought out mutual agreement followed by a sense of fairness, consideration for one another, (possibly even friendship), divorce is usually a very nasty piece of business. When it involves children, the simpler breakup becomes a deeper, more painful wound, known as the fractured family.

Divorce is the death and the demise of a dream. A grieving process to one degree or another is surely experienced. Marriage is the ultimate investment in every sense of the word. Some may argue that raising children is an even bigger investment. However, I draw the distinction that under healthy circumstances, raising children is *the most selfless act*.

The parent-child relationship dynamic is obviously a much different dynamic than a relationship between adults. Along with the natural heart-opening experience that occurs from the moment you hold your baby; caring for your child, or children, brings about an unconditional and relentless love no matter what.

When immense time, energy, faith, trust, hope, and the vision of all that marriage holds dear is annihilated or the investment does not pay off, it is certainly quite devastating. Falling out of love with one another, or knowing your spouse has fallen out of love with you, is sadly tragic. I am not sure whether the term "divorce," otherwise known as "The D Word," actually refers to the words, *draining* or *devastating* instead. Being married generally offers a certain social/emotional status. Culturally, for many women, it lends a sense of security, or mutual support, opportunity for nest building, and proof of worthiness, as well as a feeling of being desired, valued, and loved.

For most couples, the notion of marriage may mark a personal sense of having arrived, or to yourself and the outside world, you are considered more established. For some, it may feel more like being a *grown up.* There is a certain sense of safety and maturity, perhaps for setting mutual goals for family, lifestyle, and/or just growing through life together. Marriage marks a change in identity. You are now, (check the box), a married couple. You were pronounced *"man and wife and from this day forward, for richer or for poorer, in sickness and in health, until death do you part..."*

In other words, marriage may be considered a traditional mechanism for survival, personal identity, growing community, a sense of family, family legacy, and the list goes on. Unfortunately, the divorce rate has exponentially grown over the last fifty-plus years. The concept of commitment has been trivialized to one degree or another. Divorce has become all too common and socially quite acceptable.

Today, it seems many couples more easily look at opting out of marriage rather than rolling up their shirtsleeves, diving in, and working through their issues. Further, there are those who have a keen awareness of the price paid for divorce. Of course, some couples remain in unhealthy marriages for monetary reasons, feeling it is too financially costly to divorce. Many may feel "the attorneys are the only people who benefit financially," or the idea of selling their home or assets, paying spousal or child support is daunting. However, what I am referring to is the emotional price paid by the whole family.

When children are involved, it does become a family crisis, since naturally the parents are not divorcing their children, but their home-life will never be the same. Unfortunately, more often the parents are emotionally driven and not always prepared for all of the real-life negative ramifications or the drama that can occur. It can be a very trying process to co-parent, maintain relationships or decorum with previous in-laws, even long-standing mutual family friends, and most importantly provide a sense of healthy family values, environment, and connections for all the children.

Ben's Story

"AND JILL CAME TUMBLING AFTER"

Once, years ago, I attended a rather posh dinner party and happened to be seated next to an interesting man, Ben, an accomplished real estate developer. In our conversation, I mentioned my passion for letter writing and explained my letter-writing service. He was quite interested and, after dinner, he took me aside whereby he began to openly share his overwhelming sense of sadness regarding a recent situation that had transpired with his daughter. This is his story:

Ben married his college sweetheart, Jillian. Jillian was very pretty and quite intelligent. In fact, she was the valedictorian of their college. Ben and Jillian were wed soon after they graduated. However, it seemed that this couple had different agendas for what their marriage would be like. Somehow, they each assumed that the other shared their goals when, actually, Ben and Jillian had very different ideas for building a family and enjoying life experiences together.

Ben's idea was to travel, see the world, build his business, and experience life together with Jillian before settling down and starting a family. Jillian, on the other hand, wanted to start having children right away, buy a nice family home, and move forward with her teaching career. In fact, soon after their wedding, Jillian became pregnant with their daughter, Meghan, followed by two more children: their sons, Daryl and Jason. According to Ben, Jillian really enjoyed being a mother. She was absolutely dedicated to their children and preferred just staying home with them as opposed to spending quality or romantic time with Ben. Cooking and sewing were her favorite pastimes.

While Ben devoted much of his time to building a very successful business, he and Jillian rarely socialized or vacationed just as a couple together. In the years that followed, he began to despair, feeling imprisoned by what Ben described as their couch-potato lifestyle. Over time, Jillian had gained a considerable amount of weight, although their love life was starving.

Ben truly loved and adored his three children; however, he felt trapped, disillusioned, and held deep feelings of missing out on other aspects of life while condemned to living in an uninspired, boring marriage. Ben felt he was a man of honor and a loyal husband and father. Despite his complaints, Jillian seemed uninterested in changing their home-life situation.

This went on year after year. Then, after ten years of marriage, Ben decided to call it quits. He and Jillian divorced. What followed, however, was unexpected. After the divorce, and over the following ten years, Jillian completely cut Ben off. She refused to communicate with him. Moreover, she did everything in her power to sabotage Ben's relationship with their three children and strove to drive a wedge between them.

Jillian created obstacles in any way she could in order to disrupt communications between the children and their father. She hijacked his letters in the mail as well as emails and phone calls. Ben had moved to a nearby state, where he expanded his business even further. He bought a small plane and regularly flew to meet his children for visitations. However, as the kids grew older, they seemed less inclined to spend time with their father. This is quite common, since developmentally, most teenagers often prefer to hang out with their friends instead of with their parents. The connection with his kids, however, began to dwindle even further. His daughter, Meghan, came to visit him one summer; however, she was often defiant and disrespectful toward her father. Ben felt Jillian had brainwashed the kids against him.

Shortly before my meeting with Ben, he had returned from Meghan's high school graduation. He lamented that his daughter never actually invited him to her graduation ceremony, or any family celebration surrounding the event. Nevertheless, he took it upon himself to fly up and attend as he did not want to miss out on this important occasion; and he wanted his daughter to know he cared enough to be there anyway.

While Ben maintained that his daughter seemed pleased to see him, and she was polite and respectful, he felt a significant disconnect between them. Moreover, he described feeling as though he was on the outside looking in at all three of his children during this significant family celebration. Sadly, Ben claimed he did not feel as though he was really a part of the family. Ben was at a loss for words. After all, this was an important step in his daughter's life. He loved her dearly, and he desperately needed guidance for reconnecting with her.

When Ben asked me to write a letter on his behalf to his daughter, Meghan, I emphatically declined. However, I did offer to write a letter for him to his former wife, Jillian. At first, Ben seemed horrified. He explained that Jillian was extremely stubborn, recalcitrant, quite mean, and she had refused to speak to him for over ten years!

I replied by letting Ben know that in order to heal their family rift, I must write to Jillian. A window had to be opened. (It seemed to me that at the core of this fractured family scenario was Jillian's sense of total rejection from Ben and his inconsideration for leaving her to raise their children, for the most part, as a single parent.) Ben finally agreed that I should write his letter to Jillian. Here is what turned out to be a most compelling *Inspired Heart Letter*.

And Jill Came Tumbling After

Inspired Heart® Letter

Dear Jillian,

I hope you are enjoying the summer. It was good to see you at Meghan's graduation. Although attending her graduation may have been a bit of a surprise, I am so glad I was there. One thing is for sure, we have three amazing kids! I attribute much of their individual success to your strength and commitment as their mom. I realize that you have made sacrifices along the way.

Although our marriage ended, I want you to know that I have always respected you for your many positive attributes, including your well-grounded sense of integrity.

It goes without saying that you've continued to be well-liked and admired by others. Your life as a dedicated mother and teacher defines your deep level of commitment and caring. Respectfully, Jillian, and with the understanding that you also wish every happiness and continued success for our children, I am imploring upon your guidance and wisdom to help resolve the obvious rift that has occurred between Meghan and myself.

I have stepped outside of laying any judgment surrounding the strain in my relationship with Meghan over the last year. She is now a young lady, an adult, and is about to begin a new path with starting college in the fall. I have to admit, it really hurt when she did not personally invite me to her high school graduation. More than that, the thought of being excluded, or unwelcome at future important events, and of course, this includes just spending time with her, or at the very least, just talking on the phone, is unbearably sad.

Jillian, I know just how important your dad was to you. I am sure you will agree that having two loving parents who will stand by your side is pretty meaningful! I want Meghan to have healthy, loving relationships and whatever her choices are in the future, I want her to always know she means the world to me. Actions speak louder than words. That is why I had to be at her graduation. Not only am I extremely proud of her, but also it is so important that she knows I am there for her.

As difficult as this situation with Meghan has been, I guess it has really given me pause for thought. I am sincerely hoping you will join me as we mutually support one another in always being great parents for our kids. While we may have had our own differences in the past, I promise to always give you your much deserved respect as their mom. I may not have expressed it before, but as I already said, I want you to know just how much I do appreciate you for being dedicated to Meghan, Daryl, and Jason... one hundred percent! And, I am so grateful for having the opportunity to be their dad. I look forward to witnessing their futures over the years ahead as their lives unfold.

Jillian, even though you and I are not together in marriage, I wish us to be together as parents. I am sure you understand how very important that is for the kids, and for their future one day, with their own children and relationships, etc.

Thanks so much for taking the time to read this, I have wanted to write to you for some time. It is difficult to put into words that really make sense. I plan on getting in touch with Meghan, either by letter or phone, but I wanted to communicate with you first. If you'd like to call me, so we can discuss this further, I would really welcome that. I hope this letter finds you well. Let me know what your feelings are.

With love,

After receiving this *Inspired Heart Letter*, Ben telephoned me while he was at the post office. He started out by saying, *"Well, I have signed the letter, addressed the envelope, and it is stamped. I feel so nervous about sending it though."* I coached him regarding the importance of courage, making the overture, and knowing that his intentions are well founded. More importantly, the relationship between Ben and his children, as well as their life experiences with having congenial parents, was well worth his fear of rejection or more negative interference from Jillian. Ben agreed, said a quick prayer, and dropped the letter into the mailbox.

After two weeks had passed, Ben contacted me complaining that he had yet to hear a word from Jillian. I reminded him that it had been over ten years since they communicated at all and suggested he simply give it more time and let the message in the letter simmer.

The following week, Ben called me with such elation and a deep sense of relief! Jillian had contacted him. He flew up to meet with her in person. They spent over two hours discussing their children and discovered that they were both on the same page!

Four months later, I received an interesting email from Ben. He wrote that he was planning to fly up to see his two sons and take them on a golfing weekend; more importantly, it was Jillian's idea, and she actually planned the whole vacation. Naturally, Ben could not have been more pleased.

Ben's willingness to move past his fears and let go of the power struggle between himself and Jillian was a tremendous step toward healing the pain surrounding his relationship with their children. By looking at the bigger picture, considering future possibilities for creating more joyous family occasions, a more positive family legacy, and, finally, for expressing gratitude for Jillian's positive role in raising their kids, a much healthier caring and new way of relating within the family was forged.

Marilyn's Story

"UNCHAIN MY HEART"

This letter-story is about a middle-aged lady, Marilyn, who was divorced over sixteen years prior to my encounter with her. Her marriage had lasted for nearly twenty years. She and her former husband, Martin, had raised a daughter and son together. Their children were nearly grown, or teenagers, when they divorced. Marilyn described her marriage to Martin as being rather typical. She maintained that while she and Martin argued on occasion, they got along well for the most part, and there wasn't any clear-cut issue she could name that served to be the culprit for destroying their marriage. In fact, when, seemingly out of the blue, Martin decided one day to pack up his things, move out, and subsequently file for divorce, Marilyn was shocked, to say the least.

She felt like a boat without a rudder. During all those years of marriage, she relied on her husband and believed they would always be together. Within a few years after their divorce, Martin met someone, remarried, and moved on. However, sadly, Marilyn remained stuck. She was frozen in time. She could not wrap her head around the reality of her marital breakup. She felt like a failure, and what's more, she felt unclear about why their marriage did not last to begin with. She had lost her identity as a wife. She felt uncomfortable being a single, divorced woman. As a result, she succumbed to bouts of depression.

Instead of working through her feelings of grief and sadness surrounding her failed marriage, Marilyn, found herself bewildered and emotionally crippled. She did not possess the stamina to move on and create a new life on her own. In certain ways, she became co-dependent regarding her relationship with her children. They were her top priority, and she did everything she could in order to preserve their connection, even at the cost of being disrespected, unappreciated, or taken for granted. In the aftermath of the collapse of her marriage she radiated a lack of self-confidence that usurped the regard her children once had for her, and made her an unattractive prospect for future romance. *Regaining* a sense of self-worth and confidence, often initiated by a heartfelt letter, makes you more likely to *attract* a worthy partner, or *repair* a faltering relationship.

When Martin left so unexpectedly, Marilyn experienced a profound sense of rejection. Even though her children were older, she could not bring herself to entertain the idea of dating, or meeting someone new. She felt quite insecure; her heart was broken. Thereafter, Marilyn withdrew and completely shut down. In fact, since her divorce from Martin many years ago, Marilyn had only dated two men and each for only one single date. When I met Marilyn, she was miserable. After talking with her, it was clear that she had not only given her power away, but she was inadvertently punishing herself through a life bereft of romance, and drenched in absolute loneliness.

She realized she had never healed from the perceived rejection surrounding her divorce. Nor, had she honored herself by moving forward and being open to finding love again. Further, she had apparently forsaken herself from experiencing a healthy, close relationship with her children and the respect from them she deserved. Here is Marilyn's *Inspired Heart Letter*:

Unchain my Heart

Inspired Heart® Letter

Dear Martin,

Perhaps it is the season, nearing the end of another year, while the sun still shines and the leaves turn gold, that my awareness to the cycle and process of life is more profound. In the hopes of creating a long-awaited, healthy closure to an ancient wound, I request your support in my attempt to become more open and aware. I am quite certain you must be surprised to receive this letter from me. I hope you will do me the honor of reading through this inspired message.

While you have moved on with apparent ease, even after all these years, it seems that I have stumbled along awkwardly lacking the type of grace and stride that I had hoped for. I felt my world fall apart when our marriage suddenly ended so many years ago. I was devastated. I saw myself as abandoned, sabotaged, without really being given an opportunity to remedy or understand what went wrong between us.

More simply put, I have struggled to recover from the absolute grief and loss of my identity as your wife, being part of an intact family, and well-connected to the children we created together, the fond memories of our past, and the possibilities of the future. This alone has been my inner challenge.

Please know that finally, while I have not only emotionally released you, Martin, certainly, I do forgive you. More importantly, I, now, forgive myself. I understand that suppressing my feelings or resisting the emotional trauma of the past only causes more pain that is mirrored in my current relationships and other life experiences. I can no longer freeze my emotions, or be numb to the anger I have felt. Instead, I am choosing to reclaim my power. I am now willing to open my heart to the sadness, to be more vulnerable instead of masking the hurt by being defensive, and to refrain from blaming others for my life circumstance.

Reflecting on our relationship, I enjoyed the companionship you offered in those years together. I am forever grateful for our beautiful children, Christopher and Gabrielle. In another context, I have a deep appreciation for the emotional challenge this chapter has been. As difficult as it seemed, I know I am finally emerging and I bless you for being a part of my life's path.

You are no longer the rock in the road I once considered you to be. Rather, I now realize, in spite of everything, you were actually a true gift... an opportunity for me to see more clearly, to become less fearful, more intimate with my true feelings, and to be able to love so much more deeply.

I hope you receive this letter in the best light possible. I am writing this from a much better place of trust, contentment, and personal strength. I still look forward to the many happy occasions of life, including those that involve our children. I believe that with parents who maintain a healthy positive connection, although they are divorced, their children and even their grandchildren, one day, will benefit immensely.

Wishing you only the best life has to offer.

After reading this letter, Marilyn had a sudden, if not dramatic, change of heart. She commented upon how much more clearly she saw her life predicament. Marilyn had a real sense of her self-sabotaging ways and began shedding the burden and weight of the torch she allowed herself to carry all these years. What's more, she immediately joined an online-dating site and even started taking ballroom dance classes. Marilyn began meeting new men, formulating friendships, and enjoying a rich social life.

She called to thank me for her newfound sense of personal strength and *joi de vive*. She expressed a sense of power through feeling cleansed of old emotional debris and enthusiastic about new possibilities.

Shortly thereafter, she also let go of trying to please or placate her grown children whom had emotionally drained and manipulated her over the years. Marilyn was better able to redefine healthier boundaries between them. I met with Marilyn a couple months ago. She actually looked more rested, if not younger. She mentioned that while Martin had never replied to her letter, she encountered him at a recent family gathering. As Marilyn described it, "*I felt absolutely no anxiety or negative attachment. Martin seemed relaxed, open, and actually quite pleasant. It was such a relief...*"

No matter how ugly or deprecating the circumstances are, taking our power back is the kindest gesture to ourselves and to those around us that we can experience.

A Way to Salvage Your Marriage Before it Ends Up in Divorce

AN OUNCE OF PREVENTION IS WORTH A POUND OF CURE

In my experience working with couples over the many years, it seems to hold true that, typically, the wife, or female, primarily creates the template, or sets the tone, for the relationship. In other words, she signals what is or is not allowed in how the relationship functions as a whole and what role she plays in their connection. The significant other, or husband, is in the position to RSVP, or accept this invitation.

For example, as the gatekeeper to the relationship, she initiates the actual boundaries. If she considers herself as a queen, she will naturally exude a type of regal air that commands devotion and respect, if not adoration. If she believes she is a princess, the relationship may also be highlighted in certain ways. For instance, she may cue her beloved to indulge her, to be more protective, to consider her feelings more, or perhaps treat her with gobs of gentleness and care.

On the other hand, if she sees herself in the rather negative light of *chambermaid, dowager, slave girl,* or even *court jester,* she may find herself being treated as such by her hubby. By this, she may find herself with a rude, demanding, whiney, insensitive "power freak", who may exhibit any number of other *"ick factors".* Her *other-half* may even have a false sense of entitlement and not take her reactions too seriously, or have any real appreciation for all her wifely efforts.

If the couple eventually divorces, the ex-wife may drop her jaw with disbelief when, or if, her former husband moves on to another relationship or remarries and acts much differently, such as in a more loving, committed, or positive way to the new woman, or wife. Nevertheless, being aware of our personal boundaries, or what we truly know is acceptable versus unacceptable behaviors from our significant other, is one of the primary ingredients for a viable relationship foundation. To fully acknowledge our feelings and remain present in any given circumstance is a step in the right direction.

In order to remain on the path toward marital bliss, the following is true for both husband and wife: Not enough can be said for influencing and reinforcing positive or desired behaviors in one another. In order to create an effective and positive connection for *any relationship* such as for a parent-child, friendship, between co-workers, and particularly for romantic and marital partnerships, a *Positive Connection Support Plan* can be extremely useful. The following is designed, in particular, for couples who are either in a committed relationship or married:

POSITIVE CONNECTION SUPPORT PLAN

- What is the presenting problem behavior? Be clear about exactly what attitudes or behaviors you may be experiencing from your spouse, or significant other, that seem to interfere with your mutually desired relationship bliss.

- What is the obvious or underlying cause for the negative behavior?

For example, what consciously or unconsciously seems to drive the annoying or unacceptable actions that your partner exhibits? Is he or she seeking more attention, (either positive or negative), from you or others? Are the behaviors a way for avoiding certain responsibilities or marital duties that are perceived as unpleasant? Is your spouse or partner suffering from a poor self-concept, or diminished self-esteem, or perhaps, has an unconscious pattern or need for drama or conflict? Does your partner feel disempowered and resorts to controlling, deceptive, or other negative behaviors as a sort of power-play? Is there a situation outside of your marriage or relationship and independent of you that is affecting your beloved's mood or actions that is adding fuel to the fire? Try to recognize the driving force behind the undesired behavior(s).

- Ask yourself, *what is within me* or *my sphere of influence* that may contribute toward a positive change in my marriage? The following areas may be considered:

Routine: Can there be an effective change in the usual, or daily, routine? Predictable schedules or routines can offer a sense of safety and assurance. However, they can also lead to a more humdrum, boring marriage. So, consider changing out of the usual rut to experiencing something new together. This can be something as simple as going on a week-night date, finding a new restaurant, taking up a hobby or sport together, taking a gourmet cooking class or going wine tasting, walking on the beach, picnicking in the park, taking a ballroom dance class, planning a romantic get-away, or working out at the gym before going straight home after a stressful day at work. The list is endless.

Environment: Are there any irritating physical or emotional circumstances in your environment? Changing elements in the environment can include anything from extricating yourselves from meddlesome in-laws, finding more satisfying work, setting the dinner table with fine china instead of plastic plates, wearing sexy lingerie, buying luxurious new bedding, putting the kids to bed earlier, turning off the television or computer, applying some fresh paint on those drab walls, changing your color scheme, getting your teeth whitened, and upgrading your wardrobe, to decorating your home with fresh flowers, etc. Consider anything that can improve the feng shui, or noticeably be added, removed, or changed right away that enhances and provides beauty and comfort to your emotional or physical environment.

Patterns: What types of negative patterns or predictable behaviors, including typical responses, play out in your relationship? What is the couple's usual, albeit ineffective, conflict-resolution style? For example, when one partner is disappointed, since the other arrives late to an event, does that partner tend to accuse the other of being irresponsible and inconsiderate? Or, does the other partner become defensive and either argumentative, hostile or perhaps, shuts down, ignoring the situation, in a sense, runs away?

There are many ways in which couples fall into unhealthy ways of problem solving that can be either aggressive or passive aggressive. These negative power-play routines can seem like a broken record over time. The trick is to notice these miserable worn-out old tunes and consciously decide to jump to a new groove, or change to a better track. For example, if one person tends to be critical or insulting, instead of acting defensively, (which typically may result in an argument), the other partner may try a different type of response. He or she may reply in an unperturbed, yet sincere manner with, "*I am sorry you feel that way. Perhaps we can discuss this another time.*" Then, simply walk away. In other words, avoid the drama. Do not bite the bait! Refuse to participate in rude or aggressive interactions.

Rewards: What can serve to positively reinforce change? Again, look at what your husband, wife, or partner may desire for him or herself and what your goals are as a couple in order to raise the happiness quotient. Allowing or providing desired rewards or outcomes, while staying within your own boundaries or comfort level, is quite powerful. Positive rewards can be tangible or intangible as long as they impart a sense of acceptance, encouragement, gratitude, and love. A kiss alone is a tangible reward. A sense of emotional safety is not something you can see or taste, yet it may be reinforced by a tender or passionate kiss, verbal praise, or gratitude such as just saying the words, "*I love you*," or simply by holding hands. In the words of Helen Keller, "*What is most beautiful is not seen with the eyes, but is felt within the heart.*"

Acknowledging or appreciating one another reinforces that universal human need for acceptance and a sense of belonging. Performing random acts of kindness for one another without expecting it to be reciprocated, but only for the sake of honoring your beloved, are rewarding experiences in and of themselves. With added unabashed TLC, any relationship will flourish with a greater sense of joy and connection.

Give it time: Most likely, unhealthy patterns were established eons before either of you entered your marriage. Or, they might possibly stem from your family of origin and early childhood experiences. Positive change can take a while to manifest and retain. Consistency, practice, and determination over time will eventually lead to greater success.

Caution: Replacing worn-out, negative, or demoralizing patterns with positive, caring, and more loving interactions with your partner can be habit forming.

With new innovative strategies taking place, check back in a month to six weeks to see whether they are effective. Then consider how you can work toward a continued re-patterning of your interactions, or creating an incentive in one another, for even more positive results.

The Price to Pay when a Marriage Is Bankrupt

A WORD ON DIVORCE MEDIATION

I have written many *Inspired Heart Letters* calling for tactics to encourage acceptable mediation between the parents, in divorce court, to end ridiculous power-plays.

These *Inspired Heart Letters* can clearly spell out what seems obvious: such as a practical, or a less emotional, common-sense approach in the division of assets, child-custody issues, and other considerations for moving forward with finalizing the divorce. By building a sturdy "bridge over troubled waters" the healing can begin.

Todd's Story

"SUDDENLY IT DAWNED ON ME..."

Back to the notion of just how devastating divorce can be on families and how costly divorce is in every way. I was asked on another occasion to write a letter on behalf of a man, Todd, in the throes of a very protracted pending divorce from Dawn. The amount of money these two had spent on attorneys was mind boggling, not to mention, the years spent squabbling over financial concerns. Todd and Dawn had two young sons who were emotionally torn apart, while being shuffled between two households in which there was a great deal of open hostility between their parents.

They had been married for many years prior to separating. During their marriage, the couple had grown a very profitable business. After Todd filed for divorce, Dawn panicked and began asserting herself for the first time as an active business partner, despite her limited business acumen. The results of her efforts were financially disastrous.

Finally, Todd contacted me to assist in this disturbing situation. I have included parts of the following *Inspired Heart Letter*, which cast a much-needed light upon the more salient matters at hand.

Suddenly It Dawned On Me

Inspired Heart® Letter

EXCERPT

Dear Dawn,

I'm hoping we can once and for all find some peace around our stressful family circumstance. It has certainly been a sad ordeal which has taken its toll on all of us. I surely realize how difficult and damaging our divorce issues have been for the boys. It is my heart's desire, (and I am certain yours as well), to create positive experiences and fond childhood memories for them. It saddens me to know that our sons have suffered because of our problems and lack of foresight. I am not blaming you at all, Dawn. After having so many years together, I know how unsettling our separation and divorce process has been.

Dawn, I understand that you want to secure a solid future for yourself. Obviously, your efforts in managing the family business reflect that. However, I am simply taking stock of the situation at hand. It seems that instead of each of us falling prey to the whims of the costly attorneys (who have an interest in dragging cases out for years to come only for their personal profit), I am hoping you and I can salvage as much of the dwindling financial assets, repair our relationship as co-parents, and move forward in life with the energy to be more creative and successful.

With age does come wisdom; although I am certainly not getting younger, I am looking at life with greater humility. I do know we once had a real love between us. Despite our conflicts over time, I married you because you are, in fact, a good-hearted, lovely woman. I have the utmost respect for your integrity, your loyalty, and your sincerity. I am proud that you are the mother of our children. It is our responsibility to raise them into fine young men. I believe we can still do that together.

It has taken me a while to find the right words to express my feelings and concerns. I hope you will read this with a caring heart for our family and be willing to consider negotiating a financial settlement that we both can live with. Again, lining the pockets of the attorneys, and prolonging the agony of our divorce process any further, does not benefit our financial picture or the emotional welfare of our boys.

With all considered, there is much to be gained from coming to acceptable terms for resolving our financial situation and amicably focusing on raising our sons. After all, they are still young, and, together, we will see them through many events and situations over the years to come.

Thanks, Dawn, for taking the time to read this through. If you are willing and open to meet with me, please call me at your earliest convenience.

Most Sincerely,

Todd

This *Inspired Heart Letter* seemed to have a calming effect upon this couple's divorce proceedings. In fact, they agreed to seek guidance from their local minister who, in turn, referred them to a divorce mediator. This resulted in developing a more amicable co-parenting plan to the benefit of the entire family.

After the Mud-Slinging

(BEFORE THROWING IN THE TOWEL, YOU MIGHT WANT TO RINSE OFF!)

Once again, we can become shortsighted or blind to the real damage that can result when our egos get in the way, when there is a perceived loss of power, when we become afraid, or when we do not trust in life's process. Unfortunately, too often, "hindsight is 20/20" and we experience the "aha" moment from a place of dissatisfaction or regret.

When it involves trying our best to live consciously, with consideration, respect, and compassion, we must strive to be honest and maintain personal integrity toward one another. However, *we cannot be responsible* for another's success in life, or for their personal development and sense of happiness. While life happens, we each are solely and completely responsible for how we perceive and react to any given circumstance. That is a part of our soul's evolution.

When we are enmeshed in a draining relational situation of any kind, it is wise to consider not just who is to gain, but, more importantly, what are the bigger gains for happiness. Once that is established, we can each do our part to shift into a new paradigm, a new reality, and a whole new and improved circumstance.

Rejection Is God's Protection

Michael's Story

"TO EVERY SEASON: LEAVES OF GOLD"

I once wrote an *Inspired Heart Letter* for a wealthy gentleman, Michael, who had struggled for nearly two years after his life partner, Liana, had moved out. After hearing his story, it felt as though she may have held on to old resentments from her former marriage and transferred that anger onto Michael. According to Michael, she was from a certain middle eastern culture, one in which the wives were often disrespected, mistreated, and prohibited from experiencing many of the social freedoms western women enjoy.

Reportedly, Liana had been terribly abused on every level by her first husband. She managed to take her children and escape that marriage. Eventually she found a home with Michael. Tragically, ten years later, her eldest son died unexpectedly. Overcome with grief, she was unable to emotionally recover from his death. This led to years of prescription drug and alcohol abuse. After going in and out of rehab, constant upsets with never-ending emotional tirades, including physically lashing out at Michael, and reportedly emptying their bank accounts, their relationship finally ended.

Confounded by his own victimization and sadness over the loss of his partner, (although he maintained a good rapport with Liana's children), Michael continued to be bothered by her nonstop malice and profound rejection toward him. He felt he had supported her and her kids in every way he knew. Yet, for some reason, even after their relationship ended, she chastised him both to his face, to her family, and within their community of friends. This became a thorn in his side; Michael was tormented and wished to be emotionally released. Here is an excerpt from that *Inspired Heart Letter*.

To Every Season: Leaves of Gold

Inspired Heart® Letter

EXCERPT

I know how painful it is to try and pick up the pieces when it doesn't work out. Liana, I'd like you to know that you did once capture my heart in a way that made me feel both devoted and protective. The underlying truth of our relationship, as far as I was concerned, came from a sense of love, connection, and absolute commitment. I opened my arms to your children, as my dream was to be part of your family and to spend our life together. Omar's passing was surely devastating. Although I too mourned his death, I cannot imagine the sorrow you have gone through and still feel to this day.

Thanks for reading this letter. It means so much to me as I need to convey to you, with all sincerity, that I do wish you to find peace. I thought this letter might offer a declaration for finally coming to the end of the road with no further bitterness, and instead, be replaced by a truce. I am choosing to reflect upon our time together as a meaning-ful experience. The wisdom and clarity I have gained is priceless.

After receiving this letter and forwarding it to Liana, Michael was able to exhale a sigh of relief. He felt a sense of completion, knowing he was an honorable man who was able to accept the limitations of the given circumstances. Michael began an unfettered and invigorating pursuit of joy. And, oh, by the way, his golf game improved!

When a marriage or committed partnership ends, a chapter in life closes. Yet, in order to move forward, it is wise to reclaim yourself in such a way that feels cleansing and renewing. Moving on *without* a sense of emotional completion from the past, or *without* forgiving yourself and your former spouse and finding a real appreciation for the experience, is a way of anchoring yourself to the past. (You will notice that I refrain from using the term *Your X*. "X" is what you see between the skull and crossbones on a bottle of poison and has very negative connotations. Often people refer to the title "X" in a disrespectful manner. The term "Former" however, does not demean or humiliate the person you once thought the world of and were willing to share your future with. Instead, refer to them as your "former spouse," because there was a time when they truly did give form to your life.)

Often, the process of true emotional release after a parting of ways can take time. The transition from being married to being single once again is a real adjustment. We are creatures of habit, yet our personal evolvement arrives only when we dare to break out of patterns and out-worn negative habits or lifestyles. By letting go of the past and staying hopeful, we meet life head on and can courageously step, hop, run, or skip forward free falling into new possibilities.

DIVORCE AND CO-PARENTHOOD

While we must take responsibility for our own happiness, when children are involved, we cannot overlook their interpretation and experience of the divorce. Our children may not be emotionally equipped to let go, and simply move on. If the parents struggle with this endeavor, imagine how painful it is for the kids.

There are definite hardships to raising children as single parents, not to mention that the kids end up dividing their time into visitations between parents, house-hopping while being denied the experience of being all together and part of a whole family. Moreover, kids of troubled, separated, or divorced parents, may find themselves feeling caught in the middle, forced to divide their loyalties and having to choose sides while wanting to please and feel connected to both Mom and Dad.

Over time, this may lead the children to manipulate their parents as the parent(s) continue in a power struggle to win their child's affection and allegiance; each parent may even attempt to emotionally, or even physically, distance their children from the other.

It is quite common for the children to play the game of aligning with one parent or the other in order to receive more, whether it is more power, more privilege, or tangible goodies. Hence, the term Disneyland Dad. That moniker simply describes how a divorced father, for example, may pamper, or spoil, his children out of a sense of guilt, or instead of running the perceived risk of losing their parent-child bond.

Every situation surrounding divorce has its own challenges or complexities. Striving to create and maintain a sense of home for the children, no matter their ages, will pay off over time. Consider your child or children, one day, grown up, pulling out the family album, and reflecting upon their childhood experience, or adolescence. Leafing through the pages of time, just what does that look like?

We cannot erase the past or take back lost opportunities. Raising your children, guiding them through their childhood, only comes along once. Our family history is marked by events that are imprinted in our hearts. How wonderful for any child, no matter his or her age, to see both parents proudly and comfortably attending their birthday party, graduation ceremony, wedding, the birth of their grandchildren, not to mention holiday celebrations, or other family events.

In order to be part of the important, family gatherings, and not miss out on these special occasions, calls for both parents to see the advantages of maintaining a positive rapport between one another. As difficult as it may seem, maintaining a sense of unity through being part of a dual-parenting team is strongly encouraged in order for your children to be less traumatized or feel disenfranchised and miss out on being part of a more connected family experience.

With this healthier dynamic in place, parents can better negotiate their differences in parenting styles or values and decisions. Together you both can be actively engaged parents, supporting your kids through any number of childhood/adolescent, or even adult, personal challenges. Without enumerating upon the current statistics, let's just say that your children will benefit in countless ways when you, the parents, agree to put down the sword and find an amicable truce, or learn to get along, even if it is only for the sake of your kids, and especially when your children are not adults.

Most certainly, there are situations that obviate maintaining a congenial connection with your former spouse. Only emotionally reasonable, healthy, mature parents are able to put their grievances and their egos aside in order to allow for a more copacetic post-marriage parenting experience.

Maya's Story

"PEARLS IN THE SAND"

Once. I wrote an *Inspired Heart Letter* for a woman, Maya, who was about to divorce her husband, Brett. She had two young sons; the youngest, Justin, was born from their marriage, while her older son, Joshua, was born from an earlier relationship in which his father had been estranged from Joshua since his birth. Honestly, I do not recall the actual circumstance which led to this marital split, however, Maya was determined to end the relationship, seeing no chance for reconciliation. At the same time, she consciously chose to let go of, or dissolve, any negative feelings associated with her marital experience. Maya had an earnest desire to complete their divorce in a clean, honorable, and reassuring way. Here is her *Inspired Heart Letter*:

Pearls in the Sand

Inspired Heart® Letter

Brett,

Since the close of our marriage will soon be finalized in ink, I am moved to share my thoughts with you at this time. The way I see it, there are never any accidents or real mistakes, only opportunities to grow or evolve. Our marriage was certainly a catalyst for my own internal growth. I choose to see our time together as an inevitable calling from my heart's urge to heal and expand.

I say this with all sincerity... overall, Brett, you have been a precious gift to me. Through the more loving, joyful moments of splendor, and along with the more challenging times, or when you and I continued to irritate one another, a pearl was formed. This perfect pearl was spun from love and wrapped in wisdom.

Thank you for being such a loving Daddy to our Justin, and for opening your arms wide for Joshua, who cherishes the underlying truth, which is that you really care. I know there are many opportunities over the years ahead for you to form kind and special memories with the boys.

Whatever your feelings are at this point, please know that I completely understand; we each tried our best. Gratefully, I am walking away with so many treasures. While I have had to work through the sadness, it seems pointless to view our marriage as a failure or a source of disappointment.

Life seems to have its own way of awakening us so that we may find a deeper meaning within every circumstance. The key is to consider what the ultimate gift of the experience is. Again, for me, the gifts include: being blessed by our amazing Justin and your cherished relationship with both of the boys, our unforgettable connection, and my own personal growth. Brett, I wish you only more peace and love.

Always,

Maya

The sentiments expressed in this letter are a mother's heartfelt gratitude. Although their marriage was dissolving, that sense of family did not altogether end. While Maya and Brett were unable to heal their relationship, they could maintain a special bond through the children. Gratitude should be included in our daily affirmations. It truly carries a special frequency for healing and for creating more blessings.

Chapter 6

Letter Theme – Stranger No More

ESTRANGEMENT ISSUES – FAMILY FALL-OUTS
LOST CHILDREN: FROM ESTRANGEMENT TO RECONNECTING

It never ceases to amaze me just how many sad and terrible stories of parent-child estrangement I have encountered. In fact, lately, the majority of *Inspired Heart Letter* requests I receive involve this very topic, ranging from a six-month time-out, to rather shocking separations involving grown children who have not connected with their mother or father for over twenty or thirty years. Despite these difficult rifts and lengthy separations, it is quite satisfying to see how parents and their sons or daughters can start to salvage their relationships and begin to reconnect through the written word.

Whether there has been a short or longer-term disconnect, it is quite possible to eventually heal from the painful emotional wounds, terrible disappointments, and, so often, simple misunderstandings that have destroyed the precious family bond.

The parent-child relationship is a primary connection that becomes a devastating and tragic loss when there is a falling out or the bond is broken. In certain instances, the emotional and/or physical connection was never formed, or at least not in a healthy way. Often, there is a transgenerational pattern, or a history of poor or even harmful parent-child connections, within the family lineage. Still, regardless of how obvious or hidden, in every child there is a deep yearning to feel loved and nurtured, and this experience becomes an integral part of their identity.

Children, who have experienced unhealthy connections with their parent(s) growing up, often subconsciously seek adult partners who manifest some or many of the same personality traits or behaviors similar to the dysfunctional parent. This may be since unwholesome connections seem familiar or expected and because there is an underlying yearning to strive for being loved or accepted by their partner who unconsciously represents the parent-figure for whom the sense of healthy bonding was never realized.

Certain *Inspired Heart Letters* have served to help the parent and/or their children to experience a sort of reality check and finally understand, not only how unhealthy their situation is, but how they individually continue to feed the long-standing, underlying emotional pain. This new understanding allows a shift toward a closer, more satisfying blending of hearts to occur.

Just like most long-term relationships of any nature, including between parents and their offspring, how we each relate to one another is shaped and molded over time. After a while, the pattern of relating eventually runs on autopilot. Without intension or consciously considering the role each of us takes on, there is a certain predictability that evolves, both in our communications and interactions with one another.

This may not necessarily be a negative experience. For instance, if the relationship is formulated with enough respect, appreciation, kindness, and consideration, then a fairly positive predictable parent-child dynamic takes root and blossoms with an unshakable trust that encourages a more open, honest relationship. Conversely, when the dynamic is unhealthy and there is not a real sense of perceived safety in one or more areas, then obviously, a more difficult relationship is formed, often with a sense of antagonism or defensiveness

When there is a falling out or a big enough disappointment and the notion of ever salvaging the relationship seems futile, even to the point where there is a final parting of the ways, consider that the identified problem is not the actual cause, rather it is a symptom. The very nature of the particular parent-child dynamic is at the root of the issue. Taking this a step further, typically there is never a conscious decision to create any type of unwholesome relationships with our kids. However, in the words of Thomas Moore, "*Wherever you go, you take yourself with you.*" Emotionally unhealthy parents, or parents who may be trapped with feelings of unworthiness, or those who have not experienced healthy relationships with their own parents, are more likely to feel inadequate when raising their own kids.

Sometimes, a parent attempts to correct the flaws found in his or her own childhood by overcompensating in other ways, at times, to the extreme. For example, a parent who was raised in a latchkey environment or with absentee parents, may be overly protective and smothering toward his or her kids. If a parent grew up in a home where there was never enough money and the family struggled, that parent might overindulge their children. When a parent is unable to devote enough time and energy toward nurturing the relationship with their kids, or if the parent, is uncomfortable expressing love in positive ways that are emotionally supportive, the relationship will not entirely thrive.

Lowell's Story

"CHIP OFF THE OLD BLOCK"

I once wrote an *Inspired Heart Letter* for Lowell, a man in his late fifties, who had grown up as an only child in the suburbs of New York City. His father passed away when he was nine years old. His mother was overwhelmed with grief and had never held a job before. Immediately, as a young boy, Lowell went to work selling papers, stocking shelves at a hardware store, and doing other odd jobs in order to support himself and his mother. While he often cried himself to sleep at night over the loss of his dad, he was devoted to his mother and determined to make sure they survived.

Eventually, Lowell grew up, went away to college, became a financial accountant, married a lovely woman, Sharon, and enjoyed a very happy marriage. Together, they raised their two children, a girl and a boy.

Lowell was considered a very kind, caring, and generous person. Without fail, he volunteered at soup kitchens every Thanksgiving and donated his time and money to other charities as well. He was always ready to lend a helping hand to friends and neighbors, whether it was a financial loan, dog-sitting, or bringing chicken soup to a sick neighbor.

Lowell raised his children, Debora and James, with an abundance of care. He gave them everything he could to make sure they were educated and had every opportunity to build successful lives.

His daughter, Debora, had gone to college as an exchange student in Norway and happened to fall in love with a local Norwegian. She was happily married with two young children and living abroad. His son, James, who was in his mid-thirties, was climbing the corporate ladder and held an impressive position in the world of international finance. He had been living in Sweden over the last three years and during that time had not seen his parents.

Given these apparently successful outcomes, I was surprised when Lowell contacted me to write a letter to his son, James.

The previous summer, James had finally been able to take some time off and fly home to Southern California for a three-week visit with his folks. Prior to his arrival, he telephoned his father to inform him about his flight schedule. Instead of planning to meet James at the airport terminal, Lowell suggested to James that he should rent a car on his own, so he and his wife, (James' mother), could avoid all the fuss of driving down to the airport and finding parking, especially since it was a holiday weekend and it would probably be a hassle. Somehow, James forgot his father's request or did not hear that message in their phone conversation. At any rate, he telephoned his folks when he arrived, with the expectation that they were picking him up at the airport.

Lowell became somewhat perturbed and reminded James to rent a car as he had already asked him to do. James was apparently surprised his parents were not there to meet him, especially since he had taken time from his demanding job and flown all the way from Sweden just to spend time visiting with them. When James protested, letting his father know that he had not secured a rental car, and besides, it was pretty difficult to acquire a car during a busy holiday weekend, Lowell became annoyed and snidely responded by saying, "*You are a grown man, James, I am sure you can figure something out.*" Well, James was so deeply offended by his father's belligerence, he decided not to visit or contact either of his parents during his entire three-week vacation. Instead, he telephoned his maternal grandmother, who happened to be Lowell's arch enemy… nemesis, and well, rather difficult mother in-law, and spent the entire three weeks with her.

So, not only did James fail to contact his parents while he was spending time in Southern California, but choosing to spend his entire vacation with his grandmother was a real rub in Lowell's face. Lowell considered "Grandma" to be a terrible, meddlesome, and conniving mother-in-law who never treated him or his wife with any measure of respect or common courtesy.

Over the next couple months, James never once attempted to make any contact with his parents. Lowell was completely undone with anger and upset by this. He felt so indignant and could not understand why James would decide to deny an opportunity to visit with his parents and followed by choosing to ignore them altogether. Lowell felt his son, James, was impudent and ungrateful. Lowell's growing sense of rejection was matched by his outrage. As this unsettling situation preyed heavily upon Lowell, he began losing sleep and feeling overly anxious and worried. Moreover, his mother-in-law seemed to taunt Lowell as she left several long-winded voicemail messages exclaiming about the wonderful time she had spent with James while he was in California.

Exasperated, Lowell called upon my letter-writing service. He was quite distraught over the situation. He knew he needed to clear the air with his son. However, it seemed that Lowell's idea of putting an end to this nonsense was to send his son a very powerful message, a letter that would cause James to feel complete shame and guilt regarding the awful way he was treating his parents. (By the way, although their son had no direct conversation with his mom, he knew that his parents always supported one another, and that his mother would never side with anyone but his dad.)

During my conversation with Lowell regarding the letter request, he barely spoke three sentences before I stopped him in his tracks. It was abundantly clear to me that the underlying dynamic, which caused this rift, was not about the rental car. Instead, I intuitively sensed the significant historical power struggle under way. I abruptly called Lowell's attention to the fact that he and his wife should have made the effort to be there at the airport. I could not understand why, after not seeing their only son for three years, they were not there waiting at the gate armed with a WELCOME HOME poster and balloons!

Interestingly, the actual unhealthy dynamic suddenly revealed itself in a crystal-clear way. I proceeded to share more insights about how

I felt Lowell was not allowing his son to really *Man Up*. In other words, he was not respecting his son as an adult, nor as a successful business-man. I picked up that Lowell was interfering in his son's business affairs by offering unsolicited advice, (telling him what to do and how to invest his money); moreover, he was upset since his son was thirty-five and had not yet settled down and married. Lowell shared that he and his wife always put their kids first, often sacrificing their own needs financially in order that their children, no matter what age, would never go without. I also saw that James resented his father for treating him like he was still a kid, for not acknowledging his independence, or his success.

Gratefully, Lowell was open to this conversation. He paused for a few moments, and then exclaimed, "*No one has ever pointed this out to me. I grew up without a father. I missed not having my dad. I never wanted my children to feel abandoned like I did...*"

Luckily, Lowell was open to analyzing and admitting how he had contributed to the strained relationship with his son. Furthermore, Lowell was willing and motivated to change his conversation, to re-examine how judgmental and pedantic he had been and to really see his son's perspective. Once Lowell conceded to abide by certain boundaries, such as refraining from offering James further unsolicited financial advice, or meddling in his son's personal life, I agreed to compose Lowell's *Inspired Heart Letter*.

Looking at his son's contribution to this falling out with his folks, perhaps James was unable to convey his apprehension or communicate openly with his father as well. Instead of sitting down with Dear Old Dad, and working through their aggravation, James seemed to be rather difficult or punitive by withholding his real feelings and choosing to ignore his parents. In a way, this seemed quite similar to his father's communication challenge since his dad initially struggled to truly express himself. Hmmm, could this be a learned response?

Here is Lowell's *Inspired Heart Letter* to his son, James:

Chip Off the Old Block

Inspired Heart® Letter

Dear James,

I feel so very sad we were unable to spend time together when you were here in San Diego. Truthfully, your avoidance was painful enough to force me to really consider how things have gotten so out of hand that an actual opportunity to visit was altogether missed. While meandering over the "How could this happen?" and "Life is too short." conversations in my mind, I was able to finally come to terms with my own fallibility for not always looking at the situation from your eyes.

As you know, I lost my dad when I was a young boy. It was so devastating, and yet, I knew I had to pick up the pieces for my mother, find work, and help support my mom and me. There were so many times my heart ached for losing my father, and I worried all the time about my mother. I guess, when I married your mom, I easily stepped into that continuous role of just making sure everyone was okay, that my wife and children would always be taken care of. I always wanted my kids to know I was there for them.

As painful as it has been to realize you chose not to visit us, I must admit, it has forced me to really consider my own contribution to our obvious rift. I believe I tried my very best to always be considerate and caring of you and your sister... yes, your mother and I have made sacrifices. However, that is not your fault. How we raised you and Debora was our decision. You do not owe us anything. I realize now that I must be responsible for my own actions. And when I decide to give, I know I must give freely and without emotional strings; or be okay with declining to give when it places such a personal hardship for Mom and me.

In retrospect, I now know your mother and I should have met you at the airport with open arms. It must have been a letdown for you to arrive without your long-lost parents greeting you at the gate. I got hung up on the idea that you were not being respectful of our request regarding renting a car, but that is small potatoes and certainly meaningless when considering your feelings were obviously hurt, as were ours, resulting in a needless disconnect.

I also need to express that, although your grandmother and I never got along, I really do appreciate that you have a supportive, loving, and close relationship with her. As I grow older, I am looking beyond the surface, or what appears obvious, such as when someone acts indifferent, caustic or rude, and consider the real source of that behavior.

I have learned that when people act negatively or when they feel angry, in reality it is their underlying sense of fear. My anger has only been a defense mechanism, and, honestly, what I fear is losing my connection with you, my son. Moving past my ego, underneath it all, is my simple need to feel loved and appreciated. Perhaps we both want the same things.

I guess that's it, in a nutshell, James. More than anything, I must express to you from my heart, how proud I am of who you are. I always look forward to our time together. I enjoy your intelligence, witty humor, and I have known your kindness and compassion. Looking back, I never consciously meant to meddle in your life, or your affairs. When I have in the past, it came from a place of caring. Now I realize how offensive it must have felt. I promised myself that from now on, unless you openly ask for my opinion, I will allow you to make your *decisions without interfering and graciously accept your decisions without expectations or demands.*

Please know I love you dearly. You are a man for whom I have such high respect. Our door is always open to you. With time passing, I want our time together to be meaningful.

My wish is that we can start over and renew our relationship, with no other agenda except sharing quality time and even having fun together.

Love,

Dad

After receiving this, *Inspired Heart Letter*, Lowell called me the next day. He mentioned that he could not sleep all night. He felt like a light switch had been turned on. He could not explain his renewed energy and enthusiasm. It seemed that the letter had spoken to his heart. Later that day, Sharon, his wife called. She mentioned how perfect the letter was, in fact, she kept reading it over and over and each time she read it, she cried. She was compelled to send it to their daughter in Norway, who also was touched by the message and wept.

Finally, they sent it to James. A whole week went by before Lowell received a call from his son. There was a new softness in James' voice. He mentioned receiving the letter, thanked his father, then made the following comment, *"I just hope what is in the letter is true."* Lowell assured his son that, *"Yes, it is true, and son, you know I cannot write worth a lick. I actually had a lady help me to write your letter. But you need to know: Every single word in that letter came from my heart."*

A couple weeks later, James telephoned his dad; this time, he called from Paris. He was vacationing with his new fiancée. James took time out from his romantic Paris vacation to contact his dad. In his words, *"Hi, Dad, how are you? I just wanted to hear your voice…"*

Lowell was so thrilled to receive James' touching call that, after hanging up the phone, he promptly drove to my office to share the good news in person. Lowell was filled with relief and appreciation for the dramatic shift in their connection.

I helped Lowell to openly acknowledge his innermost feelings and to create healthier boundaries, which were outlined and promised in his *Inspired Heart Letter.* Lowell claims he is following my advice and now sleeps like a baby.

FOLLOWING THROUGH

Parents are their children's primary teachers and role models. By example, they teach their children how to communicate, or express their feelings and desires, in either healthy or not so healthy ways; how to show or withhold affection; how to problem solve, etc. Children grow up usually mimicking the "family style" for achieving a sense of power, safety, and for getting their needs met.

Parents who live with a sense of personal integrity or good character naturally impart those traits onto their kids. Being accountable and keeping your word are two of the most important merits you can embrace.

Some parents may fall short and not follow through with their word, creating a domino effect. Likewise, their kids may not follow through with parent/teacher directives, house rules, or other responsibilities either. When we fail to keep our word, we get to experience a multitude of repercussions when everything seems to turn sideways or goes out of control.

Yes, parenting is hard work, and often, more than a bit overwhelming. It takes a great deal of fortitude, backbone, and a willingness to be a disciplinarian, even if it hurts you more than your child. By the time the child enters adolescence, if the expectations for good behavior are not well-established and adhered to, the road to compliance can be a treacherous climb.

All kids try to push the boundaries set by parents and others in authority. That is normal. When children do locate the boundary, however unpleasant, they usually feel an inner, if not unconscious, sense of safety and relief. Parents, being the first and primary teachers to their child, teach their children directly by setting stated rules and consequences as well as indirectly through setting examples or modeling acceptable behaviors by their own actions.

Ideally, the child grows up in a healthy, intact, two-parent household. Just as in the previous letter vignette, "Chip Off the Old Block", although there were issues between Lowell and his son, James never once considered trying to convince his mother to take his side in their dispute. That is a sign of healthy parenting. Parents may certainly not agree all the time, or even half the time, but when they model themselves as a united front for their children, they hold a much stronger and effective position.

Single parents, more often, have a tougher time enforcing discipline. As previously shared, this is especially true when they are unable to co-parent, or when one parent does not agree and sabotages the efforts of the other. When we keep our word, *when we walk our talk* and *actually follow through with our commitments*, then the relationship results in a profound sense of TRUST and HONOR. Without trust, the relationship will eventually collapse.

An Unhealthy Sense of Entitlement
Sylvia's Story

"ALL THAT GLITTERS"

This brings to mind the story of Sylvia, a mother who implored upon my letter-writing skills in order to set a healthy boundary with her daughter, Brittany. Actually, Sylvia wished to teach Brittany the value of earning money and the responsibilities that go along with financial success.

In this case, Sylvia had married into an extremely wealthy family. She and her husband had raised their very beautiful, intelligent daughter, Brittany, amidst an ultra-luxurious lifestyle. Brittany had everything a girl born with a silver spoon could ever want. It seemed the word "*No*" was not part of her vocabulary when it came to spending lavishly. Brittany was in her late twenties, unmarried, but with a steady beau, well-educated, and residing in a beautiful penthouse apartment in San Francisco's very upscale, tony neighborhood, known as Pacific Heights.

Brittany possessed a rich, innovative imagination. To her credit, she had real aspirations for creating new, interesting entrepreneurial projects that, at first glance, appeared as promising ideas. However, time and time again, after sinking a ton of money into them, every business plan failed before they barely got off the ground. You see, Brittany, considered her ideas only at face value and failed to do the proper marketing analysis and research to confirm the actual feasibility of the proposed business ventures. Somehow, despite these very costly, now buried business ideas, Brittany forged on in her attempt to finally see one of her ideas through to its success.

Meanwhile, Brittany never felt the pain of an actual real-world financial loss, since her parents and grandparents continued to indulge her and front the money for every novel business whim. While Brittany was not earning any of her own money, she was supported by a hand-some trust fund that paid around $30,000.00 per month. Further, her parents paid for her luxurious apartment in the city.

This scenario played out over and over before her mother began feeling overwhelmed and quite concerned that Brittany was taking advantage of her family's financial power with little regard for the value of a well-earned dollar. However, Brittany's father was apparently not too concerned with his daughter's irresponsible spending habits and flippant business skills. As a result, there was growing tension between her parents. Moreover, Brittany's grandparents could not seem to say "No," either, and continued to generously spend heaps of money on financing their granddaughter's whimsical business ideas. Her mother was in a real pickle and knew that ultimately, by setting a limit and maintaining financial restraints on their daughter's behalf, either her husband or in-laws would somehow eventually override her efforts.

At the time Sylvia contacted me, she had finally managed to convince her husband to withhold Brittany's hefty allowance while still paying for her apartment and living expenses. Along with cutting their daughter off from her allowance, Brittany, in turn, (with apparent contempt), cut herself off from having any contact with her parents. This manipulative maneuver did create quite a bit of family tension. Once her parents agreed to significantly cut her off from their financial purse strings, they had not seen or spoken to Brittany in over six months.

Sylvia was heartbroken and, at the same time, felt that she was fighting a losing battle, although she understood that her daughter would deeply benefit from gaining the real-life experience of responsibly earning her way instead of being handed everything on a silver platter.

Sylvia requested an *Inspired Heart Letter* in order to promote Brittany's sense of awareness and maturity. This particular letter request was somewhat challenging, since there was such little support from Brittany's father and the rest of the family. Sylvia, in essence, was finally taking a stand for her daughter's sense of value, purpose, and relationship toward money. Unfortunately, Sylvia was standing alone.

While I applauded Sylvia's sensibility and desire to teach her daughter a valuable life lesson, I cautioned her, on a practical note, given the circumstance; there was a chance that Brittany might not actually be receptive or acknowledge the real message delivered within the *Inspired Heart Letter*, immediately. Realistically, it may take time, perhaps not for years to come.

All That Glitters

Inspired Heart® Letter

Dearest Brittany,

I think of you often, as you are always in my heart. I am taking this opportunity to, hopefully, shed some light upon our decision to withdraw the usual funds we have allocated to you in order to subsidize your entrepreneurial projects. You may not fully understand what I am about to share with you, therefore, I hope you will keep this letter as you may grasp its intention over time.

Please be assured that I do believe in you and fully acknowledge your innate strengths. I see you as a highly industrious, creative dynamo with a genuine desire to be amazingly successful. I also see that you must learn patience, scrutiny, and discernment in order to see your wonderful ideas come to fruition.

Your dad and I, as well as your grandparents, have subsidized your ventures without question. However, I invite you to not only view this situation, (withholding of funds), from our perspective as business investors, but I encourage you to take a moment, and perhaps consider this scenario on a much deeper level. With that in mind, I do question... Have we really been supporting your development as an aspiring entrepreneur, while at the same time, forsaking your opportunity to evolve as a formidable woman with both purpose, poise, and a foundation based upon integrity?

As you can see, I have been contemplating the whole family dynamic that surrounds what is valued compared with what is truly of value. I assert that our family theme or "love language" is rather distorted and heavily based upon the power of money; my love for you is unconditional though. To me, the measure of success is much more profound and involves such attributes as kindness, compassion, appreciation, and acceptance.

Brittany, I see your true nature, your loving heart, the delight you find in dreaming of new innovative possibilities. However, it feels quite out of balance and detrimental to your personal growth when your dad and I are relied upon to be an endless stream of financial backup. Therefore, I simply want you to realize your full potential without relying upon us. Moreover, when you align with who you truly are and when you are not striving for acceptance from others out of some sense of family expectation for a certain level of monetary status or success, you will only become stronger and feel happier.

I understand you have been angry with me, and yes, it is very hurtful to feel the distance between us. Regardless, I am so grateful to know you as my daughter. You're a beautiful young woman who is just finding her way. Without challenges, how are any of us to grow internally? I am here for you, Brittany. My hope is that you have read and understood this letter in the light of caring. Either way, I always look forward to seeing you, Darling... my heart goes with you.

Much Love,

Mom

Upon receiving this *Inspired Heart Letter*, Sylvia sighed with relief. She, somehow, felt complete by delivering this heartfelt message to her beloved daughter. Further, she was not overly attached to the outcome, or whether Brittany actually would forgive her for stopping the family's function as benefactor to an endless financial stream. Instead, the clarification expressed in the letter allowed this mother to feel secure in knowing she had stood up for her daughter in a more profound way. She had offered Brittany a chance to evolve by earning valuable life skills and an opportunity to gain the personal enrichment of finding her own way.

In essence, although it was certainly easier to give in and placate her daughter's financial demands and thereby avoid Brittany's continued anger and alienation, Sylvia chose a higher path in support of Brittany's character development.

Sylvia contacted me some weeks later, (though she had not yet had a response from Brittany), to assure me that, by seeing her concerns articulated so sensitively in the *Inspired Heart Letter*, she felt confident she had offered her daughter something of real value: an uncompromising expression of love, no matter the cost.

Forgiveness Is Truly Divine

Tanya's Story

"A MOTHER'S SORROW"

On another occasion, I was invited to write an *Inspired Heart Letter* for another mother, Tanya, who had not had contact with her three sons in at least sixteen years. I am uncertain what exactly caused Tanya to leave her marriage and abandon her young children even years earlier. Based upon our telephone interview, it was evident that this unfortunate woman had never healed from a great deal of physical and emotional trauma surrounding her childhood, including paternal incest. What was even more disturbing was the emotional distance and sense of rejection she still felt from her own mother.

When Tanya initially took off, leaving her husband and kids behind, she moved thousands of miles away to another state. Eventually, after their divorce, her husband remarried and continued to raise their three sons with his new wife. Meanwhile, Tanya struggled in life just to support herself. Beset with symptoms of anxiety and depression, she was forced to face her inner demons of guilt and remorse over many years.

At one point, after several years of living a lonely existence filled with guilt over her separation from her three sons, one son, Randy, somehow was able to invite her to his wedding. This poor lady managed to bungle that opportunity when, at the wedding, her youngest son, Eric, invited her to dance. Unfortunately, instead of relishing in this gentle overture, while they were dancing together, Tanya blurted an insult. She laughingly accused Eric of having two left feet. After hearing this disparaging remark, Eric quickly left the dance floor and never spoke to her again.

With great shame and embarrassment, Tanya flew home shortly thereafter. Of course, this careless and caustic remark was highly inappropriate and only served to further destroy a chance to connect with her sons. So, here we are, sixteen years later, after the wedding *faux pas* whereby this unfortunate soul, (now in her senior years), is ready to attempt once more to gain any measure of connection with her sons.

With years of counseling support, Tanya was willing to try once more to heal those damaged relationships. Tanya wished to begin by sending an *Inspired Heart Letter* to her son, Eric first. And here it is:

A Mother's Sorrow

Inspired Heart® Letter

Dear Eric,

First, thank you for actually opening this letter. My hope is that you will receive this message with an open mind, if not an open heart.

I am not a very brave person. So much of my life, I have spent either emotionally or physically running away. But, as they say, "You can run, but you cannot hide." Now, at this point in time, after so much sorrow, guilt, remorse, and heavy emotional baggage, I realize I can no longer withhold my truth. I must step up to the plate and try my best to convey to you just how very sorry I am for all I have done to shatter our relationship.

With all my heart, I sincerely wish you to know that I take complete responsibility for the decisions I made, which I am sure must have deeply hurt you, and perhaps, even made you feel unloved. You deserved a mother who was loving, kind, supportive, and fully present. Unfortunately, that was not who I was for you, especially after your dad and I divorced.

Although I never stopped loving you for one single moment, my own insecurities, health challenges, and, otherwise self-sabotaging ways were obviously too compelling and I ended up making some lousy choices. Over all these years of being alone, separated from my sons, and living the consequences of this separation, I have searched my soul, and continue to hope that one day we could see each other again.

With your grandmother's passing, my self-reflection has grown even stronger. You see, I never had a loving connection with my mom. I grew up feeling emotionally separated, even though we lived in the same house. I cannot discuss my relationship with my father, as it was not only distant as well, but dreadful and shaming. Sometimes, you cannot see the forest for the trees. The thought that I have passed along this unloving legacy to you and your brothers is so painful.

No matter what the future holds, (and I would give anything to talk with you again, to see you again, and to recover any measure of our relationship), I want you to know that I do love and cherish you, Eric. I have missed you dearly – your funny, witty, charming personality – and most of all your kindness. I shudder to think of the last time we saw each other at Randy's wedding. Again, I managed to take my own insecurities out on you, through an awful, undeserved insult.

I guess I am a slow learner, but through this all, I have learned to not only be accountable for my choices in life, but also to understand that unless I am willing to be open, vulnerable, and completely honest, I will not have any real peace.

I pray you receive this letter knowing it truly comes from my heart. Thank you for allowing me to air my regrets and to emotionally risk the fear and anguish of any further rejection. If you could see inside my heart and soul, you would know how much it means to allow me to share this letter. Most of all, please accept my deepest apology. I am far from perfect, Eric, but I am learning to accept myself and to be a better person.

Every day, I think of you and your brothers. I wish you only the best in life. Thank you; forgive me; I am so sorry, and I do love you.

Your mother

After receiving this letter, Tanya remarked by saying she felt like a ton of bricks had been lifted. She mentioned that, if she never received a response from her son, Eric, she could live with that, since the words expressed in her letter rang true from her soul and she was already feeling a better sense of peace. This *Inspired Heart Letter* expressed what she held in her heart for nearly two decades, (although she previously seemed to have tremendous difficulty clarifying for herself, or putting her feelings into words that evoked a sense of atonement or prayer for peace).

Once she made the overture to reach out to her son, Eric, through this *Inspired Heart Letter*, Tanya immediately experienced a newfound willingness to more boldly emerge from hiding and face the truth in the sunlight. More recently, the door opened and a healing is unfolding. After all this time, as a result of this *Inspired Heart Letter* overture, Tanya is now communicating regularly with her sons. Instead of experiencing such a devastating loss, a new way to reconnect is being discovered.

It is never too late to say you are sorry and to ask for forgiveness from those we have hurt or offended. Love is energy and resonates at a much higher frequency. It is expansive, whereas, feelings of guilt, shame, or resentment function at a much lower vibratory frequency. Those negative feelings are quite heavy to bear and hold us down, diminishing our true nature.

When we finally take those family skeletons out of the closet, we realize they are just a bunch of bones. They are only scary when we give them power or meaning.

It is a universal desire for mankind to seek acceptance from others and to feel that sense of connection and belonging. In order to rebuild a relationship that has been violated or demolished and the trust has been lost, it is tremendously important to come clean and confront one another not only by sharing the truth, and without reserve, but openly claim the part you played in creating the issue at hand. What is even more powerful, though, is to diligently work toward repairing the offense and prove, over time, that the life lesson was learned.

Our connections to others, and especially with our children, are precious. If not continually nurtured, the trust begins to lessen and the bond becomes fragile. Treating our children with respect only serves to strengthen their own self-respect. We always have the option of re-inventing who we are, or rather, how we appear. So, once again, let go of the outworn role you have cast yourself in. *Act* as though and you will *Become*.

If you have been withholding affection, instead, learn to act more loving. If you tend to be chastising or controlling, learn to soften and yield. It is never too late to raise your frequency, to be more loving and kind, and to begin to heal. Your children and your parents will love you for it.

Does time really heal all wounds? It seems that I have encountered so many people who live out their lives filled with remorse and sorrow. Sometimes, it feels as though they do not trust themselves, in a sense. They either walk around all bundled up in denial, or to one degree or another, they have turned their back on their loved one(s) and even on themselves. It takes courage to admit you were wrong, to come clean with the truth, and to extend an invitation to repair the damage. It is the transparent heart that glows brighter.

Rolling Back the Clock

Max's Story

"THE LONG AND WINDING ROAD"

Once, I was asked to write an *Inspired Heart Letter* from a father, Max, to his grown daughter, Bette, who was about to be married for the second time; and sadly, he was not invited to her wedding. Bette lived in another state and had a seven-year-old daughter, Audrey, from her first marriage.

Max and Bette's mother had divorced when she was just a toddler. Shortly thereafter, Bette and her mom moved out of state and, eventually, her mother remarried. Reportedly, along with dealing with the physical distance between them, Max had combatted years of clinical depression. Admittedly, he was not very emotionally or physically available to Bette while she was growing up. In fact, it seems that he rarely saw her over the years, although she would visit him for a time over the summers until the age of ten or eleven.

Only once, (in order to attend her Bat Mitzvah), did Max fly back to visit Bette. Moreover, since Max did not approve of his daughter's first husband, he had refused to attend their wedding ceremony. Obviously, with their difficult history and such limited investment in their relationship, I was not terribly surprised his daughter did not invite Max to her current wedding.

Interestingly, it took Max over a year, (and after many inquiries), to confirm with me that he would actually like me to move forward and compose an *Inspired Heart Letter* to his daughter. After speaking at length with Max, it seemed to me that he had great difficulty gaining clarity regarding his true feelings, including personal accountability. Instead, he appeared invested in blaming others, or holding onto certain grudges, while tending to skirt around the issue at hand. While Max kept dragging his feet, I began to feel his frustration and underlying desire to bury his head in the sand, or just ignore the situation rather than make a defined effort toward resolving the matter.

Taking the bull by the horns, I finally just wrote the letter and Max was, indeed, grateful once he received it. Hopefully, he had the courage and fortitude to send it on.

The Long and Winding Road

Inspired Heart® Letter

My Dear Bette,

I find myself fumbling around, thinking of you, and missing you terribly. I actually do love you dearly and with deep sincerity. I am so sorry, Bette, I wish we could build our relationship anew. More than anything, I want to have the most loving father-daughter connection that is possible between us.

I am trying to reach out to you in the hopes that you can feel and know my love for you is forever... no matter what. Your mother and I prayed for you. When you were born, I could not believe we created such a precious, beautiful daughter.

When Mom and I divorced, it seemed like the right thing to do at the time. When we grew apart in our marriage, I did not want you to grow up in an unhealthy environment. To be honest, I suffered with depression. I know I cried a lot when you were little. Still, looking back, after the divorce it was certainly difficult living so far away from you. I tried, in the best way I knew at the time to maintain our connection. However, the little time we actually were together over the years was hardly enough to build a relationship in a way that you could really consider me to be your dad.

I humbly apologize for not being there for you enough. Now, it feels like I am on the outside looking in. This is not a comfortable place to *be. I hope you understand that I am very sorry for letting you down. I guess it took nearly a lifetime to get to the point where I can own my regrets and irresponsibility, and at the same time, express to you where I am at, which is a place of truly honoring you.*

If I could roll back the clock, there would most certainly be so many things I would have done differently. I apologize for not attending your previous wedding to Kyle. At this time, I want to express my heartfelt wish. My wish is for you to have a blessed, loving, and ful-filling marriage this time around.

Although I was not invited to the celebration, please know, that as your father, the one who prayed to have a child and was blessed to have you, my Bette, my love goes with you always. My heart bursts with a dream of having an opportunity to start over and truly get to know you. And, I hope, whenever you are ready, you will want to know me as well.

Please give my love to little Audrey. If she is anything like you, then you too are blessed. It would mean so much to one day see my granddaughter as well. I am so happy for your new marriage. You deserve all the happiness life can offer.

Please let me know what I can do to bridge our gap. It would mean so much to hear back from you whenever you can. You might think this is too much to ask, so instead of a phone call, I thought it best to write to you at this time, dear daughter. Your heart is what I hope to capture the most.

Your loving father

Once Max was issued his *Inspired Heart Letter*, I did not hear back. Frankly, I am unsure whether he had the courage to send it to Bette. Max may have vacillated because he was stuck in a familiar comfort zone that lulled him into maintaining the *status quo*. I believe he had an unrealized fear that perhaps felt more powerful than risking possible further rejection by attempting to reconnect with his daughter. Obviously, Max was plagued by his disconnected relationship with Bette or he would not have hounded me for so long, while going back and forth over the notion of sending her an *Inspired Heart Letter*. Emotional paralysis is not without consequences, and in his case, perhaps his unwillingness to put the energy toward plugging the holes in the boat could easily have sunken any chances of keeping his relationship with his daughter afloat.

RESISTANCE

How sad it would be if we never felt the love that is available. While it is true, we cannot roll back the clock, I believe we can embrace the precious time we do have to move forward hand in hand. When there is a rift or falling out with a family member or loved one, it is important to be willing to meet the other person halfway, or more.

Searching for the truth, even when we run the risk of rejection, is a powerful way to claim our freedom. With that understanding, it is important and wise to ask the other person to inform you on just what else you can do, or otherwise, how can you best help to resolve and heal your relationship matter. Finally, letting the other person know you would really love to hear back from them is a powerful gesture that creates an opening to possibly rekindle or repair the relationship and invites the other person to share their thoughts or feelings as well.

Regarding his "The Long and Winding Road" message, Max waffled for well over a year, before committing to the letter. In my interview with him, he seemed somewhat unwilling to take ownership or even show sufficient compassion for his daughter's point of view, or for her experience of their relationship. Rather, it seemed that Max actually felt victimized, blaming his inadequacy on his history of depression. I could empathize with his daughter's position for essentially walking away from a father who was so shut-down emotionally.

Unfortunately, we remain stuck in the outer manifestation of our predicament, such as a loss of connection with a loved one, when we are unwilling to be vulnerable and expose ourselves to the truth. We can choose to open our eyes and our heart and certainly learn from the past.

Feelings such as guilt, shame, or resentment can stunt our potential for happiness. Turning those annoying feelings into opportunities to grow and to bravely strive for an emotional cleansing is to claim emotional freedom. Unearthing the motives behind our own resistance is essential if we are to find peace with ourselves and others. We can be poor editors of our own feelings. A successful letter is not about a cover-up, but about vulnerability and exposure. Max vacillated because he may have felt more comfortable being depressed and sitting on his underlying anger, as outward expressions of anger or emotional pain is often taboo in our culture.

Gary's Story

"CHASING AFTER YESTERDAY"

Another difficult letter request came from a woman, Jody, who was the sister of Gary, a man who was living on a farm in Iowa. Gary and Jody came from a large family of fifteen, (yes, this is not a typo), fifteen children. They were raised by staunchly religious Catholic parents. Gary was one of the older children. He was in his late sixties, never married, and living on farmland he inherited from his folks. When he was a young man, he had spent about a year in a Catholic seminary. Afterwards, he was eventually drafted and spent time as a combat Marine in Vietnam during the war.

When Gary returned home from the war, he was obviously distressed. According to his sister, he not only was shocked by the war experience alone, but at times had felt unappreciated if not mistreated by his fellow countrymen. It seems Gary started drinking alcohol more often and otherwise usually kept to himself. At one point, he met a young lady, Nora, and they started dating. When Nora discovered she was pregnant, Gary offered to marry her, but she refused his proposal.

Gary did financially support his baby daughter, April, and visited with her during her early and formative childhood years until Nora finally met another man and got married. According to Gary, Nora felt it was best that he move on and allow his daughter to enjoy a whole family without confusing her with two father figures. So Gary did just that. He moved to live on his parent's farm and eventually, after they passed, he remained their alone. Gary continued to be a devout Catholic and was known for being charitable toward others less fortunate in the community. However, he never saw his daughter, April, again. Now, thirty years later, Gary was suffering from liver disease. Further, his neurological functions were starting to decline.

With Gary's expressed permission, his sister, Jody, contacted me to write an *Inspired Heart Letter* from Gary to his long-lost daughter, April. He knew that with his declining health, he had just a brief window of time to share a revealing message that might alleviate the emotional pain he most likely caused by extricating himself from his daughter's life when she was not quite twelve years of age. In composing this letter, it was my sincere hope that Gary could finally tear off some of the armor surrounding his heart and find a sense of vulnerability, kindness, and a measure of relief.

To April: A Shower of Tears

Inspired Heart® Letter

Dear April,

I hope you will read my letter with an open heart. I don't have a clue as to just where to begin. With all the time that has passed between us, it is hard for me to put into words that will give you even a glimpse of understanding as to why we have not connected in over thirty years.

As I am getting on in years, and my health is pretty challenging, I now decided to finally stop hiding and pushing painful memories away.

While risking my ridiculous false pride, dear daughter, I must come to terms and face a very harsh realization... There are no real excuses that I can offer. You did not deserve the experience. The simple truth is I ran away from my responsibilities to you. No, even more, I ran away from having the opportunity to be in a loving, healthy father-daughter bonded connection.

Let me first say, in retrospect, for so many years, I did not want to look. I did not want to see what I had done or not done or even where I was going. In a way, I was lost.

When I returned from Viet Nam, I met your mother. I cared about her, and tried to make our relationship work. But, I know now, I was not ready. I was still dealing with coming out of combat. When you were conceived, I really did want to marry your mom, but I guess she saw that I was a bit broken and probably not the best catch. You were an unbelievably beautiful and cherished child. Although my memory has faded from this encephalopathy brain disease, for some reason the vision of you – my sweet little girl, April, playing ball in the yard with me – has stayed with me over the years.

I made some poor choices along the way, but I always wanted to do the right thing at the time. However, in your case, looking back, I sure wish I had not made the choice to leave you. I guess I was not strong enough. I rationalized that when your mom married, I would somehow be in the way, and that it would be too confusing for you to have both a father and a stepfather. Well, I was wrong. On some level, I knew it. I guess I could not face the heartache and I just moved on.

Prior to my military experience, I actually joined the seminary for about a year. My Catholic faith is something I have held onto my entire life. I have prayed with countless rosaries and prayed for God's mercy. Now I must ask you with such deep sadness and in all sincerity… Can you please forgive me? This does weigh so heavy on my heart. If you are unable to forgive me, I can understand, April. However, it pains me to no end to think that you may still be holding onto the deep hurt you must have felt as a young girl, knowing I left you.

My prayer for you, April, is that you will rest assured and know you are completely lovable. I hope you are happy and close with your mom and stepdad. I missed out on so much in my life. Time is precious... and goes so quickly. Let my life be a measure of that for you. Follow your heart, no matter what. Your beautiful photos you shared with my mother have stayed with me throughout the years.

If you are inclined, I would really welcome an opportunity to see you and to hug you. I would come visit you, but given my health situation, I will gladly accommodate you in any way should you wish to see me. Please know time is of the essence. My door is open, and now along with a deep reflection, admitting my regrets seems to have begun to unlock my heart.

At this stage in my life, I want you to know that even though we have not been together, I was the one that missed out on so much. I wish I could have been there for you, helping you in any way I could. April, I also want you to know that as my daughter, you are my heir. It comforts me to know that I am able to at least leave you a healthy financial legacy. While it does not replace the loss of our father-daughter connection over so very many years, hopefully you will realize that despite the pain of being separated, you are still so precious to me. Thanks for reading this letter, April.

Love,

Gary

Gary's sister, Jody, collected the letter from me; as she read it, she cried. She explained that Gary had become increasingly reclusive over the last several years. Reportedly, he had emotionally withdrawn from his siblings and their families too. Nevertheless, Jody and the rest of his siblings had a deep desire to welcome April, their niece, back into the family fold. Jody concurred that Gary most likely did suffer from bouts of post-traumatic stress disorder or PTSD that had never been psycho-therapeutically treated.

After flying back to Iowa to meet with her brother, Gary, Jody visited with him over the Father's Day holiday weekend. Gary was intently watching his usual Sunday morning Catholic television show. Interestingly, the priest hosting the show gave a compelling sermon regarding the importance of the father-daughter relationship. After the show, Jody reached into her purse, drew out the *Inspired Heart Letter*, and gave it to her brother after which she left, so he could contemplate the letter on his own. She returned about a half hour later. Tears were streaming down Gary's cheeks.

Gary received a deeply moving, honest, and quite remarkable letter from his daughter, April, in reply. In essence, she was quite grateful to have received his *Inspired Heart Letter*. She filled in the blanks of her life which included "finding God" and, as she expressed, *"leaning on Him for support."*

April shared her sense of abandonment, and loss of family connections which were conflicting and seems to have influenced her chronic anxiety, along with her difficulty trusting men or experiencing a loving relationship. However, she spoke of her deep gratitude for becoming resilient due to confronting the obstacles in her life. She is on a path toward finding more peace. Most importantly, April shared *"Please know that I read your letter and have accepted your words with an open heart. Over time, I have come to believe my mother. You did the best you could under the circumstances, and I do not believe you intended to hurt me in the process. For this, I can forgive you. I accept the past for what it was, to live the life I have today – a life full of hopes and dreams, love and happiness."*

Gary's *Inspired Heart Letter* and April's remarkable, and thoughtful response has encouraged a father-daughter reunion which on so many levels has blessed both their lives.

WHAT ELSE HOLDS US BACK?

From time to time, I receive letter requests from adult children who are estranged or feel disengaged from a parent and wish to come to terms and heal their relationship issue. It is an interesting dynamic, since often there is a lack of what is called "individuation" whereby the grown child still considers their parent to be in an exalted position or have authority over them. It takes time for people to finally come to terms with the notion that their parents are only mere mortals and not only imperfect, but no more powerful, or necessarily more knowing or right than their offspring.

Often when there is a serious rift between a parent and child, the child carries a deep imprint that may hold a belief, such as "*I am not lovable... I am not enough... or I am the problem,*" etc. It is a healthy realization to come to terms with a parent being human and subject to human frailties.

Hopefully over time, with wisdom gained and maturity, the previously angry or turned-off child can learn to accept their parents as imperfect, or unenlightened.

Trans-generational patterns are those unhealthy mindsets and/or maladaptive behaviors that are passed on from generation to generation. When one generational offspring becomes more aware of the dysfuntional patterns, they are capable of breaking them or tossing them out in exchange for a more liberated future.

Guilt & Betrayal

OTHER FALL-OUTS WITH FRIENDS & FAMILY

Often, there are long-standing issues and separations between parents and their grown children, grown siblings, or long-term friendships that stem from an earlier experience that led to feelings of guilt, resentment, or betrayal. In my letter-writing experience, often the outward manifestation has to do with MONEY issues. Common themes are often around one sibling taking financial advantage, committing fraud, and/or absconding with the elderly parents' money, cheating the parents out of their income or their sibling(s) out of their legal inheritance, or failing to repay or honor loans from family members or friends.

Frequently the victims feel it is not worth the time, effort, or legal expenses to resolve this in court, or it would be too stressful for the parents to have their children embroiled in legal matters, or they believe the friend or relative will find another way to escape from having to pay. In sum, perhaps one way or another, it is just too painful to deal with. So more often nothing is done and the financial perpetrator gets away with his or her evil deeds.

At times, adults who did not grow up in a healthy family environment may feel an acute sense of entitlement and may blame their parents for not being good parents and/or not giving them enough. Taking it a step further, they may blame their parents for their own inadequacies,or failures in life. In this case, a certain neurosis sets in and a false sense of entitlement allows the grown child to remain shortsighted, narcissistic, or self-centered.

The perpetrators obviously have real character flaws. Instead of taking the defensive position when confronted with their selfish, conniving acts, they tend to take the more powerful offensive position and may try to use guilt or shame toward someone else in order to justify their misdeeds and get away with their betrayal.

Ralph's Story

"TWISTED SISTER"

I was once asked to write a letter from a man, Ralph, to his older sister, Carol. Ralph felt terribly rejected by her and ostracized by the rest of the family. This man grew up with a physical disability; he was blind since birth. A great deal of their parent's attention was paid to him. As a result, his sister, Carol, in comparison, felt somewhat neglected. Moreover, growing up, she was expected to always be there to help her brother. It seemed there was an obvious resentment toward her disabled brother and anger toward her parents that left Carol feeling cheated during her childhood.

Carol, a devout Christian, was married, and a mother of three children. Nevertheless, long into adulthood, after their father had passed away and before their mother died, Carol had managed to get access to their mother's income and coerced their mother into signing over her house exclusively to her, leaving her poor disabled brother, Ralph, out of the equation.

Ralph was not a very materialistic person. (He held down a part-time job and received Social Security benefits.) Although he could not understand his sister's actions, Ralph accepted this injustice. Nevertheless, he also found himself being continuously ridiculed and shunned by Carol as well as many other family members.

Feeling betrayed by Carol was one thing, but to be ridiculed and rejected by others in the family was difficult to bear. Ralph's sister did take the offensive and somehow disparaged her brother to her children and other relatives. She was rude, belittling, and complained about her needy brother to others. By keeping him away, she made sure he felt unwelcome. By somehow making her brother "wrong," Carol could protect herself from having to face the truth, that she violated her mother's trust and cheated Ralph out of his inheritance.

Carol was only deluding herself, though. There was a hefty price to pay for her selfish ways and financial/emotional abuse. As time wore on, she became increasingly bitter and angry toward Ralph. This seemed to consume her energy and overshadowed her enjoyment of life, which led to more difficulty connecting with her own children and other family members. She was primarily fueled by anger and a need to justify her words and actions. While her inheritance allowed Carol to be more comfortable on a material level, she felt emotionally bankrupt; this led to her dissatisfied and miserable life.

In order to rectify their strained relationship and to seek peace within the family, Ralph asked me to write an *Inspired Heart Letter* to his sister. The following excerpt from his letter inspires more compassionate communication for a closer brother-sister bond.

Twisted Sister

Inspired Heart® Letter

EXCERPT

Carol,

In an attempt to have meaning for why we are not close, I wonder whether you might have felt left out, at times, during our childhood when so much of Mom's attention was given to me. If that is the case, then with compassion, I am very sorry for your experience. You must know, I had my own cross to bear growing up and living through life with a disability. I really hope I do not come off as though I want anyone's pity. I actually am proud of what I have overcome, where I am at, and who I am today. Truly, Carol, I want to know and understand you better. I pray to God that we can find a way to enjoy mutual respect and a closer connection.

With the intent of trying to be more open with you and because I do care, I could not let another day go by without letting you know just how I feel. Everything in life is a choice. To enjoy family ties is a blessing. My heart is open to the possibility of having a blessed relationship with you. Forgiveness is the key to redemption, which is acceptance. Thanks for allowing me to share my truth with you. Please give me a chance. It would mean the world to me.

Your brother,

Ralph

Ralph has yet to hear a direct reply. Surprisingly, Carol recently sent Ralph belated Christmas and birthday gifts in the mail. Ralph reports that other family members who have also read the letter found it to be quite commendable and impressive under the circumstance. To his credit, Ralph continues to receive increased family support and respect.

When we are not too busy judging ourselves or someone else, we may find we are open to discover a new understanding. Staying open also implies there is a certain confidence that ensures a better outlook for enjoying every moment, creating new beginnings, inviting more love to occur, and only looking back with fonder memories.

Chapter 7

Letter Theme:
In-Laws & Blended-Family Scenarios

VICTIM OF CIRCUMSTANCE: DEALING WITH
DIFFICULT IN-LAWS & BLENDED-FAMILY STRUGGLES

When we fall in love and marry, we do not consciously choose, and we certainly may not always love or accept, the in-laws we inherit. I concur, it is usually better to be loved than right especially when it comes to your beloved's family. Obviously, you don't want to placate others by enduring rude, disrespectful, or inconsiderate behaviors. However, like all relationships, putting your best foot forward, remaining open and optimistic, while forging a trustworthy foundation, goes quite a long way in the overall scheme of things.

SCHMOOZING WITH THE IN-LAWS

Most of the stories I have shared with you originated when someone had a problem that needed to be addressed and resolved with an *Inspired Heart Letter*. Being that this book revolves around healing relationships, I feel compelled to include a model to emulate.

One story comes to mind about a young woman who learned a great deal about living in grace with very lovable, interesting in-laws. This lady, let's call her, Emily, married a very handsome, ambitious young doctor named Aaron from the East Coast. Aaron was raised in a large, rather loud, boisterous family that displayed a great deal of energy and enthusiasm. In fact, according to Emily, it took a while to comprehend what was actually being said, or shared, amidst the rather "cling-clang" conversation at their dinner table. Everyone tended to converse simultaneously. She could barely get a word in edgewise.

Instantly, Emily saw where Aaron received his incredible energy and gusto for life. Emily described Aaron's parents as both being in amazing physical shape for their age. In many respects, they had a traditional family. Aaron's father was from London originally. He was highly educated as both a medical doctor and financial accountant. Aaron's mother kept herself busy taking care of the household. She was physically quite small, yet she was a tiny ball of fire and cute as a button. Yes, she was truly a dedicated wife, and their children were the center of her world. Further, Aaron's mom grew up in Baltimore and was the youngest of nine children. Her parents were poor and struggled to raise so many children. Tragically, both her parents passed away when she was still a child.

The first time Emily met Aaron's parents and four siblings, she and her future fiancé had flown in from Los Angeles to visit them at their home in Maine, over Thanksgiving. This was over a year prior to their engagement. In fact, Aaron went to the trouble of purchasing a very thick tome entitled *Hoorah for Yiddish* for her to read on the plane. He thought it might be helpful if his girlfriend, (who was raised in an Irish Catholic family), could glean a better understanding for his family's Jewish culture prior to meeting everyone. Emily found this particular book quite entertaining, if not humorous, as it was replete with probably every Jewish colloquialism. The book also familiarized her to an ethnically fun sense of chiding. (Apparently, Aaron worried that his folks would not accept Emily, his *Gentile* girlfriend.) Despite all of Aaron's hand wringing on the airplane, Emily kept affirming aloud, with confidence, that Aaron's parents would simply adore her no matter what.

Aaron's family lived in a large, graceful, New England-style home, in an older, established neighborhood. Naturally, while they were certainly kind and welcoming upon meeting this true native Southern Californian, she knew she was under their shrewd inspection.

The first evening, they all dressed to go out to a fine restaurant for dinner. As Emily walked down the staircase, Aaron's mother came around the corner, looked at her, and exclaimed, *"Oh my, that's such a beautiful dress!"* Emily laughed in response and said, *"What … this schmatta?"* Upon hearing that remark, everyone burst into laughter. Emily's use of this humorous Jewish saying, which translates to *"What … this rag?"* was a definite icebreaker.

For the rest of their visit, Emily volunteered to help his mom, including with serving the Thanksgiving meal. She was polite and genuinely interested in learning about their family; she did her best to be as charming and ingratiating as possible. At the end of their visit, his mother shared with her son Aaron, *"This one… you can bring back!"*

Well, Aaron and Emily married about a year later. Emily was naturally quite insightful, and a caring soul. She was also emotionally intelligent. Emily did not readily take offense or go to battle over her new in-laws' tendency to be controlling or pushy. Instead, Emily took stock of the family history and dynamics.

Given Aaron's mother's insecure childhood history and his father's need to protect, it seems that maintaining their family connection was a major priority. Instead of battling with her in-laws just to prove a point, Emily tried to be compassionate and kind toward them. As their daughter-in-law, she remained openly honest and direct, yet sensitive to their position even when she, or she and Aaron, both disagreed. Remember, it is not what you say, but how you say it.

You see, it was more powerful for Emily to remain aware and discerning, or to honor her in-laws' positive traits, and not take their differences of opinion too seriously.

Over time, Emily and her in-laws grew to trust one another and bond deeply. They ultimately appreciated her candor, respect, and light-hearted humor, and she truly looked forward to their visits. One time, Aaron's parents wrote a beautiful letter to Emily in which she was honored with an amazing compliment. In that letter, his folks expressed just how much they always enjoyed spending time with Emily on their visits to the West Coast. Moreover, they considered her much more than just their daughter-in-law, but more as though she was their actual daughter.

Sometimes, the daughter, or son-in-law, is better able to draw back and analyze the family dynamics and, therefore, recognize certain set patterns or vulnerabilities such as a type of enmeshed, long-standing power play between their spouse and his or her parents. Getting to really know your in-laws also gives an opportunity to further explore and understand how your spouse's behaviors or attitudes may have been influenced or formed.

I am led to share this sweet story, since Emily developed a wonderfully close and loving relationship with her in-laws over the years. At times, it seemed Aaron's parents' meddlesome behaviors were difficult to bear. However, Emily wisely understood their true essence, their ultimate caring, and their heartfelt intentions.

THE BUCK STOPS HERE

Once, I was asked to help with an *Inspired Heart Letter* on behalf of a newly married couple, Jeff and Vanessa, whereby the new wife was feeling quite slighted by her new parent-in-laws. This was her husband's second marriage. While Jeff had been divorced for nearly five years, he and his first wife continued to struggle with co-parenting their two young daughters, who were around the ages of ten and twelve. Jeff's parents were quite wealthy due to their prosperous family business as vintners, a business that would eventually be handed down to their grown children.

Shortly after this couple became engaged, they traveled across the state to meet his parents. The couple was quite surprised when they noticed an abundant array of photographs in his parent's home depicting their son's first wife displayed on nearly every wall throughout the house. In fact, the elaborate photo exhibit could almost be considered as sort of a shrine, in dedication to their former daughter-in-law.

Upon viewing this, Jeff actually felt more insulted and bothered than did his new fiancée, Vanessa. He later questioned his parents about the strange photo display. However, his parents remained obtuse to his inquiry or remarks. It seemed that this was just the beginning of many bold acts of passive aggression perpetrated by his parents and Vanessa's soon-to-be in-laws.

Before they wed, while this couple was engaged, they decided to live together. At this time, while visiting his folks, the parents hosted an elaborate party with music and wine tasting. During this event, Jeff's mother insisted that her son's fiancée be formally introduced to their friends and relatives who were in attendance. However, for some reason, after making this grand overture, his mother suddenly could not recall Vanessas name. Instead, after hemming and hawing, she simply said, "*Well uh, this is, uh... is the woman who my son is living with.*" Obviously, this rather awkward strike below the belt was understood to be a demonstration of just how little his mother accepted or approved of her future daughter in-law.

Even after this couple was married, his parents continued to be rude while openly praising Jeff's first wife, and only finding fault with his new one. Yes, it appeared that his parents were conspiring against this couple, seemingly determined to try and break up their marriage. Incidentally, Jeff was due to inherit a significant amount of wealth one day from his parents. Over the years, his folks discussed their family will openly with their grown children, including the details of what was to be inherited by whom. Conceivably, this was a way to assert or maintain power and control over them.

I was very clear with my advice to this couple. I agreed an *Inspired Heart Letter* was a powerful gesture, and was definitely in order if they were to level the playing field and begin to develop a respectful, if not harmonious, rapport between the new wife and her in-laws. However, I was adamant that the letter should come only from the son and not from the newlyweds together. It is important for adult children to assert their independence and establish a sense of honor for their spouse and children with their family of origin.

It is not wise for the new spouse to be placed in the middle and be expected to defend his or herself when they are being disrespected. Clearly, marking boundaries by making sure of your specific role as daughter- or son-in-law, or your role as a parent-in-law, will help the relationships within the family to be defined and respected without stepping on anyone's toes.

After listening to their story and delving deeper into Jeff's family background, it was apparent to me that his parents were most likely still grieving over their son's previous divorce and the perceived loss of their first daughter-in-law. They were unable to cope with their defiled family identity and the meaning that a divorce in the family held for them.

I learned Jeff's parents had been married for nearly fifty years, raised two children, built a successful family business, and enjoyed spoiling their grandchildren. Furthermore, they were devout Catholics, and the concept of divorce is not considered religiously holy, or in accordance with the sacrament of marriage. What's more, second marriages in the eyes of the Catholic church are most often not even validated or recognized. Therefore, these devoutly religious parents, presumably, must have felt their family was completely torn apart. Moreover, they may have blamed themselves in some way for not raising their son to honor his marriage vows, especially for the sake of his children, not to mention his soul.

Jeff's parents' cultural and religious values, their sense of morality, and perhaps their belief regarding their son's "sinful" divorce, most likely had preyed upon their heart and sense of family tradition. Now that he was remarried, any secret hope that their son one day would reconcile his marriage to his first wife was lost forever.

This couple listened to my appraisal and found a deeper empathy and understanding toward his parents' perspective. The letter was written in a forthright manner that clearly laid down Jeff's desire for new, healthy, acceptable boundaries between his parents and his new wife, Vanessa, and their treatment of her. Just as significant, however, was the letter's revelation and sharing for recognizing his parents' idea of family values and even social acceptance. The *Inspired Heart Letter*, most importantly, conveyed Jeff's awareness of how his parents must truly feel and thereby acknowledged their pain and deep disappointment.

In this powerful *Inspired Heart Letter*, Jeff was perfectly willing to assert his manhood and independence at all cost, even if it meant jeopardizing his inheritance. Obviously, he knew he could not be responsible for, or control, his mother's or father's point of view. However, the letter itself let it be known that unless they were willing to allow him to live his life without asserting their judgment, rudeness, or reprimands, and instead act graciously toward his new wife, he must walk away.

Jeff's parents seemed astonished after receiving this letter. They contacted him immediately. And so began their journey to recover their family virtue through a deeper clarity, acceptance, and a way of finding forgiveness. This was, indeed, a blessing.

Adding to the Mix

STEPPARENTS AND STEPKIDS

It can be quite challenging to suddenly step into the role of step-mother or stepfather, let alone suddenly become someone else's new stepchild when your parent decides to re-marry. This is especially true when a child begins to realize that one or both of his or her parents has not only not reconciled their marriage, but, instead, has found a replacement for what the child may feel could never ever be replaced: their whole family being together again with their real mother or father! This is very tender territory for any new stepparent to tread upon.

I have spoken with many stepparents over the years, even the significant others of divorced parents, and commonly they feel the same way: pretty much stuck in the middle of someone else's family drama with plenty of egg shells to walk upon. This predicament is felt while trying to maintain the adult romance and partnership, (and get through all the awkward stuff, such as finding your place in the new family paradigm), while at the same time needing to figure out just how to grow a sense of comfort between you and your new stepkids.

What may complicate matters even more is if there are children from both adults who must now, also, contend with accepting their new stepsiblings. What's more, there can be another layer of confusion or even further relationship challenges when both original parents re-marry and dual sets of stepparents, and even dual sets of stepsiblings, arrive. Yikes! Now that does sound complex. This is not to mention a mix of histories, parenting styles, and child-parent dynamics that is somehow expected to blend into a viable extended family constellation. Whew! I get exhausted just thinking of that!

Looking a bit closer at the potential for overwhelm and upset, children are, for the most part, egocentric beings who are in serious need of wholesome parenting. Being a parent is the most responsible, dutiful act you can ever imagine. It is twenty-four-seven nonstop care, worry, organizing, and planning.

While wholesome parents offer so much unconditional love to their children, they also need to harness enough energy to keep up with so many obligations. As you know, it is the parents' responsibility to impart healthy values, set rules and expectations for good character-shaping, and instill other virtues, (such as responsibility, respect, patience, kindness, appreciation, consideration, and simple social decorum), not to mention, at times, play the referee in their children's conflicts with others. Moreover, parents must make sure their children are physically safe and their needs for proper nutrition are met as well as provide clothing, shelter, medical care, including tending to their psychological or emotional needs. Parenting is a commitment and a journey in and of itself. It can be both satisfying and draining on every level.

TERMS FOR ENDEARMENT

Looking, once again, upon the blended-family challenges, it is often too seductive for the stepchild, or children, to refrain from asserting a newfound sense of power through manipulating the situation at hand. It does not usually take too long to discover whether they can get what they want through certain maneuvers such as guilt, rejection, intimidation, or other manipulative tactics. The new stepparent suddenly finds he or she is *shaken* until the *not-so-blended* issues finally become intolerable. At that time, usually all Hell breaks loose and the new blended-family parents, who are completely undone with frustration, find themselves running to their next therapy session.

I recently heard from a dear friend, Rosa, who remarried less than a year ago. Her new husband is a wealthy, retired gentleman, with two grown daughters. Unfortunately, according to my friend, his two daughters have vowed to make certain their dad's new marriage does not last. With that in mind, they have vigilantly campaigned against their new stepmother with ongoing spiteful acts of subterfuge. Reportedly, these stepdaughters are exceedingly gracious, and complimentary, and they actually fawn over Rosa… only in the presence of their father and only while Rosa is in the room. The rest of the time, they constantly complain about her to their father and have made up vicious stories seemingly in order to create a wedge between their dad and his new bride. (Presumably, the stepdaughters are set on making sure their dad's new marriage does not last so his new wife won't be given the chance to spend their inheritance).

Unfortunately, Rosa's new hubby remains in denial and refuses to believe these shenanigans are really happening. For Christmas, one of his daughters gave Rosa a toilet bowl brush as a gift! When Rosa tried to comment about how awful, insulting, and ridiculous the gift was, her husband replied, *"Now, Honey, do not say a word; Stephanie spent a lot of time researching that bathroom cleaning gadget on the internet."*

Let's face it, in today's modern world, blended families are common-place and are fast becoming a whole new popular paradigm for family structures. My advice is to remain prudent and to err on the side of caution. In other words, be prepared and stay open and flexible to new conditions or emotional situations that may arise. Again, consider the Positive Connection Support Plan strategy previously discussed, and see whether you can introduce new concepts for transforming your new blended family into a more wholesome, viable arena for raising healthy kids, sustaining a sense of family, and maintaining your bliss.

Yes, indeed, it can be incredibly challenging when you find your-self smack dab in the middle of a whole new family system. A family that you did not start and you did not plan for, yet, you have now married into. It may be tempting to compromise your sense of right or wrong when it comes to lowering the bar for being respected by the new, perhaps unfamiliar, stepfamily members or in-laws. Concessions are often made for the sake of peace or your desire to feel accepted. Ideally, it is best to know your limits and maintain clear-cut boundaries as you may be tested in this regard. Stay calm, be cool, just relax… since you and your new family members will, most likely, adjust to one another over time.

COMPASSION

There is always a back story, or underlying self-conscious, precon-ceived reason for maladjusted behaviors. Consider the sentiments of author, Byron Katie, *"Don't cuss them out; Bless them out!"*

I am not suggesting that we defend our honor to the point of hostility, or run and hide, refusing to spend time with the evil stepmother, the spoiled, conniving stepchild, or the domineering father-in-law. However, I am suggesting one try to restore and remain balanced instead. Your spouse, or partner, is not likely to divorce his parents, or ever desert the children. Therefore, it is certainly not wise to force your beloved to choose between you and his/her parents or kids.

Take the high road and do not take others' negativity personally. Rather, try to focus on whatever redeeming value your new family members have. If there is a family rift, make sure you are not the cause of it. Otherwise, you may not be forgiven.

Should you find yourself stuck in a miserable situation whereby you find your new in-laws or stepkids to be unbearable, while it may not seem fair, change your thoughts and attitude anyway. If you see that your actual power to influence is fairly limited and you see that it is only your ego that can be bruised, overlook the boorish behaviors, develop a sense of humor, and stop trying to change anyone else. That is why I have cautioned you already to check the landscape before you invest in the property. In other words, before you commit to another in marriage, know that their family is part of the deed... I mean deal!

When we try too hard to win the affection or approval from others, it can backfire as well. Like the elusive butterfly, the more we chase it, the more it flies from our reach. Nor can we demand that anyone love, appreciate, or even respect us. We can each become a magnet for loving connections through our actions and attitudes. Take very good care of yourself. Decide to see difficult people as simply people in need of more love, instead. Remember, sincerity must be recognized and trust is built over time.

If you have learned to expect the worst from others, you will find yourself always waiting for the other shoe to drop. If you are able to step back and begin to recognize just how your thoughts, attitudes, and patterned reactions maintain the current dysfunction, then you can choose to be and act differently.

FAMILY-LETTER EXERCISE

Teaching your children better communication skills, or developing their emotional intelligence, will serve them immensely throughout their lives. The merits of the written word should never be underestimated. Just as reading stories to your young children at bedtime encourages them to take an interest and become better readers themselves, writing our thoughts, wishes, and desires can help to internally organize our feelings and concerns in a visible form. Giving your children diaries, or journals, and also journaling your own thoughts, can be a surprising way to problem solve.

By journaling, which will hone your abilities to convert your feelings into language, you'll be able to re-read and rewrite as your emotions shift and the circumstances at hand change. This is also a good way to measure your progress, stagnation, or regression, as you flip back to pages that may not reflect what you are currently thinking or feeling. Furthermore, when you keep a working record of progress and change, you can see which strategies work, and which do not.

Writing down your thoughts before speaking encourages more thoughtful introspection or deliberation, as opposed to speaking on impulse. Just as when we receive those endearing cards on Mother or Father's Day from our kids, we see that they are often better able to express what is truly in their heart in a card rather than through verbal dialogue.

I encourage family members to write down their thoughts before communicating with one another, especially when the subject matter may be sensitive or too difficult to verbally express. These "family letters" can actually become part of the ritual for your family meetings. Each member can begin their input by giving their letter to another, or reading it aloud. Or, the letters can be placed into a box and read by one parent to the rest of the family before opening up to a family topical discussion. This can be an effective way to begin a family conversation whereby each member has an opportunity to express themselves and be heard. Just as importantly, family members, (whether the family is blended or in its original form), will learn from one another and may eventually discover an improved or lasting connection.

Alison's Story

"DADDY'S GIRL"

I once wrote an *Inspired Heart Letter* for a woman, Alison, who had suddenly become part of a blended family, inheriting the role of stepmother to her new husband's sixteen-year-old daughter, Sarah. Sarah normally lived in Miami, Florida with her mother, and visited her father, Tony, during Thanksgiving and every other Christmas; they also often traveled on vacation together for two weeks during the summer.

Tony coveted his time with his daughter. He was concerned that they lived so far from one another, and so he always tried to make up for lost time by giving her everything she ever wanted, sparing no expense, whenever possible.

More than that, Tony and Sarah enjoyed a variety of sporting activities. They loved scuba diving, water skiing, sailing, and even hang-gliding together. Prior to her marriage to Tony, Alison and Sarah had met one another once during the Christmas holiday as Alison rendez-voused with them in New York City to do some last-minute Christmas shopping and for an enjoyable sleigh ride through Central Park. Their short encounter, at that time, was quite pleasant. Alison thought Sarah was a delightfully charming girl. Moreover, she simply adored Tony for being such a sweet, considerate, and gentle father.

Alison and Tony truly fell in love with one another. Once, on a weekend trip to Las Vegas, Tony won a small fortune at the blackjack table. On a lark, the couple grabbed a taxi and headed to the "Chapel of the Bells." The next day, they flew to Hawaii as the new "Mister and Misses" to enjoy a romantic honeymoon.

When they arrived at their hotel suite on Kauai, Tony broke the exciting news to his daughter. However, after hanging up the phone, Tony sighed and put his head in his hands. Alison had never seen him so glum. He repeated what Sarah had said during their phone conversation, *"Sarah seemed somewhat stunned. She told me that her heart just sank and she did not know exactly what to say. She accused me of being impetuous, not even considering her feelings, then, she just said, 'Well, have a nice life', and hung up."*

Although the couple managed to get through their honeymoon, Alison could see that Tony had become somewhat emotionally distant and preoccupied by his thoughts. Shortly afterwards, they flew to Miami to visit Sarah. Alison made sure Tony had plenty of exclusive father-daughter time. Alison even gave Sarah a beautiful, expensive, lavender jade pendant she purchased while they were in Hawaii. Before they left for the airport, Sarah whispered to Alison, *"Why did you take my dad from me? Now you have ruined everything."* Sarah was crying when she hugged her father goodbye.

Over the following year, Sarah became increasingly rude toward Alison. She criticized her in every way to her father and confronted Alison with sarcasm, accusing her of being a gold-digger wife and other nasty comments, such as *"Only a real bimbo would have a quickie wedding in Vegas."* The situation had spiraled downward to the point where Tony refused to discuss his daughter and would not bother to tell Alison about his phone conversations with her. Finally, Tony decided to take Sarah on a European vacation as a high school graduation gift.

They planned to be gone for nearly the entire summer, leaving Alison at home. By the time Alison contacted me, she was at her wits end. It seemed the harder she tried to be congenial and understanding of her husband's need to protect his relationship with his only daughter, the more Alison felt like an unappreciated interloper, dishonored, and left out in the cold. In fact, she noticed some of the original sweetness and passion between she and her husband had dissipated.

Alison asked me to write a compelling letter from her to Tony's daughter, so she could assure Sarah that she would never get in the way of Sarah's relationship with her dad and to help clean up any misunderstandings that might have caused Sarah to treat Alison with such disdain.

Alison was hoping an *Inspired Heart Letter* would somehow magically fix their relationship, so she and Tony could find the happiness they deserved. I responded by advising her that her true sphere of influence was not with Sarah, rather, she needed to resolve this ugly matter with her husband, establish new boundaries for her role as stepmother, and more importantly, as his wife. Alison needed to move forward on solid ground. I convinced her to address her concerns directly with Tony.

Daddy's Girl

Inspired Heart® Letter

Dear Tony,

Just so you know the angels were looking out for me the day I met you. Our wonderful connection and the incredible love we've been blessed with has been what I have always dreamed of.

What we have together is so completely precious to me. I would certainly not want to lose sight of our love and devotion. Yet, I do feel the winds are changing. Before that unique and radiant light that has held our hearts as one fades away, I need to express all that you are to me, Darling, and my deep desire to recapture that vision of who "we" are.

You have so many endearing attributes that make me smile just thinking of you. For starters, I adore your sense of adventure, your thoughtful, caring nature, your gentle touch, and your contagious laugh. When I saw the beautiful father - daughter bond you share with Sarah, it just made me fall in love with you even more. Yes, when we married, I was not the blushing bride, I was the glowing bride. I felt aglow with such joy that you and I would walk through life, hand in hand. Although, I was not really prepared for what has occurred in the aftermath.

It goes without saying, I have never wished to interfere in anyway with your relationship and decisions around your daughter. However, just as you love Sarah with all your heart, and she can certainly count on you as her dad, well… I, too, am someone's daughter. One day, Sarah will fall in love, marry, and build a life with her new husband. Please, let me know – if she married into a predicament such as the one I find myself in now, where she is not only considered a villain, but her husband seems to have abandoned her, would this be okay with you? What would you advise Sarah to do under those circumstances? Well then, is this a good enough situation for me?

The last thing I want is for you to feel torn in the middle between your wife and your daughter. Perhaps it is time to take yourself out of that dynamic. I am not suggesting that you choose between us. I am hoping you will realize that we can all start over and build a respectable, if not amicable, relationship. However, it really is up to you.

My role, of course, is not to replace her mother, or take you away from your daughter. My place is by your side, as your wife. Truthfully, Sarah will not love you any less whether you are married. So, whatever fear may be at the root of this difficulty, you and I both know it is not based in reality. As your wife, I am asking you to please consider taking yourself off the hook.

Perhaps you feel you owe your allegiance to Sarah to the extent that you are willing to forsake your own happiness with me. What I am suggesting is to grasp a clearer perspective.

Yes, I am quite disappointed. You must know that by now. In a way, I am glad you and Sarah will have an opportunity to spend quality time together soon, in Europe. Perhaps this will give you enough time to really consider all that is at stake. It feels to me that learning to cope through the challenging times is a skill that we learn to master when we are able to let go of fear. After all, isn't that what growing together is all about?

I am so thankful I met you, Tony. We sure know how to have fun together. Let's see how compatible we really are when/if we can handle the difficult times together as well. No matter how much I love you, I must be treated with honor and respect. I cannot settle for less. Let me know your thoughts and what is in your heart.

Love,

Alison

This was a bold, however, much-needed plea for Tony to finally confront the unhealthy situation and come to terms with his long-standing fear, perhaps, even guilt, regarding his long-distance relationship over the years with Sarah. Unless Tony asserted that he was now married, (and Alison, must be treated with respect, at the very least), the chances of endless opportunities for manipulation, scorn, and other power plays would surely destroy Tony and Alison's chance for real happiness.

Alison slipped this letter into Tony's carry-on luggage. In fact, she placed it inside a novel he purchased to read on the plane. She hoped he would have the opportunity to contemplate its message during the long flight to Europe.

Two days later, she received a gorgeous box of long-stemmed roses. With a simple note from Tony, "*Alison, you are my love, my friend, my adorable wife, please forgive me.*" It was signed… *Forever, Tony.*

Tony called Alison every night just to express his love and to wish her sweet dreams. When he returned home, he shared that he was able to take the time and instead of just "doing" things with Sarah, they actually relaxed together and had deep, meaningful conversations.

During their time in Europe, Tony was able to let his daughter know how much he really missed her and felt sad he missed out on watching her grow up by living so far away. Sarah in turn, let her dad know how stressful and sad it was for her, when her family was torn apart after her parents divorced. Most importantly, Tony, in his own gentle way, did an excellent job of listening to his daughter as she opened up to her deeper feelings. He was then able to confirm to her that Alison was now his wife and he was entrusted to keep her safe in his heart. What's more, there was plenty of room in his heart for everyone. A letter in and of itself is not a panacea, but is often the first step for a way to recalibrate and strive for a better connection.

The Aftermath of the Crumbled Family

Joan's Story

"UN-BLENDING & SIFTING THROUGH THE PAIN"

I was asked to compose an *Inspired Heart Letter* for Joan, who decided to break off an engagement, after a rather long-term relationship with a man who had three lovely daughters.

The daughters, Danielle, Donna, and Daphne, ranged in age between sixteen and twenty-two. Joan's letter request sought to lend both her acknowledgment and desire to preserve the endearing connection between her and now her ex-fiancé's daughters, which had been forged over time. It was a difficult realization for Joan to cope with the sense of failure and loss for a vision of being part of this family. Moreover, she wished to spare these young ladies any undo emotional stress or confusion. Therefore, while she decided the prospective marriage was never going to work, Joan wanted to move on in peace without incurring a sense of bitterness or betrayal for ending the engagement. Here is the letter.

Un-Blending & Sifting Through the Pain

Inspired Heart® Letter

Dear Danielle, Donna, and Daphne,

I am sure you must know by now that your dad and I are no longer planning to be married. Although I am still sorting this out emotionally, I just want to take this opportunity to express to each of you how very dear you are to me. At the same time, honestly, I feel quite sad at the thought of losing our connection. More importantly, I need you to know that I have grown to love you and always will; and while it is not working out for your dad and me, I still feel a special love for your father too.

In my heart, I truly see each of you as amazing young women. While you are beautiful, bright stars now, I can only imagine what the future holds for you as the accomplished, insightful, caring, and internally strong women you are becoming. Each of you is so wonderfully unique. And, you are very fortunate to have been raised by such thoughtful, loving, and wise parents. I always dreamed of having a daughter. Through knowing your dad, I have to thank him for the pleasure of allowing me to share special times with you, his beautiful daughters.

I hope you understand, I am not writing this note just to honor you, but I truly wish that your impression regarding the shift in my relationship with your dad as well as my connection with all of you is seen in the best light possible, however confusing it may seem right now.

I absolutely cherished the time I did have feeling as though I was becoming a part of your family. Again, each of you will always remain in my heart. I hope, in some way that is comforting for you. Hopefully, we can stay in touch. Please understand that I am truly sorry for the circumstances that compelled me to write at this time and know that I miss you already.

No matter what, please know that I am just a phone call away should you ever need someone to listen, or if I can help you in any way.

Love always,

Joan

When you are entwined in a blended-family scenario, know there is more to consider since there are other relevant people involved. You may not initially realize, or grasp, the real significance of the family paradigm before the die is cast and introductions between any new partner and yours or their children are made. Under the best circumstance, the children are not set up for heartache or confusion when the new relationship does not gel. Kids should be spared introductions or opportunities to bond with a parent's new significant other only after the relationship is definitely bound for marriage, or a lifetime partnership.

Sometimes, despite how careful and mindful the couple is, disaster strikes, things go haywire, it does not work out, and there is no one person to lay blame upon. Most often, the other blended-family members, in the event of divorce, separation, or when a serious relationship falls through the cracks, maintain their loyalty to their blood relatives, whether it be the father, mother, sister, brother, child, regardless of who is being dumped, or is extricating his or herself from the relationship.

Typically, any connection with the blended spouse, or significant other, outside of the primary family or bloodline is relinquished, or at least noticeably distanced to one degree or another. The loyalty to parents and children usually outweighs the connection to the stepparent, step-child, or in-law(s).

I am not certain whether any or all of the three daughters continued to communicate with their "almost-stepmother" despite the content and intention of the inspired letter. Nevertheless, Joan's letter was a compassionate and very caring gesture, and was a kinder way to help these girls adjust and move on with less emotional trauma or resentment. In essence, this *Inspired Heart Letter* allowed Joan to move forward gracefully with an honorable exit.

Dwayne's Story

"YOU'RE NOT MY REAL DAD"

Dwayne, an eager young salesman, had been living with his long-term girlfriend, Tanisha, and her ten-year-old old son, Tyrell. He was seriously considering proposing marriage. However, although Dwayne truly loved her, he was hesitant to make a life-long marital commitment since he felt Tanisha was often indulgent and way too lenient toward her son. This was evidenced since Tyrell usually was able to talk his mom out of following through with discipline. In essence, Dwayne felt the boy was running the show. Dwayne also thought Tanisha had a tendency to overindulge her son with extravagant gifts and lavish celebrations for birthdays and such. Moreover, while Tanisha claimed that she wanted Dwayne to play the role of father figure toward her son, when Dwayne attempted to impose more structure and accountability upon Tyrell, Tanisha usually overrode Dwayne's authority, backed down on previously set consequences, and caved in to Tyrell's oppositional defiance or demands.

Dwayne was not a meek or mild-mannered individual. Although he thought Tyrell was basically a good kid, who was intelligent and had excellent athletic potential, he had visions of Tyrell possibly acting out even more and getting into real trouble, (since he was already spoiled and defiant), by the time he reached his teen years. Dwayne held deep concern that their home-life, especially his relationship with Tanisha, would end up in disaster.

I respected Dwayne's apprehension and concern. At the same time, I shared with him (especially given Tyrell's age), how important it was for Tanisha, <u>at this time</u>, to take the lead when disciplining her child. Otherwise, with Tanisha's tendency to cave in to her son's manipulative tactics, chances are Tyrell would only grow to resent Dwayne over the years, and he very well might create a wedge between Dwayne and his mom. Given the family history, should they marry, it would be wise for Tanisha to assert her position as lead parent in their home and provide firm, consistent guidance for Tyrell. Moreover, like all parents, ideally, they should aim to develop a more collaborative parenting style and work as a solid team.

Both parents in the home will experience more success if they commit to share and maintain a code for expected, acceptable behaviors, and follow through with enforcing reasonable consequences. Most of all, Tyrell will ultimately benefit from their dual-parenting efforts.

Fortunately, Dwayne was able to initiate the process of communicating his fears and trepidations as well as gain a better focus for solving the matter of co-parenting through an *Inspired Heart Letter* I wrote for him to Tanisha. This resulted in Dwayne and Tanisha's agreement to begin couple's counseling with an emphasis on effective parenting.

We're Off to See The Wizard
(WHO IS HIDING BEHIND THE CURTAIN?)

One woman I recently met, who struggles with her role as a stepmother, complained that she continues to feel quite belittled by her stepdaughter, who is twenty-one years old. She described her plight by saying, "*Even after nearly five years, I feel as though she considers me to be "The Wicked Witch of the West."* referring to the classic *Wizard of Oz* story.

My advice to her was to change her emotional image. In a chiding way, I suggested that instead of being cast in the role of the *Wicked Witch of the West,* only to be spat upon or doused with water and melt away, she might take on the more gracious, benevolent persona of *Glinda,* the *Good Witch of the North.*

Glinda was known for her kind, caring sweetness. While she was admired and quite powerful, Glinda floated above it all in a sort of

protected bubble. After casting sweet smiles and words of encouragement, Glinda simply faded away. She never seemed to become personally
involved with the worry, drama, or fears of the other characters.

Quite unlike the evil *Wicked Witch*, Glinda remained neutral,
unscathed, and unfettered. She was not one to engage in aggression,
vindictiveness, or other altercations. Once again, she managed to remain
above it all. More importantly, and without any interference, *Glinda*
allowed everyone else to walk their own yellow brick road, or path, in
order to resolve their issues or reach their goals.

Remember the adage, *Act as though and you will become.* Once
again, try to remain poised, beautiful, kind, and with a more gentle,
unruffled demeanor. Staying neutral and remaining lovingly detached is
a skill well worth building. In order to maintain finesse and composure
though, you must remember to take very good care of yourself.

It hurts when we feel rejected or disrespected by others, especially
by those we inherit into our family circle. Rather than becoming
emotionally defensive or depleted, it is much wiser to remain lovingly
detached, to resist going into battle, and not energize the vindictive or
aggressive attacks from others. Whatever internal drama other blended-
family members may be experiencing, do not allow them to drag you down.

Emotional strain, including resentment, is a very common dilemma
among blended families. For the sake of peace and harmony, the new
stepparent often wishes to step in and confront, or even write a letter
to their stepkid(s), in the hopes of alleviating their misgivings or angst.
If you are a stepparent, you should not have to openly plead your case.
Instead, it is the spouse, the child's natural parent, who ought to rise to
the occasion and set the ground rules for maintaining respect and polite
decorum toward the new stepparent. Moreover, the natural parent
should explain that any rude behaviors toward their new spouse will not
be tolerated. By doing so, the natural parent is taking responsibility for
nurturing and protecting their new marriage or partnership. Therefore:
Dear stepparent, gently back off and enjoy your marriage. And, perhaps
pray for Divine intervention.

My Letter Story

"BRINGING CHILDREN INTO YOUR NEW RELATIONSHIP"

I must re-emphasize, it is usually pretty tricky to know exactly when to introduce your child to your potential new partner. Since we are the role models for our kids when it comes to teaching them how to build and maintain committed relationships, it is unwise to introduce your children prematurely before knowing whether your choice of partner will be there for the long haul.

I was once in a relationship in which I understood that we were both absolutely committed to one another and planned to grow old together. My daughter was already grown and living away from home. My significant other shared regular custody or visitation with his ten-year-old daughter, Anna. Over time, I was eventually introduced to Anna and we easily formed a very close, bonded relationship. Anna confided in me, sharing her secret wishes and worries. I found her to be such a lovable, sweet-natured young girl. Moreover, I appreciated witnessing how well her father treated her, which only made me feel closer to him.

Unfortunately, the relationship did not last and I was heartbroken. Not only for the loss of what I had envisioned as my future with this man, but I grieved deeply for the loss of connection with his daughter, Anna. It saddened me to consider that Anna may have thought she was somehow to blame or that I had abandoned her without a care. Therefore, I wrote the following letter.

A Heart Connection With His Daughter

Inspired Heart® Letter

Dear Anna,

I am thinking of you, and just wanted to send you this note. I hope you enjoyed a very special Christmas and celebrated the New Year in style. I know we have not seen each other in a while. I have been wondering just how you are doing. I heard your Christmas song recital was fabulous!

As you must know, your dad and I have taken a break. I think he has a lot on his mind. So we may not see each other. I just needed you to know how wonderful, beautiful, and impressive you are. I adore your creative imagination. You truly are a brilliant conversationalist as well. More important, Anna, you are your own person. And as you said, you "are not going to pretend to be anyone else than who you are." I wish everyone on the planet had your attitude!

It was my pleasure to meet you and to know you, Anna Banana. I know sometimes it can be hard dealing with some of the kids at school. Just remember, only miserable people say "mean" things. No matter what, stay the beautiful, and the kind princess you are. I wish only the best for you. Take care, precious.

Much Love,

Kristine

Initially I contacted her father, my former boyfriend, to give him the letter first, leaving it up to him as to whether he would share it with Anna. He agreed to give it to her and felt it was a positive message. I recently saw Anna again. It was a very happy reunion.

A SMOOTHER BLEND

Should you remain dissatisfied with how you are being treated by your stepchildren or in-laws, convey your feelings to your spouse and encourage them to set new boundaries with their family members on your behalf. Be mindful of just where you are placing your thoughts or focus. Being defensive or offensive toward blended-family members is hardly a guarantee for winning anyone's respect or admiration. However, it is a good way to sabotage your primary relationship with your spouse!

In short, while you are never responsible for another's happiness, or whether anyone else likes or accepts you, be sure to honor yourself. Again, locate and acknowledge your true sphere of influence regarding others, without needlessly overstepping your bounds. Most often, it is best not to fan the flames, or make an issue an even bigger deal. If the situation at hand is not fueled with drama or increased anxiety, chances are eventually it will exhaust itself and fade away.

Usually when we experience rejection from others, it is based upon their feelings of anger and resentment, which is rooted in a deeper sense of fear. For many, the prospect of change or the unknown is stressful. It may take time to adjust and accept a new family member or circumstance. As I have mentioned over and over throughout this book, trust is the foundation for which successful relationships are built upon, and that does call for an investment of caring and reliability over time.

Stay focused upon the progress you've made, breathe deeply, open your heart even more, and become exceedingly compassionate. Then, be thankful, since conditions inevitably do change as we change our perspective.

Chapter 8

Letter Theme: Friendships

HONORING OUR FRIENDS
AND
WHEN FRIENDSHIPS GET IN THE WAY

Do you find yourself to be attractive? I am not referring to looking in the mirror. Rather, do you consider yourself to be the kind of person you would easily befriend? Forming and maintaining friendships is somewhat of a skill, yet it is a natural talent for those who consider themselves to be a wonderful friend already. In other words, if you would like to have a friend who is similar to you, bestowed with those certain ingratiating attributes that you already own and are difficult to ignore, then you most likely are a sought-after friend. You are a keeper.

EXPLORING THE MEANING OF FRIENDSHIP

There is a universal need for feeling accepted by others. Most of us have experienced feeling lonely at one point or another. On those occasions, having a friend, a supportive connection with another can be so very comforting. As children, once we begin to socialize outside of our family circle, typically, we soon understand how to navigate our way through our attractions for desired entertainment, need for playmates, or otherwise satisfy our urge to fit in and feel part of the social milieu. Our friendships tend to further feed our sense of identity. Developmentally, if a child somehow fails to grasp how to successfully navigate the social terrain or awkwardly misses the "friendship boat", they may tend to either socially withdraw or act out with their peers in more aggressive ways.

SCARRED FOR LIFE

Children are essentially egocentric. They initially tend to base their friendships on whether they really belong or are accepted by their peers. Unfortunately, children can suffer life-long emotional scars when they have participated in any form of relational aggression during their formative years. These emotional imprints may stem from either being a bully, a target, or a bystander, which refers to someone who did not stand up for another kid who was being mistreated. This subject is so close to my heart due to my daughter's horrific encounter with bullying when she was in middle school that I wrote the "Be Friendship Focused" children's self-empowerment/anti-bullying program along with creating the "A-Z Power Cards", which helps children to learn about what character or integrity really means.

As we mature, we grow to feel our friends not only support our values, interests, and social status, but they provide a safe space for revealing ourselves and our innermost feelings when we feel we have been mistreated, find ourselves feeling out of sync, or when we are filled with regret. We turn to our friends for emotional support and guidance. We seek our friends to share our interests and, at times, to fill a void, so we do not feel so alone.

Friendships can also enhance our memories. As we recall special moments in time or other lovely sentimental experiences, what about that collection of photos or the memorabilia we've saved over the years? If we do not have a meaningful person such as a family member or a friend seen in that photo who shared the moment with us, well, it is just not as treasured.

An important feature involving the concept of friendships is that our friends often tend to reflect back to us a sense of group identity, or we are, in a way, defined through our friendships, such as the adage: *Birds of a feather flock together*. In essence, we hang out with certain friends, since through our rapport, we can feel understood, or we just relate to one another based on common values, or shared interests. However, let's face it; friendships do occur in matters of degrees.

What qualifies as a true *BFF* or life-long friendship, just like any other meaningful relationship, is an underlying, undeniable sense of trust. While we may have a large social circle, replete with scads of acquaintances for whom we may refer to as our "friends," real friendships are born on a much deeper, much more honest level that is developed with the investment of time and experience.

Sometimes, our dearest friends show up in the strangest places. They appear out of the blue in uncanny, surprising ways and step forward to help us in our times of need. Other times, upon meeting someone, we are intuitively drawn to become one another's friend as there is an unspoken energetic affinity and connection. This lends a sense of belonging to the same tribe.

As I look back on my life and muse over the most important alliances with others, I am struck by the knowingness that there was never a per chance meeting. Rather, our friendship connection emerged out of an urge to experience a certain life lesson or feel connected either directly or through our mutual sense of resonance and care.

GENDER-MIXED PLATONIC FRIENDS

It is quite common for gay men and any gender-preferenced woman to form an endearing friendship. In fact, this type of friendly mix can be quite fun and supportive. However, true platonic friendships between straight males and females is somewhat more unique. If there is a physical attraction by either party, then the friendship may be gratifying, yet somewhat stressful on some level. However, for those men and women who just *click* as good friends, their connection can be immensely rewarding.

A friend of mine, Trish, discussed one of her dearest and most treasured friendships with a fellow named Hank, who happened to be her next-door neighbor. They have known one another for over ten years. Trish is quite convinced that Hank is an incarnated angel who was Divinely sent to her on a mission from Heaven. Hank has generously demonstrated such a pure and genuine kindness and care toward Trish and her family over the years that it would be difficult to list all the wonderful, supportive gifts he has brought to their lives.

In fact, Hank has performed so many random acts of kindness that Trish initially began wondering how she would ever be able to repay him.

Since she felt so beholden to this man, she asked my advice. After some consideration, I suggested that she allow herself to, unequivocally, be a recipient of his kindness. Further, in a playful way, I advised her to make the following pronouncement to Hank:

Surely, Hank, I must have been an amazing friend of yours in a previous lifetime. In fact, I am quite certain I was so selflessly kind, generous, and supportive toward you that you absolutely must owe me in this lifetime! I am actually allowing you to return the favors and pay me back abundantly as my good karma has graced me to receive so many gifts from you.

My friend Trish followed my advice and quoted my verbal rhetoric verbatim. Thereby, she gave Hank complete carte blanche to be relentlessly good to her and her family as long as he is compelled to do so. Dear Hank's immediate response to her proclamation, *"Great... that works for me."*

You see, there is a gift found in giving to others that is uplifting and fulfilling. Actually, whether in a romantic, familial, or neighborly fashion, the act of kindness or being generous toward another, and knowing you have made a charitable or positive difference in their life, is quite gratifying. The gift received by giving to another can simply be enough. Sometimes, just accepting kindness in the spirit of friendship is another way of living in grace and promoting the cycle of giving and receiving. Truly unabashed, platonic friendship between men and women is like a rare jewel – less abundant, and quite exquisite.

Donald's Story

"TRUE BLUE FRIEND"

I once wrote an inspired letter to be given from a young man, Donald, who had found true friendship with a woman, Patti, whom he had, once upon a time, briefly dated. While their initial encounter did not culminate in romance, they discovered a deep, mutual understanding and caring whereby they grew to rely upon the emotional support found in the comfort of their trusted friendship. They were able to openly share about personal experiences and concerns and respected one another's acceptance and/or guidance.

At one point, Patti had been experiencing some emotional difficulty with one of her family members. Donald wanted to emotionally lift her up and felt compelled to acknowledge Patti as well as his appreciation of their special connection through an *Inspired Heart Letter.*

I felt quite complimented to be asked to compose such an honorable letter and wonderful tribute to their friendship. Along with the letter, Donald personally picked each flower from a specialty florist shop and created an amazing bouquet, which accompanied the stylishly delivered *Inspired Heart Letter.* What a lovely gesture! The following is an excerpt from this sweet message:

True Blue Friend

Inspired Heart® Letter

EXCERPT

Patti,

It was wonderful to see you for lunch yesterday. As you know, your friendship means so much to me, and for whatever reason, I am simply compelled to share some thoughts. Actually, it feels like our friendship was somehow destined. I say that, since I seem to have matured emotionally since we first met four years ago.

You have given me a truly amazing gift just by being who you are... very caring and accepting. I feel that our connection is so healthy and natural that certainly God played a role in putting you in my life. Thank you for trusting me with your cares and concerns.

My hope for you, Patti, is that you fully understand how completely precious and worthwhile you are. If I were your fairy godmother (or godfather I should say), I would wave a magic wand and you could see yourself through my eyes. You would see how kind, lovely, gracious, and beautiful you are. You would know and understand your true power and essence.

It has been written that "love is letting go of fear". Through knowing you, I am starting to allow myself to share parts of me that I have not revealed before. Thanks for listening to not only what my ups and downs in life are, but how those experiences make me feel. Thank you for giving me permission to be more of who I truly am. There is no better gift.

Your friend,

Donald

Another beautiful component to friendship is that we do not tend to hold our friends to the same standards as we would a romantic partner or life-mate. We are usually much more forgiving or allowing of strange habits, peccadilloes, or even eccentricity or weirdness, that we may tend to chalk up as being flamboyant, dramatic, awkward, shy, ungrounded, a bit serious, impulsive, grandiose... yah-be-de-yah-be-de-yah... all the while exclaiming upon and defending their endearing attributes such as sweet-natured, kind, great sense of humor, talented, generous, wise, sensitive, astute intelligence, creative, fun, reliable, thoughtful, etc.

I may not be part of the norm, but I do enjoy having a colorful array of friends. Like any other relationship though, true friendship is formed over time with tender loving care, sincerity, acceptance, forgiveness, honesty, and, of course, plenty of laughter and good memories.

GIVE AND TAKE

Generosity is a key component for authentic friendships. However, it is a different brand of generosity opposed to the type of selfless giving that may be called upon for enduring romance, marriage, parenting, and other family matters. In friendship, there is less of a personal agenda. Friends can be a bit more objective when peeking into one another's lives and offering their support.

A true friend has nothing more to gain than the sense of affinity and connection, based upon mutual understanding and caring. There are no romantic or family entanglements to move through or protect. Often, our friends vicariously experience our joy or pain with no personal agenda aside from their desire to be a good friend and to wish us well.

I recently had a conversation with a wise friend who is looking forward to starting her life anew with her new fiancé, after experiencing a divorce and raising her two children. She and her hubby-to-be recently returned from an amazing vacation, including a first-class European cruise and trip to Dubai. Their vacation lasted nearly a month. With real gladness over how well they got along given the amount of time spent with each other, she reported that now, more than ever, she knew they could endure a longer-term, uninterrupted lifetime together with ease and flow.

You see, most important to her was how special it was to not only travel together, but to spend so much constant time exclusively with one another while remaining harmoniously connected.

Laughingly, she commented how, sometimes, even when traveling with a platonic friend, there can be friction. For this lady, the friendship quality of their experience while traveling – and within their relationship as a whole – was at least as important and gratifying as their romantic liaison. At the close of their vacation, she asked her beloved what he considered to be the most wonderful part of their extravagant travel experience. Without hesitation, he replied, "*Spending quality time with my partner.*"

As a world traveler myself, I can attest that there is nothing compared to experiencing new cultures, new landscapes, and the sheer joy of discovery found in traveling with a positive, flexible, fun-loving companion. The more salient message her fiancé conveyed was the value of experiencing friendship within the context of a supportive partnership and simply enjoying time together without an agenda. So, being married to your best friend is the happiest place to be on earth; besides, whom else would you consider marrying?

KEEPING IT REAL

The saying, *A friend in need is a friend indeed* translates to the idea that acceptance and support, blended with a true sense of honesty, while having each other's best interests at heart, is undeniably important for real friendship to be felt. However, absolute honesty must be conveyed with sensitivity. Without enough sensitivity and compassion, just like any other relationship, it can backfire. Just like all other meaningful relationships, there is a genuine investment of time, caring, and respect called for before the friendship can deepen and solidify into an everlasting, sincere foundation of trust. Referring to friendships, I believe that is how the philosophical thought regarding *quality versus quantity* was realized

Sometimes, although we grow apart from what initially brought us together – whether it might be a mutual interest or life experience, predicament, or passage – we may find that we no longer relate to our friends in the same way, as our lives transform and evolve over time. Still, our long-term friends shared our history and bore witness to our own life transitions. These time-honored connections we have built remain so dear to us simply based on our mutual history and experiences as well as our true knowing and acceptance of one another.

That level of friendship may even be more deeply honest than how we are known by our parents, siblings, even our spouse or children. To feel known, or understood by others, is truly a blessing. Our long-term true friends were there perhaps before our current life circumstance. They knew us when we were younger or in a previous stage of life. They have seen us through the road of life while continuing, unconditionally, to love and accept us, no matter what. I am personally quite blessed to have several enduring, valued friendships.

I contend that part of my friendship success is due to a lack of measurement for the give and take involved. It is an unquantifiable flow of love, acceptance, allowance, and concern. A balanced connection is experienced over time. For instance, there may be times when you rely upon the support of a friend, whereas, other times, the same friend sought your advice or help. Friends more easily forgive one another. A real friend does not usually freak-out if something important arises and you have to cancel your time together. If you call them late at night when you are feeling emotionally needy, they pick up the phone. Genuine friendship is based on caring, interest, and concern for one another.

You may have friends who are geographically distant or have family or work obligations that interfere with spending regular time together. In that case, it is always reassuring that despite the distance or time apart, when you do connect, it is as though there was no lapse in time. You can simply take up where you left off and are just grateful for an opportunity to share. There is a simple, underlying understanding. The role of friendship is to stand by and support one another across all circumstances, whether in celebration or in times of need.

Yes, while true friends unconditionally stand by one another and do not abandon each other no matter what, they may not always approve of a friend's decisions or actions. In reality, *standing by* means that a real friend will support their friend's best interests, even if that calls for being bluntly honest, simply disagreeing with their perspective, discouraging them from making a mistake, and giving practical advice. In those moments, a real friend will encourage you to stand in your power and experience more success even when a situation calls for courage or sacrifice.

Anyone can get lost in the land of assumptions, for example, when you encounter a situation that disappoints you, or if someone says something to you that you interpret as negative. With true friends, you can easily give honest feedback and seek clarifications for your feelings in order to clear up misunderstandings. This level of deeply honest, open communication is earned and enjoyed over the test of time. Therefore, it stands to reason that you must choose your friends wisely.

I would be lying if I said no friendship ever encounters any difficulty or unsavory rifts; however, friendships that are built upon a deeper understanding and sense of trust do eventually spring back or withstand the emotional upheaval, often reinforcing the friendship after a good cry or hearty laugh. It is important to own your mistakes, or to freely come forward with clear issues or questions concerning your friendship. Be willing to openly share any thoughts or feelings that feel out of alignment with your friendship experience. Like any other relationship, it is unwise to ignore or minimize issues that question the integrity of your connections with others.

Maintaining healthy boundaries with balanced friendships is essential for positive life experiences. Let go of "fake friends" or those that continue to violate your trust, have an alternative agenda that is more self-serving than mutually supportive, or who perpetuate a negative power struggle with you. A toxic friendship may not readily be noticed, but once it has surfaced, do yourself a favor and exit stage left. This is the type of negative drama to avoid at all cost. Let go of any resentments as well. Instead, be the wiser for the encounter.

As social beings, we all have superficial friendships or associations. These include people whom you may socialize with, or engage with in your work environment, school, church, social clubs, or other mutual areas of interest, yet they are not necessarily individuals whom you have developed that bond of trust you can openly confide in.

Remember the saying, *Water seeks its own level.* The quality of your friendships may reflect back to you your own level of transparency or willingness to be vulnerable. Moreover, in order to form true friendships with others, it is important to be open or present to having that experience. Be outwardly and genuinely interested, reach out to others, be less egocentric, and have a positive demeanor.

By becoming more involved and socially available, whether through clubs, charities, sports, art, music, educational pursuits, or trying out something altogether new like a sailing class, yoga retreat, or any Meet-Up experience, your chances of widening your social circle and building new friendships will most likely be enhanced.

MALE VERSUS FEMALE FRIENDSHIPS

When it comes to true blue friendships, often there are apparent differences between same-gender male and female relationships. The male perspective for friendships, as I have come to understand, just as all real friendships, are built over time. Perhaps it is true, in general, friendships between males are comparatively less judgmental than friendships between females. Friendships between males are seemingly less complicated, less interpersonal, and more rudimentary. Men can vacillate between their interpersonal and basic needs. While men may need a dose of interpersonal relating or desire to connect in a more authentic way from time to time as problems arise, they also tend to disconnect once the problem is solved. What is important to most men is simply how they view the other person and whether they enjoy spending time together as buddies.

Initially, when making superficial social contacts, and possibly forming new friendships, men tend to experience *shoulder-to-shoulder* connections, whereas women usually have *face-to-face* girlfriend experiences. Women are usually quite comfortable facing one another over coffee and direct conversations with fewer distractions; there is no goal other than to catch up or discuss their lives exploring both the emotional and physical realms. Men, however, are not usually seeking friendships to explore their personal issues or interests; instead men generally maintain a more aloof or superficial rapport. As an example, at dinner parties or social engagements, it seems that a man, more often, identifies himself or expresses an interest to his male counterparts by discussing how each makes a living, whether he made a profit on his last investment, who won the last football game, perhaps where one or the other enjoys playing golf, tennis, or likes to surf.

It appears the male interest starts off with exploring and relating to the human *doing*-ness rather than the *being*-ness of life when forming new alliances that possibly lead to friendships. In other words, males tend to define themselves and assess one another on their measure of social status by what they each have accomplished.

I am told that men are usually more comfortable interacting with their male friends in planned events, such as getting together in order to socialize or compete through structured activities. Conversely, women seek connections with other women with a tendency to evaluate each other on a variety of levels. They often assess each other's outward appearance and sense of style; social status, such as *married, single, divorced,* or *widowed*; and whether they *feel* a sense of safety and trust with one another.

Female friendships may be considered more multi-dimensional, such as offering support to one another for every emotional encounter. From a wide array of interpersonal relationship issues, women do seem to have more intimate communications. They will talk endlessly, recharging their cell phones during conversation while helping one another to analyze and problem solve. They will offer solace when there is a relationship breakup or other challenge. Girlfriends will often rally around one friend undergoing a crisis perhaps by hosting a pajama party whereby they stay up until the wee hours listening to emotional ranting or venting, all the while supporting their friend through the thick and thin of life's treasures and travails.

While women cry upon each other's shoulders, traditionally, men tend to shoulder their emotional pain through actions. Perhaps with a *stiff upper lip*, men are driven to just deal with life as it shows up.

I see that men are evolving, however, and more men are opening up toward being more emotionally vulnerable and balanced when expressing their thoughts and feelings with friends. You can google an onslaught of men's groups in your community. Many of these are support groups that deal with an array of social/emotional challenges. These male-oriented support groups are becoming vastly popular. I once led a men's support group entitled, "Burst Your Own Bubble." This group of men had been meeting regularly for over seven years. They formed a very tightly knit bond whereby their meetings were considered a sort of escape valve, or a place where they could openly discuss their most personal issues seeking the wisdom and support of their fellow brothers. At one point, they felt it would be an asset to have a female perspective. Thereby, they sought my guidance. I represented the *Yin* to their *Yang*. This was a rich experience for me as I found this particular group to be quite forthcoming and realistic in their approach for identifying feelings and problem solving.

Other group encounters can form solid friendships that can last a lifetime, regardless of gender. These are often developed through team efforts or common goals. When the goals include danger, risk, or exerted mutual efforts for a common cause, the group identity is often profound. There is a wonderful camaraderie in groups, such as among war veterans, firemen and policemen, a scientific expedition, volunteers for search and rescue efforts, survivors of natural disasters, any type of sport team, and the list goes on. It includes any type of group focus involving interdependency and strivings for a common purpose. Yes, there is a special empathy and bonding for shared experiences.

Lydia's Story

"CLEANING OUT THE CLOSET"

I once knew a woman, Lydia, who was a real clean freak. In fact, as a sideline, she advertised her service for being a "Professional Closet Organizer." She preferred everything that was outmoded or unused to be recycled or discarded altogether. She was the antithesis of the *pack rat*. Moreover, she did not like having any aspect of her life to be considered undefined, unresolved, or well... cluttered.

At times, she deeply agonized over challenges or disputes within her romantic relationships or disappointments regarding the behaviors of family members, issues with her neighbors, and any other perceived problem that she considered out of alignment with how she believed it should be. Lydia kept an impeccable appearance, enjoyed daily exercise routines, and was devoutly religious.

As an observer, it seemed that her sense of order and routine supported a fundamental sense of safety or certainty, whereby I came to learn she was actually internally battling messy emotional issues that were kept at bay with regular doses of mood-altering medication.

At one point, Lydia decided to create a better sense of order in her life by addressing certain disappointing or unfinished relationship matters and cleaning up any attached or unsettled emotional debris. She was aware that she still hung onto past situations that had preyed upon her heart and which she felt needed to finally be released. Consequently, Lydia called me to write an *Inspired Heart Letter* regarding an old friendship that dissolved in a mysterious way.

Lydia previously had a very close female friendship with Kerry lasting over five years. The two ladies enjoyed a mutually supportive and positive rapport with tons of beach walks, Sunday brunches, and hosting gourmet dinner parties together. They spent time with one another while viewing independent films, visiting museums, double dating, shopping, and even celebrating certain holidays together.

At one point, Lydia met a wealthy widower and soon, after a rather brief period of dating, they married. Actually, she was introduced to her husband by her dear friend, Kerry. Unfortunately, their marriage was doomed from the start. It seems that they were unable to consummate their marriage with any satisfaction. Lydia felt tremendously confused and unable to cope with her muddled marriage situation effectively.

Apparently, she could not control her growing resentment for her husband and their lack of a satisfying physical love life. Within a year, the couple had their marriage annulled. Lydia found herself in another cluttered and confusing relationship soon after. This time, she became involved with a man who was not only financially struggling, but was a single father with two young children. And, according to Lydia, what a mess that turned out to be!

Returning to the unsettled friendship or falling out with Kerry, it seems that once she divorced her husband, her friend, Kerry, also left the scene. She quit returning Lydia's phone calls and would not respond to her emails. Lydia felt as though she had been "dropped like a hot potato" when she actually needed the emotional support from her friend.

One might surmise that perhaps Kerry felt that Lydia was out of integrity regarding her treatment of her husband; or she thought Lydia did not work hard enough to repair or heal their marital difficulties. Whatever the case may be, Lydia continued to struggle with her disenfranchised friendship and grew to consider it as part of her hidden, yet unresolved, emotional baggage.

When she asked me to write an *Inspired Heart Letter* to her long-lost friend, Kerry, Lydia's goal was to clean up any misgivings and to clear out the obviously untidy, outworn friendship with a better sense of closure. Yes, she wanted to make a clean break while basically letting her old friend know how much their friendship had meant to her and to wish her well.

Cleaning Out the Closet

Inspired Heart® Letter

Dear Kerry,

What I am about to share with you has lain heavy on my heart. I have thought of you over the last few years since we have been out of touch with one another. More recently, as my life circumstance has shifted yet again, I feel sad that we are disconnected. Although my life's journey has been fraught with so many emotional challenges, hopefully, I am the wiser for it.

Our friendship was very special to me. I do miss the closeness we shared as "sisters." With all my heart, I wish you well. We never know what the future holds. With that, I want you to know that I do hold you as a dear soul in my heart. I apologize for anything I might have said or done that caused you to walk away from our friendship. I am far from perfect; my life is a demonstration of that. I do continue to hold the love we shared as such good friends in a perfect light, and it will stay there forever in my heart.

If you are moved to forgive me, I thank you. Either way, Kerry, I have been feeling a real need to clear the air and express these sentiments. Please give my love to your sweet daughter, Amanda. I understand she is now married and received her PhD. How wonderful is that!

Blessings to you both,

Lydia

Interestingly, Lydia is the only client, so far, who wanted the closing contents of her letter changed in a rather peculiar way. When I read the initial *Inspired Heart Letter* to her over the phone, she exclaimed with delight that it sounded perfect, well almost perfect. Her one and only concern was that near the close of the original letter, it seemed that her old friend, Kerry, may be inspired to contact her. My response to Lydia was to explain that the latter part of the initial letter was written with that very intention. I truly felt she would welcome the opportunity to hear from her old friend. However, Lydia insisted that she only wanted to clean matters up and move on. She emphatically insisted she had no compunction or desire to ever engage with Kerry again. With that, I re-wrote the close of her letter in such a way that it sealed their history and certainly discouraged any invitation to regain their friendship or even have a conversation regarding their falling out.

After a few months had passed, I heard from Lydia again on another letter matter. During our conversation, she happened to mention with considerable dismay that she had never heard a response to the *Inspired Heart Letter* she had commissioned me to write to her old friend, Kerry. What can I say? At times, it feels like I *keep writing the books and they tear out the pages.* In other words, I intuitively knew her heart's intention, yet, it seems she had a tendency to be an emotional hoarder. Ultimately, her ego's defensiveness got in the way.

DRAWING THE LINE ON FRIENDSHIP

I helped a lovely couple from Australia, Katrina and Dennis, by writing an *Inspired Heart Letter* to one of their friends, Tiffany, who seemed quite unaware of her intrusiveness, or how she often took on the role of being the third wheel encroaching on this married couple's lifestyle.

To lend a bit of history, this couple first met through Katrina's mother during her visit to the Hawaiian Islands while she was there to see her sons who were famous surfers. She met their surfing buddy, Dennis, from Australia, and her mother astutely mentioned that he should meet her daughter, Katrina, as she was sure he would absolutely fall in love with her.

Well, they did meet, per chance, soon after, when Katrina was nearly finished with high school, and Dennis happened to visit the California coast on another surfing expedition. They had an amicable meeting and he left a week or so later to return to Australia.

Twenty years later, Dennis happened to travel to Los Angeles again for a job interview and while he was there, he looked up his old surfing buddies, Katrina's brothers. They mentioned Katrina had never married and had recently returned to the Los Angeles area, after working in New York for several years. Dennis had never married either as he had other family obligations in Australia. Well, the couple did re-meet after two decades of separation and felt an instant and powerful attraction. Two months later, Dennis sent Katrina a plane ticket to visit him in Australia. She returned from down-under as an engaged woman, and they were married shortly thereafter. Yes, all those years later, and Katrina has been happily living the life of an Aussie with her loving hubby Dennis.

Regarding the intrusive Tiffany, she was not an intentional inter-loper nor was she a difficult or negative person. She was just clingy, rather obtuse, and perhaps lonely. Katrina and Dennis are very kindhearted, caring people. They did not wish to offend their friend. However, they relished their time together as a couple, and their patience for sharing so much of their time with Tiffany was beginning to wear thin.

Apparently, Tiffany invited herself, or stopped by uninvited, to their home nearly on a daily basis. Dennis and Katrina were always gracious, although often they privately felt a bit indignant toward this awkwardly unaware friend. Through my suggested *Inspired Heart Letter* for enlightening her, they were able to send Tiffany a message that expressed their position as well as acknowledge the wholesome parts of their friendship. At the same time, Katrina and Dennis laid down the prerequisite behaviors for sharing time together with her. This couple was very grateful for my letter-writing intervention and, later on, reported that the issue was easily resolved with a better sense of mutual respect and awareness.

VIRTUAL FRIENDSHIP

With all of the current social media at play, I must comment regarding virtual versus actual friendships. One cannot fully realize the value of friendship solely based on internet introductions. There is so much to be gained for growing friendships through actual, real-life encounters and shared experiences. It is sad when I hear people boast of having so many online friends whom they have never actually met in person. There is a great deal of manipulation that can occur; it is far too easy to create a pretend life experience, or hide behind your true feelings and identity, as opposed to getting out there and mingling with real people and finding your tribe.

Get out of the safety zone and live in the reality zone. Besides, no matter what might be said or revealed, one cannot feel an actual friendly hug over the computer.

Joyce's Story

"GIRL TALK"

Once there were two friends, Lilly and Joyce, who had grown up together in a small town, in rural Iowa. They met in the second grade and grew to be inseparable best friends all the way through high school and beyond. The two had shared so many life experiences growing up, from playing with Barbie dolls and joining Girl Scouts, to becoming high school cheerleaders and models for the local department stores. They spent endless hours fantasizing about how their lives would turn out. Yes, they were both quite lovely, beautiful young ladies.

They shared their dreams of becoming well-paid, celebrated fashion models, marrying handsome men, and having exactly two adorable children. Of course, they planned to declare each other as the godmother to each other's children. The two friends relied upon one another for emotional support and assumed they would be a part of each other's life forever. After high school, both young ladies desperately wished to move to either New York or Los Angeles and get away from the humdrum predictable, small-town existence that seemed to entrap so many of their peers.

The two friends knew that by sticking together they could more easily fly away and discover a whole new and exciting destiny. Lilly had an aunt and uncle who happened to live in Queens, New York. Joyce and Lilly agreed that instead of applying to college, their best bet was to move to New York and find some type of work while attending modeling school. Lilly's aunt and uncle agreed to let the girls live in their spare room for up to three months while they looked for work If they wished to stay in New York beyond that, Lilly's aunt and uncle would charge them reasonable rent.

And so it was. Lilly and Joyce took off on their grand adventure. Their parents each provided enough money for their daughters to attend a rather prestigious modeling school. They were proud of their daughters, and at the very least, agreed that by giving them this "once in a lifetime" opportunity, if the girls failed, they could always return home and make other plans.

The condensed version of this story goes like this. Lilly and Joyce each found employment. Initially, Lilly worked in a bookstore, and Joyce worked at Nordstrom's cosmetics counter. Lilly stayed and worked overtime whenever the bookstore hosted an event for book signings or lectures. She actually found herself soaking up the knowledge and enjoying the social rapport that went along with these events. Over time, she found herself participating in book clubs, attending poetry recitals, and even joining a "New Writers" workshop. On the other hand, Joyce found herself filling endless hours applying makeup on aging New York housewives, and working as a makeup artist for a variety of events from bridal showers, college graduations, weddings, and anniversaries, to in-house fashion events. These young ladies tried out for numerous modeling opportunities. The competition was fierce.

Lilly was fortunate at the time. Not only was she hired to model for a prestigious fashion magazine, but she met the man of her dreams, a very successful, dedicated author, at a book signing she attended. The couple married within a year. Of course, Joyce was her Maid of Honor. Three years later, Lilly gave birth to their daughter, Brianna. Then, two years after that, their other daughter, Jocelyn, was born.

Joyce, however, was having a different life experience, not exactly what she had originally planned. Joyce procured a limited number of print-ad modeling jobs. Further, through her work experience at Nordstrom's, she had been hired from time to time to model at storewide fashion events. However, she never landed the type of fashion career she originally dreamed of. Her love life was less than satisfactory as well. She just never seemed to connect with a man who felt altogether right for her. Lilly and Joyce remained dear friends, but Joyce felt somewhat disenfranchised, or out of rhythm, with Lilly and her lifestyle.

After years of struggling to make it in New York City, Joyce still could not bring herself to return to her humble roots in Iowa. However, she intuitively knew that she needed to make a radical change in her life and try something new. She decided to try her luck by moving to the West Coast. Joyce thought Lilly would surely understand that she needed to move on in her life. However, surprisingly, Lilly must have been shocked and somewhat let down at the thought of her long-time friend moving so far away.

Instead of feeling understood, Joyce got the impression that Lilly, in essence, "cut her off." Joyce recalled Lilly's reaction to the news that Joyce was flying to the West Coast as being indifferent, if not chastising. According to Joyce, Lilly said:

> Well, Joyce, I helped you all I could. My aunt and uncle were kind enough to give you a chance in the beginning. All these years later, you still can't seem to make your life work. Now, you are blaming New York? Please, Joyce, get your head out of the sand. Maybe it is time you grew up and just found someone you can settle down with. Life is moving forward. Running away to "La-La Land" is not going to solve anything.

Joyce felt unsupported, if not abandoned, by her best friend. However, she was growing tired of feeling like the fifth wheel when she got together with Lilly and her growing family. Although Lilly tried several times to introduce her to her husband's eligible bachelor friends, it just never worked out. Besides, her job at the department store was starting to feel like a real burn out. Those endless hours standing in high heels at the makeup counter were becoming unbearable. Every day, as time moved on, Joyce was growing past the prime age for being discovered and finally making it big in the modeling world. It felt like her life was collapsing and that she was not living her own life, but someone else's. Joyce had no choice but to let go of her girlhood dreams, try to find her own way, and venture forth into unknown territory.

After relocating to Los Angeles, Joyce struggled for a few years, working at various jobs in sales and marketing. Finally, she decided to expand her education in the growing field of arts and technology. Joyce ended up at the Brook Institute for Photography. In short, she finally found her niche and became an established videographer. She even worked on a few fashion shows. Joyce's life seemed to open up in new and gratifying ways.

When Joyce met me, she spoke of how her life had taken some "dog-leg turns", and in spite of all the many disappointments life in New York left her with, she was proud of her growing accomplishments in LA. Regarding her friendship with Lilly, Joyce felt they no longer fit into each other's world. It was as if they lived on two separate planets. Lilly was busy raising her kids and going on book tours with her husband. Their social circle was comprised mostly of other married couples and their families.

Still, Joyce admitted she really missed having the closeness, the shared history, and the sisterhood she had felt with Lilly in the past. She was grateful since Lilly had recently called her leaving a voice message announcing she was expecting a baby boy. However, although the message sounded friendly, it did not seem terribly warm or engaging. Joyce thought it sounded somewhat stiff, or formal, as though she was just part of a list of numbers to call. It really bothered Joyce; she felt so sad that their connection had dwindled. After hearing of my letter-writing service, Joyce asked me to write an *Inspired Heart Letter* to Lilly in hopes of regaining their special bond of friendship.

Girl Talk

Inspired Heart® Letter

Hi Lilly,

It was great hearing from you last week; thanks for your call. I am sorry we did not have a chance to actually talk. We should not let so much time pass without catching up. I cannot believe the good news... baby number three on his way! Actually, you have been on my mind so much lately.

When I received the latest photos of your darling girls, it brought me back in time to those days when you and I used to have so much fun playing with our dolls and having pretend tea parties. Now you have your very own real-life dolls!

How fortunate you are. It seems that you have lived out what the two of us only dreamed of: a career in modeling, marrying the handsome guy, and being blessed with beautiful children. It took quite a lot for me to let go of a part of that dream. I spent so much time just trying to find my path. To be honest, Lilly, it was not always easy for me to stand on the sidelines as you stepped into your destiny as though it were just waiting for you.

I am beginning to understand that certain sense of clarity and ease with the feeling that I am finally enjoying my life with purpose, and being aligned with the natural flow of my destiny. So finally, my own life is beginning to show up for me. Of course, I had to pull up stakes and pave my way out here on the West Coast. It has turned out to be the best decision though. Instead of feeling like I was paddling against the tide, thankfully, new and wonderful opportunities are coming my way. Next week, I will be flying to Catalina Island to videotape a sunset wedding on a sailboat. Doesn't that sound romantic?

Lilly, although there are twenty-five hundred miles between us, and we haven't really connected in a while, I still consider you my absolute dearest friend in the world. It was not easy, tossing it all away, waving goodbye to New York, and moving across the country without a real plan, not knowing a soul, and leaving you, my best friend. I am so sorry if you ever felt that I let you down. You see, I gambled on creating a bigger life. After all, that is why you and I left Iowa in the first place, to take a chance in the Big Apple.

Life offers so many moments or opportunities for jumping on or off. For me, changing lanes when I did felt right, and I am finally at a point where I feel I am on track and coming out of the woods. Instead of trying to explain myself to everyone, now I feel so excited, actually passionate, about my career path. I still want the handsome husband and the two gorgeous kids. It is interesting though, with my life situation finally improving, I actually have so much more energy. My outlook is so much brighter. Rather than searching for love, I have a sense true love and romance may just find me.

Please kiss my beautiful goddaughters for me. I would love to see you all. Perhaps a family vacation to visit "Aunt Joyce", along with seeing Disneyland, is something to consider for next summer. Either way, Lilly, please know how very proud of you I have always felt, if not a bit envious at times. You have always fulfilled your convictions and followed your dreams. I realize now how very lucky we both are in so many ways, starting with our indelible friendship. I look forward to hearing from you

Much love,

Joyce

Soon after sending this letter, Joyce received a call from Lilly. This phone conversation was more than two hours. It was just a bit of catching up and a great deal of clearing up the misgivings over the last few years. Joyce was somewhat surprised that Lilly remarked, in retrospect, upon her feelings of sadness for her friend's struggles, if not guilt, regarding how easily her own life had turned out in comparison.

At the time, Lilly did not realize just how painful it was for her dearest friend, Joyce, to encounter so much disappointment in New York while on her own. Further, Lilly could not fathom how Joyce could drastically move across country with no definite plan. In a way, Lilly admired Joyce's bravery and independence. While Lilly's life now seemed somewhat safe or predictable, she recalled the sweet sense of adventure that spurred the two friends to move to New York City to begin with.

Although their lives seemed, at this time, to contrast, the friends reveled in their special connection and enduring friendship through familiarity, developmental history, life passages, and shared values. Joyce soon became godmother, once again, to Lilly's son, Cameron.

More often than we may like to admit, our dear friends may actually feel more like our true family than the family we were born into. Those of us who do not enjoy deep connections with our immediate family of origin would probably never consciously select any of them to be our mother, father, brother or sister. Actually, in those instances, individuals are drawn to more deeply loving *family-like* connections with others through outer-world experiences. It feels to me that our soul ultimately decides who we decide to call family and hone our sense of identity from. However, as we grow up, we may eventually feel more understood, nurtured, and even accepted, or respected, by our friends, or those special individuals who are connected to us through our hearts and not necessarily through bloodlines.

Hypothetically, while some people are incredibly lucky to be nurtured and raised within healthy families, for those who did not experience a particularly warm fuzzy, nurturing home-life, there is a different soul contract or expression, a different destiny, that perhaps encourages one to leave the family nest early and look for more loving, wholesome connections with others out in the world where they can connect on a deeper level rather than conveniently relying upon the consistently dependable genetic family roots.

FEARLESS FRIENDSHIPS

What do you do when you see your friend is overwhelmed or is acting in harmful, self-destructive ways, or you have knowledge that they are somehow being duped or disrespected? True friends will step in and try to do the right thing, even though they may run the risk of anger or rejection from the friend they are actually trying to protect.

Years ago, when my daughter was quite young, and I had been studying rigorously in order to pass the licensure exams for becoming a family therapist. I will never forget my dear friends, Kim, Maureen, and Ciel, who not only surprised me, but actually rescued me from feeling so wrung out, tired, and consumed with stress and responsibility. Without my prior knowledge, one day right after sitting for my board exams, my friends arrived at my home, popped me into the car, and we all drove to a relaxing resort south of the border. They had planned this for weeks, even my husband was in on this.

What a delightful surprise! Everything, including childcare was pre-arranged by these dear friends. I slept the whole way there. It was transformational to just sleep on the beach, laugh, get a massage, and have our girl-time to totally unwind. Yes, it was wonderful to feel nurtured and cared for in such a supportive way. While I would not purposely have taken the time out for me, my friends cared enough to step in and support my need for a well-earned rest and relaxing time out.

BEING THE BEARER OF BAD TIDINGS

There are times true friends run the risk of receiving negative emotional backlash when they confront a friend regarding difficult or even terrible matters. It takes a great deal of love and devotion to confront a friend with the truth, especially when there is much at stake. Personally, for example, I have known women whose friends chose not to alert them when they knew about their cheating spouse. In other similar instances, friends that knew about a spouse's infidelity and informed their friend were often contradicted or pushed away, at least initially, while the friend worked through their shock or denial.

Nevertheless, when friends do decide not to reveal this type of critical information, then once it is discovered and is out in the open, there is a great deal of anger toward those friends that chose to withhold their prior knowledge. It may feel like a *damned if you do and damned if you don't* predicament. However, just step into your friend's shoes – if there was a dishonest situation that was happening to you behind your back – then decide whether or not you would want to know the truth.

By sharing the truth, you do not have to lay judgment or give any unsolicited advice on how your friend should deal with the information. However, you can let your friend know you are there for them should they need to talk. You are open to listen and offer your insights or advice only if asked. Butting in to your friend's life should not be your intention. Yet alerting them to known, verified information or even to inform them about local gossip when it may be damaging is being responsible.

RESCUING FRIENDS

When friends are acting in self-destructive ways or living an unhealthy lifestyle in one way or another, I feel as a friend, you are obligated to bring the situation to light and offer to help in any way you realistically can. This also can be tricky, as often people are in denial and they can construe a friend's care as being meddlesome or judgmental. So tread carefully, but be honest. You are not there to *fix* anyone as that is most likely beyond your capabilities. Although through love and concern, you can guide your friend to acknowledge the problem, get the right help, or find the answers.

As far as being a good friend to another, ask yourself whether you would want someone *just like you* to be your own friend. Consider the following concept: *Be Friendship Focused, Be a Friend First.*

Chapter 9

Letter Theme: Eulogies

CELEBRATION OF LIFE:
EULOGIES FOR BITTER & SWEET GOODBYES

When I am requested to write an *Inspired Heart Eulogy*, I am deeply honored. Eulogies mark the culmination of one's heartfelt feelings that serve to honor the life of a loved one. It is the final publicly pronounced farewell. In the event of an unexpected passing, the loved ones left behind may be shocked, overwhelmed, and unprepared. Their own mourning consumes them, leaving them little time or energy to actually contemplate just how to say goodbye in the most meaningful, loving way.

To me, the most unbearable circumstance occurs when a parent loses a child. I once volunteered to write a prayer for a six-year-old girl with a serious illness. She was undergoing a bone-marrow transplant, and I just had a feeling she was going to transition soon after, which she did. I was so intrigued by her name. That little girl's name was Patience. I found myself contemplating the meaning of her name and in what way it may have symbolized an unrealized gift to her family in terms of teaching them the true meaning of patience, which is graceful endurance. I wrote this short poem in her honor:

Patience

(Poem)

Patience is a virtue.
Patience is kind
Have mercy on me Dear Heart
Only sweetness you will find

As you fly away like a dove
You always live in my heart
Where I hold you dearly, My Love
We will never be apart

Your life held such meaning
It was my blessing just to know you
With Patience, My Little Darling,
You will see my love is true

From the mighty heavens above
I know, for sure, we will endure
Patience,
An expression of Love.

Learning patience is often more challenging than one can imagine. It can be devastating to stand by feeling helpless while our world falls apart and unfortunate, sad, inexplicable events occur. However, to be patient, more importantly, includes maintaining a deep, unshakable trust. When we can trust that there is a Divine plan, and to all things that occur, there is a purpose – whether or not that purpose eludes us and remains a mystery – then we can let go of fear. Even when an innocent child transitions in death, leaving the parents overcome with grief to mourn and then to try to pick up the pieces in order to move on in that unfathomable experience, there is a profound lesson that challenges our faith.

This creates an opportunity for those left behind to expand their aching hearts, to come to terms with their own vulnerability, and, in time, to succumb to life's precarious, unpredictable, if not shocking, situations with a final acceptance that all is in *Divine* order. The one constant in life's process, what we can rely upon, is inevitable change. Over time, there is an opportunity to heal and give thanks for the precious gifts received by stretching past our sadness or disappointments, hopefully to finally understand that our love has no limits. Every life is meaningful, no matter how long or brief.

Our emotional connection to others can cause a myriad of experiences from joy and ecstasy all the way to anger, sadness, and despair. Yet, there is always the gift or the possibility to realize our own capacity to love more.

"TRIBUTE OF HONOR"

On one occasion, I received an urgent phone call from Janet, a woman, clearly in distress. It seems her husband's stepfather, Jerry, had suddenly passed away from an unexpected massive coronary. The shocking news was overwhelming. The grieving couple was in the process of making harried plans to travel out of state for the family gathering and funeral. Janet's husband, Greg, was having a difficult time dealing with the news and emotionally pulling it together.

When Janet called me, she sounded very distraught, to say the least. Greg was relying on her to write a eulogy for his stepfather, as he was too stricken with emotion to even clear his thoughts. Janet mentioned just how urgent, if not unreasonable, this eulogy request was, as they were leaving for the airport soon, and she actually needed to have the eulogy packed and ready to go in a mere fifteen minutes!

I grabbed my notebook and asked her to take a couple deep breaths. Then, I asked her to recall anything at all regarding the history and nature of her husband's stepfather. I asked if there were any constant references or things that highlighted Jerry as a person and as a father figure. In other words, what did her husband share most often about his relationship with his stepdad?

Janet quickly explained that, although Jerry was not blood related, Greg adored him and considered him to be his actual father. Jerry had become Greg's stepfather when he was only three and his sister was only two. Their natural father had passed away and there was no recollection of him. Jerry was a retired military man. He enjoyed country western music. He was warm, kind, loving, and cherished his stepchildren; and he always wore cowboy boots.

The urgent demand for this *Inspired Heart Eulogy* required little thought and much intuition. I interviewed Janet for a mere five minutes, jotted down some notes, and began to write this important family eulogy. I was able to deliver Jerry's eulogy that would be given by his son ten minutes later:

A Tribute of Honor

Inspired Heart® Eulogy

On a day such as today it is not ever a moment in time you can totally be prepared for. However, I must admit, I am honored to bid farewell to Jerry, a man who helped to shape my life and for whom I always felt a certain affinity or deep connection.

Jerry came into our lives when Mary and I were such young children. This was at a time when we really needed to feel like a whole family. Without any hesitation, Jerry filled a space in our home with love and genuine caring. Truth be known, Jerry is the reason I started collecting those GI Joe's when I was a little boy. His love has obviously left quite an imprint since I aspired to be a man, like Jerry, honorable and in uniform. He raised my sister and me in such a natural way, never making us feel like a burden, or an extra responsibility. Instead, his arms were wide open. What we did not necessarily say, we felt. And it was endearing.

I guess, as a child, I may have taken Jerry for granted and just figured he was a great guy, who liked to wear cowboy boots, listen to Elvis, and sing Johnny Cash songs while he was in the shower. When I grew up, though, I clearly understood that I had the distinct privilege of being in the company of a bona fide hero. As part of the US Navy Seal Team One, Jerry received more medals and honors than I can mention.

Who you see standing here today, me – Jerry's stepson, and I consider myself to be his actual son – is one who is still trying to live up to the man Jerry was. I try every day, to follow in his amazing footsteps... not such an easy trail, but one worth mentioning and one worth honoring. Jerry, with grace, I send you so much love, and I thank you.

His wife called me later that evening from the airport. She was quite amazed at her husband's reaction to the eulogy I had sent. For starters, her husband read the eulogy and instantly wept. While drying his tears, he exclaimed to his wife, *"How did you know Jerry sang along to Johnny Cash in the shower? I know I never shared that with you, and yet, just reading that brought back so many wonderful memories of growing up."*

When I wrote Jerry's eulogy, I was inexplicably compelled to write down the part about singing to Johnny Cash's music. I had a clear vision of this man singing along with a real sense of contentment, feeling proud and good about his life. Again, it is truly my privilege to be a part of these enlightened writings that help to express and rejoice in heartfelt experiences with others.

Eulogies essentially are performed for the benefit of those family members, friends, and loved ones who need to pay homage and are seeking to assuage their personal sorrow and ease their sense of grief and loss. When those we love pass on, they do not ever leave our hearts. They are always with us. However, it is coming to terms with, or accepting, that they have transitioned and their physical presence is transformed, that is difficult.

Speaking from personal experience, my older brother, Bob, passed away from a long-term illness when he was only thirty-six. During the final three years of his life, I spent a great deal of time caring for and comforting him. My boyfriend at the time invited me to go on a very special vacation over the Christmas holiday, an African photo safari. I knew my brother's health was declining rapidly. I pondered for weeks over whether I should go so far away at this critical time. I decided to ask my brother for his permission. Without the least bit of hesitation, my brother adamantly remarked, *"Life is for the living. You absolutely must go on this trip."* So, I did.

The safari was quite amazing, to say the least. In fact, my boyfriend proposed in the most romantic way shortly after a hot air balloon ride over the Serengeti. I could not have been happier. However, one day, while on this extravagant vacation safari, my new fiancé looked at me and exclaimed, *"What is the matter? You seem quite different; there is something going on with you."*

I turned to him and quietly said, *"I believe my brother just passed."*

When we returned home, I learned that my brother, Bobby, had indeed passed away. Actually, he transitioned at the same time I had felt his departure on an energetic level. I am told the funeral was spectacular. The procession of cars leading to the church was no less than a mile and a half long. Friends and family gathered in a profound, memorable way.

I was sad to have missed his funeral, the illustrious tribute in celebration of his life. However, I also knew the importance of my personal contribution, the love and caring, the time spent with my brother, including all the laughter and tears that could never be reclaimed by anyone who had not really been there with him through the ordeal of his final life chapter.

The lesson is found in the quality of time we spend with those we love while they are still alive. Life we share with others is quite precious. Our connections with others may be long-term, or fleeting, if not fragile. Acknowledging the value of our relationships, appreciating the time we have to spend with one another, is important. We cannot take life for granted. Appreciating those we care for, spending time with those we love, and taking the time to honestly confront and clear up emotionally charged issues, is time well spent, not only for those we feel challenged by, but for those we may be worried about, and, most importantly, for our own sense of inner peace.

"UNFINISHED BUSINESS WITH MOM"

I wrote a eulogy for a woman, Sally, whose elderly mother had passed away. This client was the eldest of three children. Her father had passed away several years prior.

Unfortunately, apart from more recent years, Sally had not spent much time with her mother. As it was initially shared with me, their relationship was rather damaged and disconnected as far back as Sally could recall. In particular, Sally felt as though she was the "black sheep" while growing up in her family.

She often felt a keen sense of rejection, emotional neglect, even disdain from her mother. By continually giving her personal power and sense of self-worth away, Sally dealt with a great deal of internal anguish and depression throughout most of her lifetime. Therefore, most likely stemming from this deep sense of disapproval from her mother, she had difficulty building and maintaining worthwhile relationships with others. In fact, Sally struggled for years to enjoy a loving, healthy relationship with herself as well.

When she contacted me to help her write a meaningful eulogy, we had to process a great deal of her painful childhood memories and conflicts regarding feeling lovable, accepted, or worthy of receiving love from anyone. I felt such compassion for Sally who had forsaken her sense of belonging and had given her power away for most of her lifetime.

I understood Sally's long-term struggle with self-acceptance and her profound sense of rejection, especially since she had finally started to move past the pain and was in the process of healing her relationship with her mom. Unfortunately, time had run out before Sally could finally communicate her feelings and openly resolve her long-term emotional issues with her mother. Now she was forced to deal with her mother's passing.

Honestly, we spent a great deal of time reminiscing about Sally's childhood and life. Intuitively, it seemed important for her to finally lay to rest her grievances and to acknowledge the gift offered in this moment, which was to move past her self-sabotaging tendencies, forgive her mother, accept herself, and finally be able to fly free.

An interesting sidebar is that she commented how she often dreamed of her mother since her mother's passing. At times, she heard her mother's voice within, whispering to her, "*I am okay. I love you.*"

Mother-Daughter Connection

Mother's Inspired Heart® Eulogy

I stand before you all today with my heart in my hand. Life is full of missed opportunities, but if you look closer, we can all consider the bigger gift in the lesson learned. My dear mother was often a mystery to me. She was truly a lady of southern charm and iridescent composure. I know with all my heart, she devoted herself to being a wonderful homemaker, made sure her children were always well cared for and never went hungry, or lacked for the proper attire.

Mom was very artistic and creative. She was a talented decorator, fabulous cook, classic dinner-party hostess, and an amazing costume designer and seamstress. At times, if I was lucky, she would let me help her in the kitchen. Once, I recall, she made this amazing birthday cake for my father that looked exactly like a shirt folded in a box!

Mom loved clothes, and she loved to dress very stylishly. I remember the matching mother-daughter dresses she made for herself, my sister, Nancy, and me. Mom embodied the ideal role of Queen of her Castle. Or, you might say, she gave new meaning to the title, Domestic

Engineer. She took pride in her home and aspired to always try to do the right thing. Some of my fondest memories, though, were seeing Mom dance about the house, or listening to her sing her favorite ditty, a Polka-type song, "Put your little foot here..."

My mother was born here in Kentucky. She came into this world sharing, as she was born an identical twin to her sister, Sally, my namesake. I know she missed Aunt Sally so very much when she passed on a few years ago. It makes me smile to think of my mother laughing with Aunt Sally again. Mom lived a fairly long life; she was ninety-one-years young at her passing. She was just a little thing, a pretty, gentle lady, who had endured a great deal emotionally.

I wish she could have shared her innermost feelings, although I believe she chose to protect us, her children, by remaining stoic, reliable, and determined to always keep moving forward no matter what. I will never forget how kind and helpful she was when my children were born. Without a second thought, my mother dropped everything to come and help me with the babies.

We actually grew closer over time although I had lived so far away from her. In the autumn years of her life, Mom was more able to be open and express her love for me. And, for that, I have found a greater sense of peace. In fact, I know she is with me now. She watches over me and whispers to me in a way that, in my heart of hearts, lets me know all is well.

I reflect upon this proud, refined lady I knew as my mother, and I bless her for all of her sacrifices. Perhaps there were not enough opportunities taken to share the truth, be more forgiving, and love more. Now and forever, may her light truly shine in Heaven and upon us here today; and may she freely dance, sing, and be at peace.

So, Mom, just know that everything is okay, and I am okay.
I love you.

Upon receiving this *Inspired Heart Eulogy* for her mother, Sally was immensely grateful. She delivered it to a hearty round of applause and felt as though it signified more than a proper send-off, but a real emotional clearing, a place to move forward, or to step off from, and more importantly, a ceremonial way to embrace the goodness, let go of the pain, and find a way to heal.

With the notion that funerals are now popularly considered or referred to as Celebrations of Life, it seems reasonable we should make our own precious life one to actually celebrate.

HOW WE GRIEVE

It is interesting to note that not everyone grieves in the same manner. Some people can easily emote and tears flow like the river, while other people may hide out, not wanting to draw attention to their emotional distress. And others are somehow able to remain very stoic, if not seemingly detached, from the sadness of losing their loved one. I can recall when I was only about five years of age, my dear grandmother, "Grandma Lovey" (short for Lovinia), passed. I can still remember her singing, playing piano, baking pies, and driving her old Hudson Hornet car. I recall arguing with my cousins about just how old she was... as we thought surely she had to be well over one hundred years of age! Nevertheless, since she had raised several children and had many grand-children and other extended family, her funeral was very well attended.

My dad was the eldest of her five children. He had identical twin brothers, my uncles, who were affectionately referred to as "Uncle Pinky and Uncle Bluey." Well, these two uncles, much to everyone's surprise and my father's chagrin, began hysterically laughing at their mother's funeral. They were both hunched over in complete belly rolls of laughter. It was not for years later that I learned that laughter is often just a stress relief. And for some people, who cannot succumb to tears... well, they laugh.

Gail's Story

"DIGGING UP BURIED MEMORIES"

This brings me to another *Inspired Heart Letter* that I wrote for Gail, a young woman whose husband's father recently passed away. Gail's husband, Matthew, was a caring man who worked as a paramedic. At his father's funeral, reportedly Gail not only acted rudely and aloof toward his family members, but belittled her husband in front of them. It was no surprise that after his father's funeral service and family wake ended, Matthew became distraught with anger at his wife. In fact, he made her sleep on the couch!

Gail realized her behavior was not only inappropriate, but cruel. She expressed to me how funerals seem to trigger the worst in her since she had lost her father at a very young age. Truly, she felt remorseful. She asked for my help. Here is her apology.

What a Fool I've Been

Inspired Heart® Letter

Darling,

My heart truly goes out to you. Sometimes, life is so overwhelming. I cannot imagine how you must be feeling. Please hear me. I really need to get this off my chest. I am so very sorry. It has always been difficult for me to express myself under duress. I am not sure why I came off in such an aloof and caustic way at your dad's memorial service, since I do really care. I, too, feel so sad for your father's passing.

I think I was feeling a bit overwhelmed. Obviously, you are better at handling crisis situations just by the nature of your work. As it turns out, it is a real shortcoming for me. Honestly, I just found myself at a loss for what to say or even how to comfort you. The last thing I want is to see you or your family hurting in anyway.

During the funeral service, inside, I felt like Jell-O. Although I wanted to, I realize now that I was not being very strong for you. I know it must have felt like I abandoned you emotionally at your time of grief. All I can say again is I am truly sorry, My Love. I am reaching out to you now. I want to hold you close to me. I hope you will find it in your heart to forgive me. Let me know how I can help to soothe your pain.

Know that I loved your dad, and I understand how you must miss him. He was there for us and always such a good father to you. It still hurts when I think of my own father's passing. All I can say is... please know, I am trying and I love you so much.

I truly love you,

Gail

Understandably, Gail's husband must have been crushed by her lashing out at him with such outrageous, terrible behaviors and awful insults, especially on the day of his father's funeral. Yet issuing an *Inspired Heart Letter* did give him a chance to read and re-read her plea for forgiveness. Reading the letter and between the lines, Mathew knew his wife's behavior was certainly out of character, and he soon realized how traumatized she had been over her own father's demise. She was such a little girl when her father passed, and Gail had never really processed the emotional shock that she felt. Needless to say, Matthew did forgive her with true compassion for her loss. Gail felt so relieved by her husband's response, she was able to forgive herself as well.

"ODE TO HANNA, MY *OTHER MOTHER*"

On another occasion, I was asked to write a eulogy for a woman who had absolutely no family members left to mourn her, or say goodbye. Hanna was a refugee from Hungary who married, was widowed, and never had children. She had lived a life of tribulation as a post-traumatic victim who had witnessed many horrors and atrocities during World War Two and during the Hungarian Revolution. Her life was largely one of hardship, deprivation, and, often, a sense of anguishing despair.

Despite her tortured past, Hanna was a sensible, somewhat stern, yet a good-hearted, religious woman, who enjoyed helping others in need. She found contentment within devoted friendships that, more often, felt like family. One of her dearest friends happened to be her family physician, a man about thirty years her junior. Her connection to him grew so deep over the years that she considered him in the same way a mother would care for a grown son. In fact, her loyal doctor/friend appreciated her endearing motherly kindness so much that he introduced her to his parents and siblings.

He actually flew her across country to attend his family's gatherings, as well as included her in most of his significant local family celebrations. Furthermore, he continued to oversee her healthcare well past his time working as a physician. They enjoyed a wonderful family-like, if not karmic, connection. This is an excerpt from Hanna's eulogy I was inspired to write.

Ode to Hanna, My "OtherMother"

Inspired Heart® Eulogy

Hanna and I go way back. She was not only one of my first patients when I arrived here as a young, new doctor, but she was also one of my very first friends, one of my dearest friends – no, actually more than that – she became part of my family. She provided an endless supply of delicious dinners, lunches, home-made soups, cookies, cakes, pies, and strudels… all made with love and care. She not only kept me well fed over the twenty years I was in practice here, but also made me feel especially nurtured and embraced by a real kindness and caring that I was quite fortunate to receive and came to rely upon.

Hanna's lifetime is celebrated for her selfless generosity and kindness to others. She loved animals, sewing, cooking, gardening, and just being helpful in any way she could. Her genuine hospitality was endearing as her door was always open, and she made everyone who visited her feel like royalty.

However, when she spoke of the many trials and tribulations of her past, especially growing up during the Hungarian Revolution, living on trains over stretches of time between Germany and Hungary, bearing witness to the brutality and poverty of war, and surviving many terrible, heartbreaking circumstances, she certainly grieved. And my heart went out to her as those sad memories were obviously quite difficult for her to bear.

While I will surely miss her, it is not very easy to say goodbye to someone who was such a loyal, steadfast friend, one who truly loved me as though I were her son. In my heart, I cannot help but feel that she is now free. With an open heart, under the grace of God, she can dance, laugh, sing, and finally find serenity amidst the angels. I feel so immeasurably grateful and blessed to have known you. Dear Hanna, I love you."

"MY BIG BROTHER"

Another beautiful Celebration of Life funeral that I was graced with the opportunity to write for was the passing of a dear friend's older brother, Richard. Although he was in his early sixties when he passed, as a very young man Richard had been rendered severely disabled, both mentally and physically, as the result of a brain surgery that unfortunately went wrong. The family had encountered many years of grieving and coping with her brother's resultant traumatic brain injury. There was a quality to Richard's life as an intellectually disabled invalid that dramatically contrasted to his earlier life when he was healthy and robust. Nevertheless, there was a gift realized over time that gave his entire life such beautiful value and precious meaning to his family. Here it is …

For my Big Brother

Inspired Heart® Eulogy

My dearest brother, Richard, was such a gift to our family. Some of my most special childhood memories were of having this amazing big brother who was not only strikingly handsome – with icy-blue eyes and thick dark hair – but he had this luminous personality.

Richard was always so completely gentle, so caring, and so very lovable. I adored the sound of his soft voice and how easily he flowed with life. He seemed to take everything in stride. He was so composed, so satisfied. And, he truly lived life in the moment.

Yet we could never hold onto him for long. He would usually arrive unexpectedly, always bringing wonderful gifts and never expecting anything in return. As a little girl, I remember Richard sitting me down next to him while he magically played the piano and sang songs such as "You've really got a hold on me." Then, poof! He would hop in his car and ride off into the sunset with his pet dog, free as a bird, and I would instantly miss him.

Yes, it was tragic to see Richard undergo the physical pain and awful results from a medical procedure to his brain that went awry. After that, he would never physically leave us again… not until now. He was such an endearing soul and, once again, a truly precious gift to our family.

Richard taught us how to treasure life in the moment, to let go of expectations, to be more caring, more generous, and to be kind. My family has grieved for Richard over the decades, since his health challenge left him with no other choice but to be on the receiving end of our care. Our beautiful mother never left his side.

So now, with deep gratitude for the experience of knowing Richard, we say "Aloha." As he finds his way into the arms of the angels, and as they carry him into the gates of Heaven to claim him as one of their own, we send our never-ending stream of joyful tears, knowing he is completely free, surrendered in everlasting love and light.

I love you, Richard. Be at peace.

When those we love move on in death, it causes a way to consider and reflect upon their life, almost as if we are reading a novel or watching a movie and they are the star or main feature. In other words, our lives seem to move and transform as though in chapters or scenes. There is a beginning, middle, and the final curtain, when our loved one has completed their story or life purpose and moves on. It is an opportunity to deeply ponder what their lessons and contributions may have been in this lifetime. We can also consider our connection to them. Hopefully, we can find a sense of peace surrounded in gratitude for the opportunity and experience of knowing them.

If there are unsettled emotional disputes, or painful memories, that were never consciously resolved, look to that pain and see the lessons learned or the gifts received. Or, begin to find a way to be at peace in spite of the painful relationship. The meaning their life held for them is their soul's sojourn, their story or life plan.

Considering how the connection with the deceased creates a meaningful experience in the lives of those left behind, or how they may have contributed to your life path, is a beautiful way to locate a better sense of acceptance. Rest assured that we can change the outcome of any story simply by what we focus upon or give meaning to. Yes, indeed *Life is for the living*. Therefore, be happy. Be satisfied. Choose a brighter path and enjoy your life *on purpose!*

What else can be said, except to revel in the joy that life offers? Make our lives as meaningful as we dare, and let go of any fear, shame, or guilt that prevents our divinity from shining brightly. Yes, understanding and claiming ourselves in the light of God, as being truly Divine, is an underestimated gift: an honoring, a tribute, and homage to our contribution as part of our own Divinely spiritual evolution.

Amen.

Chapter 10

Other Inspired Messages & Letter Applications for Writing with an Inspired Heart®

DYNAMIC DATING PROFILES

INSPIRED WEDDING VOWS

POWERFUL COVER LETTERS

A UNIQUE LETTER TO ONESELF

This chapter offers a brief commentary on other ways *Inspired Letters* or other writing applications can be effectively used that are outside of the healing realms that focus upon matters of the heart.

The following topics refer to creative and/or compelling personal profiles or letters that promote our best selves, or offer other possibilities such as for dating, landing job interviews, or resolving legal or business matters. This next section focuses upon creating your best dating profile.

In today's world, it can be challenging to meet prospective "soul mates" or love interests, without resorting to internet or other commercial means. In fact, this has become so popular that the majority of couples who marry today actually met through the internet or through other dating services. Therefore, this is where we begin.

DYNAMIC DATING PROFILES

Coming back around full circle to nearly the beginning of this book, Chapter 3, *Dating Dilemmas... Singles Looking for Love*, I now offer some useful commentary and advice for anyone contemplating finding a love connection via an online-dating service, or if they are working directly with a coach or matchmaker. Matchmaking services, including online dating, can feel awkward and quite unnatural. Nevertheless, it has been a growing industry and offers a viable alternative to a serendipitous meeting of the *right one.*

Frustrated clients have told me that the photos presented on an individual's profile often are not current or have been Photoshopped considerably. Obviously, the most flattering photos should be shown, yet they should be a fair representation of how you currently appear. Moreover, the written introduction should add enough zest, or appeal, to capture the interest of healthy, respectable, if not fabulous, suitors.

I have helped several friends and clients by writing their profile for them. After all, in essence, your dating profile is a way to promote yourself in the best light possible. It is your calling card, and must be crafted and delivered in a way that compels the interest of an appealing and suitable "other." Based upon my experience in helping singles to shine online, the following is sound advice:

Photos: This may be the most important feature of your online profile, especially if you are seeking a love match. Look directly into the camera and offer at least one photo with a full smile, exposing your pearly whites. A more direct open gaze and soft smile elicit a sense of confident, relaxed sincerity. Dress appropriately as though you were meeting another attractive person for the very first time. Again, there is a meta-message depicted in your attire as well as in your stance, or body language. If you appear too seductive, or look like you are trying out for a center-fold, just realize the type of dating experiences you will most likely attract.

On the other hand, poor or stiff posture, closed grins, or arms folded or pressed to your side, may convey a more emotionally shut down, unfriendly, or persnickety personality.

Only include photos of yourself, although a photo with your pet(s) may be appealing. A full photo from head to toe increases your chances for being pursued as well. Hats, sunglasses, and photos in Halloween costumes are discouraged. Also, sharing photos of landscapes, sceneries, a sunset view from your balcony, or random photos of rabbits on your front lawn, can be detrimental for attracting dates. Photos of your possessions, or toys, such as sports cars, motorcycles, jet skis, sailboats, or your home in particular, without your photo in the same shot, may be perceived as superficial or in poor taste.

Content: Our values or preferences, immediate and future goals, and what we consider meaningful or important, may change depending on our social/emotional status or stage in life. Be clear, be open, and be flexible. This takes a great deal of contemplation. The better you recognize your "must haves" for your vision of lasting love and satisfaction, the more magnetized you will become for meeting the best match for you. Be honest with yourself so you can be honest creating an authentic profile for a successful outcome.

This is an opportunity to put your best foot forward and improve your chances of attracting someone special and well-matched to you. It is your personal advertisement, and you should present a dynamic profile that will cause a stir in the viewing audience.

Flashy bells and whistles are fine if they convey an interesting, fun, or lovable aspect of who you genuinely are. However, "come-on" gimmicks, or tricks, should be avoided. That will surely backfire, and you will waste your time. Your content should be interesting, yet brief. Remember, *Less is more*, so get to the punch line.

Flavor: Your profile should inspire a sense of intrigue, or mystery that can be alluring. Keep your message positive, and add a little sparkle to be remembered by. In writing your content, try to dial in on a sense of just who you would like to attract, and write as though you are talking directly to him or her.

Initial Contact: Having decent conversational skills is a must for capturing the interest of a prospective date. Most people will be inspired to actually meet in person if the phone dialogue is relaxed, easy, and comfortable. It is important to read the entire profile of the online contact prior to having that first telephone conversation. Remarking upon some of the highlights viewed on their profile may be flattering.

The art of conversation can be amplified when it is positive or complimentary about the other person. Keep the initial phone contact short and sweet. I suggest keeping it less than twenty minutes. Further, I recommend only one initial phone contact prior to meeting. More importantly, avoid text messages unless it is to confirm a meeting place or time; hearing someone's voice via a telephone call or voicemail conveys not only their personality, but their authenticity, which is a more considerate way to communicate.

The Date: Wherever you plan your first meeting, choose a comfortable spot where you can converse without too much environmental distraction, whether visual or auditory. If you happen to enjoy a wonderful connection and are attracted enough to see each other again, be aware that your first date will always be remembered. Therefore, while it does not have to be a five-star restaurant, or somewhere too extravagant, it should be inviting and lovely, if not romantic in some way: perhaps a café overlooking the ocean, a downtown bistro, or a rustic supper club with soft lighting and a cozy ambiance. Good table manners and any other touch of class can earn more points as well.

Remember, the first impression is just that. Many people sum up their meeting within the first few minutes and in those first minutes decide whether there is enough attraction. The actual chemistry or what may be considered one another's *energetic field,* either mutually resonates or does not. Regardless, enjoying time getting to know someone new, despite the romantic outcome, can be part of the fun involved in the dating-service experience.

The Interview: Often, when meeting someone interesting for the first time, there may be an inclination to sell ourselves by impressing the other person with our talents, accomplishments, possessions, or other dazzling life experiences. Maintain an even exchange. This is more than a date; it is an interview. Be mindful to share conversation. You may consider creating a mental list of appropriate, open-ended questions that you can ask your date. Other tacky or boorish behaviors are noticed when the conversation turns to current problems you may be facing or past relationship matters.

There is nothing worse than setting the tone for your date on a low note based upon what has not worked for you either in divorce court, problems with your children, conflicts at work, or any life experiences that you regret. Your date will consider this egocentric and unappetizing. It is much better to wet your lips with flirtatious, upbeat, tantalizing, and congenial conversation. Less is more regarding the art of conversation. Monologues can feel overwhelming and stifle the mutual social reciprocity that creates an amicable flow.

Another point to consider: Some people have trouble maintaining good eye contact. Personally, I find that poor eye contact is disconcerting, if not uncomfortable.

If the eyes are the windows to the soul, then open them for a direct, clear view. This alone will invite your date to want to know you better. First conversations can be awkward for both of you; eye contact is a genuine effort to convey who you are and shows your appreciation for this first opportunity to get to know the person across the table from you.

Taking it Further: Should you decide to continue dating, take the time to really get to know the other person before becoming physically involved. I realize it can be quite difficult to hold off becoming sexually intimate, especially when your attraction and hormones are amped-up. However, if you are sincerely interested in creating a lasting romance, then take the time to build a credible, viable foundation.

Spend enough time together to get a sense of how your prospective partner deals with conflict or upsets. If you eventually become a couple, no doubt fresh conflicts will arise, and seeing how your new love interest has responded to past bumps in the road may give you an idea of what to expect as you navigate your future together. Did they invest sincere effort to resolve conflicts in their past relationships, or did they, in your opinion, walk prematurely?

The most important aspects of a relationship are how, as a couple, you tackle the day-to-day annoyances and the ups and downs of life, and do you feel you have each other's permission to actually be who you really are. Can you express to one another your authentic and transparent selves safely and without fear or recrimination?

A Final Note: If you don't feel a special connection or, for whatever reason, decide you do not wish to see the person again – be honest. It is considerate and polite to let that person know truthfully, that while you enjoyed meeting them, you are not interested in subsequent dates. You don't really need to provide much detail; it is enough to let them know that you don't feel the chemistry.

Online-Dating Profiles

The Calling Card

"BOYFRIEND FOREVER"

Once, Lynn, approaching her sixtieth birthday, contacted me to help her write a more dynamic online-dating profile as she was not getting much attention with what she had written on her own behalf so far. After reading what she had already submitted, it was very clear to me that she had written a short novel instead of simply capturing her essence and creating a friendly, and certainly <u>not</u> *long-winded*, invitation for a suitable, (if not the "right" man), to capture her interest.

When writing a personal profile for online dating, a great photo and a simple to read, yet striking message that elicits what your personality and true nature are, as well as the essential traits you seek in a romantic partnership, can be easily highlighted and conveyed. Lynn was gregarious, sweet-natured, warmhearted, and wholesome. As an example, this is the online-dating profile that I created for her:

Are You my BFF? (Boy-Friend Forever!)

Dating Profile

Are you ready to meet a fun-loving redhead with a kind heart and plenty of sex appeal? I am a lover not a fighter. My life has been blessed by my three amazing (grown) children, endearing friendships, a loving family, and enriching life experiences.

I happen to be a supremely talented gourmet cook and love to entertain. I enjoy being creative and I have a real zest for life. Some of my favorite activities are tennis, hiking, cycling, traveling, (the list goes on). And, I am proud of my success as a businesswoman.

I am available to fall in love with the right man for me. He still believes in romance, is fun to be with, and easy to talk to. I am "true blue" and am only seeking an exclusive romantic partnership. I am looking forward to meeting my "Mister Right" who has a keen sense of integrity, is confident, maintains a healthy lifestyle, and is a man who happens to have a joyful, open heart."

This was a far cry compared to her former online profile, which read like an autobiography and contained quite a hefty laundry list of physical, emotional, and situational traits and preferences she desired in a prospective partner. It was much too wordy, too particular, and, frankly, too boring and contrived.

This new profile lends a sincere yet open, if not somewhat corny, light-heartedness that is more attractive and inviting. It seems to have captured the essence, or personality of the client. Most people are not willing to wade through long-winded content and too many adjectives listed after "What I am seeking in a partner is… " It can be intimidating and may just scare them off. With her dating profile makeover, the thought comes to mind: *So many men, so little time!* It worked!

"DANCE FEVER"

On another occasion, I helped a terrific guy, Tim, rewrite his dating profile. Tim was an attractive, good-natured gentleman, who not only had a solid career as an educator, but, among his many hobbies and interests, he was quite a talented ballroom dancer. However, creating a provocative, alluring online-dating profile for himself was definitely not his strong suit. In fact, when he requested that I rewrite or enhance his current personal ad, I found myself chuckling over some of what he had already written. Within his original profile script, he actually had included some of the following described enticements:

"I have a high threshold for boredom. (I will go shopping with you.)" and *"I can carry heavy items as well as twist tight caps off of jars."* Truly, these elements were included in his profile, I am not kidding!

To verbally converse with this charming man, one would never guess how he came up with these rather offbeat claims or attributes, never mind believing they would capture the interest of a fabulous woman. At any rate, here is his revised dating profile.

Dance Fever

Dating Profile

I would love to waltz into the life of my most perfect partner. Actually, I prefer swing dancing, but do enjoy any style of dance, including West Coast, Salsa, and even the Two-Step. Life is what we make it, and while I am quite active for fun on the dance floor, I also enjoy spending time hiking in nature, exploring local cultural events, meeting new people, fine dining, (I am told I am a pretty amazing cook at home as well), and enjoying quality time with family and friends. I love good conversation, am pretty health-conscious, and try to stay fit.

Yes, I do have a pretty great life; honestly though, the first thing on my bucket list is to meet a quality lady who is already a happy, balanced person, someone to laugh with and who enjoys my witty humor. She has an open, kind, and caring heart and is wanting to share her life with an easy-going, very romantic, thoughtful, and solid, down to earth guy,(one who is seriously open to finding real love, partnership, or marriage), who really wants someone to share life with while staying in rhythm one step at a time.

The feedback I received from this client was amazing. In one day, this man went from zero to thirty women responding to his profile. Not too surprising, he is now enjoying a wonderful, budding romance with a lovely woman whom he described in the following admirable way, "*She fits so well, holding her in my arms on the dance floor.*"

"WOMAN OF YOUR DREAMS"

A very sexy, attractive, middle-aged woman with a fabulous sense of humor asked me to help her to rewrite her dating profile. While her current profile was capturing the interest of scores of men, in fact, too many prospective suitors to keep up with, her dating experiences were disappointing. It seemed that the men contacting her were mainly interested in having a fling, and not really interested in the possibility of finding love. Not surprising, after reading what she had written, her profile was decidedly quite flirty and alluring. Flirtatiousness and sex appeal are great for capturing a man's attention, but in order to sort out the frogs from the princes, it is also important to highlight what you value and desire to create with your online personal ad.

This woman had no problems attracting men, even just by walking down the street, yet she seriously wanted to find a satisfying relationship with a committed partner and avoid wasting any more time with shallow, unfulfilling dating experiences. Here is her new, revised dating profile:

Woman of Your Dreams

Dating Profile

I believe dreams do come true.

What if I am the one you've been waiting for?

Writing about myself is not so easy for me. However, I am willing to give it a shot. If you are looking for a real woman and are sincere about finding romance, partnership, and an enduring connection, then I encourage you to read on.

I am already a very happy person, and yet I know, I am not alone when I say I want to fall in love with the right man for me. He will enjoy my spontaneity and, sometimes, outrageous sense of humor. I am very creative and have a rich imagination. I am also fun to hang out with and very outgoing.

I admit, I am drawn to glamour, social events, traveling, and wonder-ful surprises, (although I love to be the one who surprises the man in my life even more… and in thoughtful, caring, good ways, of course). I am pretty health-conscious as well. I enjoy working out and staying fit. I also love to cook, from burgers to gourmet. I am told I look pretty good in an apron too. :).

Seriously though, I only want to meet you if you, too, are sincere. That is, I am looking for a real man who is willing to take enough time to get to know me and who is open, confident, and not afraid to show his vulnerable side.

I am not on this site to just meet a ton of guys and date. Therefore, if you are not a serial dater, but are a classy guy who really wants to find the right woman, you are successful in life, have a strong character, are fun to be with, kind hearted, affectionate, considerate, and romantic, then I hope to hear from you. I am very accepting by nature, but the traits I have listed are necessary for anyone I could fall in love with. Hmm... still reading? What if you are the one I am waiting for?

As a result of this newly revised dating profile, the number of interested men dropped dramatically. However, my client was very pleased. The men who did respond were much more sincere and suitable. She no longer was wading through reams of emails from *Mister All Wrong*. What's more, she felt that she had formulated a clear intention for what she really wanted in a relationship and was taking action by declaring it on paper. Again, the law of attraction manifests through our intention and willingness to take action. Within a couple of months of running this profile, she met someone quite wonderful. They have fallen deeply in love, and he just recently asked for her hand in marriage.

Waiting by the Phone

Cary's Story

"LAST CHANCE, LAST DANCE"

I once received an *Inspired Heart Letter* request from Cary, a man in his mid-thirties. Cary had met a woman through an online-dating service. Her name was Lisa. During their first date, despite her youthful looks, Lisa revealed her true age (not what was stated on her profile), and to Cary's surprise, Lisa was ten years his senior. Nevertheless, Cary was instantly infatuated with her. He enjoyed her confidence, her style, and considered her to be quite charming with a rare seductive earthiness that seemed to radiate a strong sense of passion.

In no time flat, Cary became quite smitten with Lisa and could not deny or hold back his fiery lust for her. By the third date, they were consumed by their obvious sexual attraction and found themselves in bed together by the end of the evening.

The following morning, Lisa had to leave quite early as she had a meeting with a client at work. Cary found he was constantly thinking about her and wanting to spend more time with her. They continued to see one another over the next couple months, when, suddenly, Lisa stopped returning Cary's phone calls and disconnected herself without any explanation whatsoever.

Cary was struggling to cope with this unanticipated rejection. He felt very confused and emotionally torn up. More than his ego was bruised, he worried that he had said something wrong or had somehow offended her. Overtime, he became angry and felt she had "used him" and tossed him out when she was done.

He could not understand how she could just cut him out of her life and move on. She was not the *hot tamale* after all. Instead she was a cold fish! Cary was pretty emotionally spent when I spoke with him. He requested that I write an *Inspired Heart Letter* to Lisa as he wanted to take a stand for himself and have the last word. After consulting with Cary further and sorting out the pieces, I wrote the following *Inspired Heart Letter* to Lisa.

The Last Chance: Last Dance

Inspired Heart® Letter

Hi Lisa,

I just want to touch base with you, since we have not connected in some time. It's pretty disappointing when someone crosses your path and leaves such a positive impression, and then for no apparent reason fades away. I'd like to take this opportunity to share my perspective with the hope of clearing up any misgivings and to arrive at a better understanding.

For starters, I'd like to acknowledge you not only for your beauty, intelligence, and sensuality, but I see your caring nature with others. When we met, I felt a solid connection to you. This special feeling does not occur for me too often. You might imagine how perplexing it is to try and understand why we are not seeing each other now.

Perhaps things happened too quickly for us, such as being physically intimate or acting on our attractions before we really got to know one another on a deeper level. While I certainly enjoyed being physically close with you, it is more important to me to feel emotionally connected. I feel sad that we are not seeing each other, when there may be a real possibility for creating an amazing relationship.

Just so you know I sincerely want to be in a committed relationship with a special woman. I look forward to one day sharing my future with a partner, or a wife. During the time we have been apart, I could not help but ponder over what actually happened. I realize there is an age difference between us, but quite honestly this is not of any concern to me. I only bring this up, since I cannot fathom what occurred, or what you might be thinking or feeling that is keeping us apart. I really do miss you... having fun with you and just being together.

I hope you can contemplate my message, Lisa. No matter what the future brings, just know our connection has been truly meaningful to me. I really hope that by sharing my thoughts and feelings a door can open to more conversation. I would appreciate an honest reply.

Either way, I wish you all the best.

After reading this letter, Cary felt emotionally cleansed and proud that he was able to share his true feelings for her no matter the outcome. It took over a week before Cary received a reply from Lisa. She sent him a brief text message:

"Hi Cary Thanks so much for the awesome letter. It is not you. It is me; I have moved on. Take care. Lisa."

Ouch! Despite his willingness to put his heart on the line with no guarantee for a reciprocal reply, nevertheless, his hopes were dashed and Cary was quite taken by surprise. He was still licking his wounds when he telephoned me to share Lisa's response to his letter. However, through this emotional ordeal, Cary began to develop a much better sense of awareness regarding the importance of taking the time to know someone's character, values, communication style, and their capacity for being open, honest, and trustworthy. Feeling truly safe in one another's arms is where the heart can rest with assurance that we are where we belong.

Unfortunately, Cary's expectations for a committed relationship were, most likely, in contrast to Lisa's romantic blueprint. Intuitively, I surmised that Lisa may have seen that Cary was more interested and willing to woo, invest, and commit, however, they were emotionally misaligned. Ultimately, it seemed they each had different desires or expectations. The internal flaw is when we are not aware of the hints, or clues that were there, to one extent or another, yet went unnoticed or discounted.

Too often, when you are infatuated or smitten by a new love interest, the tendency is to be consumed with the romance while convincing yourself that everything is wonderful. Unfortunately, while skipping down this primrose path, we tend to ignore or minimize obvious or subtle actions, communications, or feelings that are disjointed or out of sync.

Finding out what each other's agendas are, and being clever enough to fully interview a prospective partner with open, honest exchange at the risk of disappointment, is being responsible and prudent. *Discretion is the better part of valor.*

The wind can surely be taken out of your sails when your hopes are high for a reciprocal love connection and caring and, instead, they are thwarted. When we feel a friend or loved one suddenly disappears off the radar, or when a prospective love interest promises to call and they don't, we are often left feeling bewildered, indignant, or even deeply hurt.

What would the world be like if we were able to express our feelings with gentle honesty? Sharing the truth of how we feel is learned with courage, confidence, and practice over time.

Often people are more focused upon the *idea* of being "in love" rather than taking a conscientious perspective and exploring whether the foundation is solid enough to build upon. They may have difficulty with defining exactly what a loving, healthy relationship truly means. Or, on a subconscious level, they are afraid to come to terms with the truth, which may be that they have simply deluded themselves.

Relationships of any nature allow ongoing opportunities to learn about ourselves. Looking back on those relationships that just didn't work out often, eventually, causes a sigh of relief. Who we are attracted to today may not be the same caliber or type of person we were attracted to in the past.

As difficult as it may be, try to capture the silver lining and learn the lesson well. Working through the pain, instead of refusing to acknowledge what part we may have played in the situation, is a way to keep the denial at bay. When we consider disappointing patterns in our experiences with others, it causes a deeper understanding and cautions us to move forward without repeating the same mistakes or misunderstandings.

Seeking a competent guide, whether a therapist, coach, or other mentor, and finding natural support systems, such as a hobby or interest that uplifts you, enjoying supportive family or friendships, and, most importantly, seeking the support that you find through spiritual or religious teachings or community, are ways to honor and nurture your beloved self.

NUPTIALS… TO RING YOUR BELL

Not only is it quite an honor, but what absolute fun it has been for me to write beautiful, inspired wedding vows. I have presided over several weddings as a Universal Life Minister since 1993. I never consciously aspired to be a reverend or perform weddings; however, while I was interning for my marriage and family therapist's license, I developed a very keen interest in subtle-energy healing practices. Often, in the midst of a psychotherapeutic counseling session, I would sense the client's energetic, or *auric* field. Moreover, I could see where they were stuck or where their energetic body was suppressed and otherwise not flowing fully with the rest of their life-force circuitry. The results offered through subtle-energy work are often quite impressive.

I began to explore the world of alternative healing and shamanism with intrigue and awe. Eventually, I became certified in several energetic healing therapies, many of which included healing touch or *laying on of hands* modalities. The most profound energetic healing work I facilitated was when I put all formal training aside and just helped clients by relying on my own inner guidance. Soon, I began to develop a new, separate clientele as a *Healing-Arts* practitioner.

For legal purposes, it was important to maintain strict professional guidelines and not co-mingle my psychotherapeutic clients with those seeking alternative healing through energetic clearings. A dear friend of mine, who taught hypnotherapy and was a former Roman Catholic nun, suggested I apply for a mail-order minister's license in order to further protect myself, should I happen to informally counsel a client who was slated for the healing-arts practice and not "talk therapy." Under a pastoral license, healing approaches with *laying on of hands* interventions are permissible.

Once my friends learned of my minister's license, I began receiving requests for writing wedding vows as well as for presiding over weddings.

My initial experience with this was when a dear friend, Michele, was planning her wedding to Emil, and she asked me to help write their vows and perform the service. Emil was a devout Roman Catholic; he was not comfortable with the idea and insisted that only a Roman Catholic priest must marry them. Nevertheless, Michele was adamant that I should be included in performing their nuptials; therefore, a compromise was finally made. Both the priest and I, together, would officiate over the service.

Preceding their wedding, I met with the future bride and groom to further plan the ceremony as well as to interview them regarding the various elements to be presented in their vows. This included what their heart desires were for building a life together, what they reminisced upon regarding their mutual love and experience as a couple, certain ideas for metaphors to be included in the ceremony, as well as preferred philosophical points to be made.

The wedding itself was performed in the couple's beautiful backyard garden in the charming seaside community of Laguna Beach, California. I had taken a great deal of time to focus and prepare their spiritual ceremony before sharing in the experience of presenting Emil and Michele as man and wife. I recall certain aspects of their vows, such as the wedding rings representing a never-ending circle of golden light and love as well as reciting certain chosen quotes about eternal love from their preferred author of The Prophet, Kahlil Gibran. I even wore a beautiful silk ceremonial type robe that I had purchased during a vacation in Hawaii. I meditated and prayed for their marriage to be blissful and blessed for weeks prior to their wedding. In short, I envisioned myself in the most spiritually reverent space I could muster.

Interestingly, the priest who was co-facilitating this ceremony was not what I had expected. Rumor has it that he had presided over one of Hugh Hefner's weddings. In fact, while he did not appear particularly pious, and his manner appeared very casual with a rather off-the-cuff demeanor, he was certainly humorous and brought a delightful sense of levity to the occasion.

The most memorable part of the ceremony for me, however, occurred at one point while I was delivering their nuptials; I was suddenly overcome with the true meaning of their vows and their souls' promises. At that point, I happened to look directly at the wedding couple and was struck by the radiant light of love that was beaming from both of them through their beautiful blue eyes. I could no longer contain myself as my own eyes flooded with tears.

I am happy to announce that this couple has enjoyed over twenty-four years of marital satisfaction. Now, in their older years, they have a son who is off to college; (Michele also has two other sons from her first marriage). Together, they enjoy a relaxed lifestyle at their lovely beachside home, a shared mutual interest in the arts, and a never-ending bond of love and partnership. As an interesting side note, I recently presided over the wedding of Michele's son, Hunter, to his lovely wife, Maria. Perhaps I am becoming a family tradition.

EXCEPTIONALLY POWERFUL BUSINESS LETTERS

While writing for business-related concerns is not my primary focus for *Inspired Heart Letters*, at times I am asked to help out with writing cover letters: letters of recommendation and letters relating to a variety of legal matters, including lawsuits, marriage settlements, child-custody mediation, and letters of rebuttal or grievance dealing with matters of employment. Again, since I am not personally involved in the situation at hand, I seem to have a certain knack for creating well-organized, logical letters that refrain from an emotional context while focusing upon resolving a business-related or legal matter.

One instance comes to mind regarding a request for a cover letter for a woman seeking employment for a very lucrative position in sales and marketing within the beauty industry. She was quite attractive, motivated, and possessed an engaging personality. She was in her mid-forties and had been dealing with health challenges and marital issues over the previous five years. As a result, she had been mostly out of the work force for quite some time. She had been combing the classified section for weeks before she saw the ad for this particular sales position.

The cover letter that I wrote, according to her, was quite astounding. It exuded self-confidence, polish, and social/emotional intelligence. In essence, it was a great "closer" letter for selling herself. It turned out there were over three hundred applicants vying for this particular position. However, she was the very first applicant chosen to interview for the job. In fact, the prospective employer, (a plastic surgeon), commented that out of all the applicants, it was her very impressive letter that compelled him to meet with her first.

Although she did not get hired, as it seemed the doctor was looking for a much younger woman to fill the position, (go figure), nevertheless, my client felt proud that she was the very first to be considered. Moreover, the cover letter showed her just how powerful and competent she really was for the right job.

So often we do not see ourselves for who we truly are. When we are forced to describe ourselves, write about ourselves, discuss our merits, be logical and fair, or simply put our best foot forward in order to claim a desired outcome, we sell ourselves short. Or, we may be so self-absorbed that what we personally write or express seems boastful, self-indulgent, or one-sided. Our insecurities regarding previous perceived failures, or our worry over negative future outcomes, prevent us from creating and actually having what we want.

A letter coach with the capacity for tapping into your higher or "best" self can serve as a personal savior, helping to create more clarity, define goals compassionately and realistically, and help manifest your vision whatever it may be.

A Love Letter to Yourself

"CELEBRATING LAURA"

Once, I had the unique opportunity to gift an *Inspired Heart Letter* to the talented winner of a short-story writer's contest. After pondering what relationship matter she would like to address, the contest winner, Laura, graciously requested that I write a love letter from her soul, or her unconscious self, to Laura, her conscious, or aware self.

If you the reader, agree that there is a purpose for our lives, that there is a personal and spiritual plan for our own soul's evolution, then you will more easily grasp the meaning of this letter request. Laura had been going through a deeply transformational episode in her personal life. She had recently gotten a divorce and was now a single mother of a young daughter trying to make her way in the world as a novelist with the wish of discovering true peace, happiness, and fulfillment. Here is her letter:

Celebrating Laura

Inspired Heart® Letter

This is the time of new beginnings. Stepping out on my own, I choose happiness. I easily center myself as though floating down a tranquil river, allowing my being to be gently caressed and easily guided by warm pools of Divine liquid and light; I surrender into bliss. I am truly connected to all life and to all love. My mind travels freely without obstacles. Wisdom unfurls through the sweet integration of mental, material, and spiritual worlds. Intuitively, I know there is no need to worry, only a need to accept. With full acceptance, I experience an open heart, an abundant life, and a joyful soul.

As my heart opens wide, I radiate love and love is returned to me tenfold. My path is that of an artist who gives beauty, grace, and sublime metaphor to those who wish to resonate with the kinder side of the human heart and to those who are curious to know the hidden mysteries of life. Angels surround me wherever I go. Their laughter expressed in the irony, and the magic, the coincidence, and all other cosmic jokes.

Now my angelic guides and I laugh together as I grow lighter and more ethereal in thought and deed. I am more than enough... I am beauty and grace, and I walk in the joyful majesty of the Divine... to have, to be, to know... all that I AM... I AM BLESSED.

After reading this letter, and with her permission, Laura wrote the following response:

You have a supreme talent of intuition, creativity, loving kindness, and, of course, a poetic passion for the word. This is a love letter, and in a way, a magic spell or a prayer, that I can read again and again, and one I can share with the world as I let its subtle energy transform and affirm to my soul and to what is already there.

EPILOGUE

My
Inspired Heart® Letter
to You

Dear Friends,

Thoughts that are written down become a declaration that conveys a stronger sense of purpose and meaning. That is why important documents are always stated in writing and call for signatures for the sake of authenticity, and/or agreement. It is our record of proof. From ancient writings on cave walls, to transcribing the bible, to engraving a sentiment onto a piece of jewelry, unearthing a message from a time capsule, or even viewing graffiti, when something is written, it takes on a life of its own. It carries a new level of importance.

I do hope that my letter writing tips and guidance shared throughout this book has helped you to gain meaningful insights with actual tools to compose your own amazing letters. Ultimately, with the wisdom of an awakened heart, you can better heal and deepen your connections with others. This book is my opportunity to encourage your heart to open so you may find your more loving self start to emerge.

I have come to understand my gift for writing intuitive letters as sheer alchemy. One definition of alchemy is: "Consciously choosing the higher vibrations of words, altering the harmonics of matter, and by the element of Love... creating the desired outcome." I am only an instrument for the heart's translation that inspires a positive shift.

I share the many parables for overcoming a variety of relationship struggles illustrated throughout this book in order to demonstrate the value of Inspired Heart letters. Clearly this sampling of letters showcases the often intense, emotional experiences that are commonly shared as part of our human condition.

The heartfelt themes presented in this book, hopefully, serve to illuminate how fragile we can be, yet how powerful we are when we shed those shackles that engender fear or misunderstandings.

Feelings such as disappointment, sadness, betrayal, rejection, or at the very least, confusion, can wound the heart. Nevertheless, we can always choose differently. Instead of remaining disempowered or stuck in emotional pain, there is the opportunity to embrace the actual gift.

As we courageously take hold of the challenge at hand, unwrap what has been covered by dread or fear, the illusion starts to fade, replaced by a new shining light of compassionate understanding. Once we emerge from our soul's struggle, then we can revel in a better sense of emotional safety and serenity and with that, yes, fully breathe.

It is a gratifying feeling to finally release the trying experience enmeshed by an unhealthy connection. That is when we finally discover the transformational truth. The ultimate meaning that eventually unfolds in our life journey is none other than to experience our own healing. When we surrender in Grace to all that is Divine we evolve. Then doors open, our heart deeply connects, and all is possible.

The initiation process for realizing the truth of our divinity is called "Life". The actual challenge is to know, see, and truly love ourselves at the core of our being. Our life experiences, whether loving or difficult, simply reflect back to us our own story, or where we are on our journey. This informs us of just how we are being and what we are doing or creating.

Living in gratitude not only causes us to be thankful for health, happiness, and wellbeing, it also means we are deeply grateful for the struggle and process by which we blossom and grow. Those trying life lessons gift us with a deeper appreciation for what is precious. Life is precious and Life is a gift.

When we turn our heart to God or a higher power, we are illuminated. We become aware and can truly see the God ever present in one another. It is a shimmering ray of kindness and love, the colors of who we truly are. When we stand in our truth and stretch ourselves well beyond what we have known or experienced, we are open, our heart does glow, and we are met in a loving embrace. It is not the ego but our souls that are Divinely connected to one another.

When we walk together and are consciously present within the realm of spirit, there is an affinity, a sense of belonging, an absolute trust. At that moment, we understand. God has expressed what is written in our hearts.

After threatening to write this book for years, one day it was finally completed. Or so I thought. A most curious happenstance occurred that very same day which caused me to add this brief, but quite intriguing, entry. With the notion that, indeed, the book was finished, I decided to celebrate with a delightful stroll on the beach.

It was my favorite time of the day. The sun was just beginning to yawn, as the clouds shyly blushed in their own radiance while shaping stories in the air. The opalescent blue sky was darkening as though a lace curtain was being drawn and Mother Nature's lullaby became so soothing. Warm breezes caressed my neck and shoulders and softly kissed my cheeks. The rolling sounds of blue-velvet waves crashed with percussion as the seagulls were trumpeting.

My feet felt embraced by the warm, luxurious wet sand bathed in blue-green suds that lapped and swirled with each step. Wispy thoughts freely floated while I became fully submerged in this canvas painted by the angels. Yes, I felt truly immersed in this lovingly sublime peace, attuned to Gaia's tranquility.

Suddenly, out of the blue, I felt this awful sensation as my foot was being battered. "Oh, WHAT the *#+^! Ouch! Ow! Ow! Ow! My toe hurts!" I cried. I was immediately hurled from a state of utopia with the songs of nature into this cacophonous dirge, of shock and pain – what an intrusion upon my serenity! As my foot clanked upon the hard glass that rudely pushed its way up from the frothy sea, I crouched down in order to check for any bleeding. "Of all things, how careless," I muttered as I retrieved what appeared to be an old wine bottle. I noticed it was not only sealed, but there was a rolled-up paper inside. I thought to myself, "Whatever were the chances... how amazing!" I then froze for a moment in awe... a LETTER?!

Wishing you love in all your relationships,

PS: I'd love to hear from you. Here's how we can stay in touch. Join me at www.inspiredheartletters.com

Endorsements & Testimonials

"Kristine, your book is a treasure for many people to have. It is a caring, clear, loving, and compassionate guide in covering most of the important issues of life. Congratulations! Ghost letter writing has been an artful and necessary tradition through the centuries for many cultures.

Kristine has taken this form of letter writing to an evolutionary conscious-ness, not only reflecting people's thoughts, but to help them bring out the core feelings in purity for conflict resolution, without being muddled in power struggle, blame, manipulation, confusion, or desperation.

This "letter-intuitive" book is Kristine's healing gift to all people who want to express themselves in healthy ways. It is a welcome treasure, especially in this technological age of blip-attentiveness."

~ Jacqueline Sa, author *Exultation: Erotic Tales of the Divine Union*

"Kristine Grant is a fantastic letter writer. In my case, she helped me to express my thoughts and feelings via a letter written to my girlfriend. I thought her interview process was thorough and, in a way, it had me re-examine what I thought about my relationship and interactions with my girlfriend.

For anyone needing a relationship letter (whether it's for starting or ending), thanking someone, a condolence, and so forth, Kristine's skills at interviewing, writing, and supplying feedback as needed make her service indispensable for those of us wanting to express ourselves in more meaningful ways that do make a difference in our experience."

~ Adam Snider

"I had the most profound experience when I was guided to write a meaningful letter to my dad. The results allowed us to connect in a deeper way than we had ever really experienced before. Letter writing is a tremen-dously helpful way to heal any type of relationship difficulty. Kristine is the "real deal." I highly recommend her letter-writing guidance… or with her intuition and experience, having her personally write your Inspired Heart Letter for you."

~ Rich German, author and co-founder, JV Insider Circle

"Kristine has helped me over the years to understand myself and to understand how to manifest a really healthy relationship. A couple years ago, I was in a long-term, painful relationship. Kristine wrote an Inspired Heart Letter that I gave to my ex upon our breakup. All I can say is after reading the letter I felt a huge sense of relief. It sounded sincere and genuine, and it was a huge help when it was hard for me to find the right words on my own at the time. The words were powerful, truthful, and not spiteful or mean. I knew I was making the absolute right decision to get out of a relationship that kept me down. Now a couple years later, I am truly in love and planning my wedding to my amazing soul mate! I recommend Kristine's coaching and inspired letters to anyone wishing to heal their heart."

     ~ Jackie R.

"I am a professional and have a hard time expressing myself when it comes to my feelings to my family, and this is where it really matters the most. I gave Kristine the facts that were contributing to the rift between my son and myself, which was quite concerning at the time for both of us. I did not want to lose him. Kristine took the time and formulated a wonderful letter, which led to an opening for us to start a healing process between the two of us. Without this letter, I saw no way of breaking – truly breaking – the ice and to start to heal the rift that had evolved between the two of us. The letter Kristine wrote for me on my behalf to my son was poignant, to the point, and could have not been more to the point of what I wanted to say but could not express in my own words. I am not the best communicator. My son knew at once that I did not write the letter but he was touched and glad I made the effort. The letter opened up the healing process that has taken time to heal, but it had taken a long time to develop the rift that was getting big between the two of us. Thanks again, Kristine, for being there and helping start the rebuilding of my relationship with my son and my family."

     ~ Joel Volsky

"Rogers and Hammerstein wrote a song in the late forties called "I'm Gonna Wash That Man Right out of My Hair" for the play, South Pacific. *Sometimes it is not that easy to do, especially when you have had many past lives with a man... as in my case. After a bitter divorce that left me penniless, alone, and raising two children on my own, I had an extremely difficult time moving on in life. Our children suffered terribly in their own ways even after they were grown and moved on to college.*

After going to psychologists, psychics, holistic health providers, shamans, and the reconnection healing sessions, I still felt an unhealthy sense of connection to this man. Not a love, hate, or anger, but something was preventing me from disseminating myself from this man even after 15 years. However, during this time, I restructured my finances, found a rewarding profession, and got my children through high school and college.

It was not until I had Kristine write an Inspired Heart Letter for me that I felt a relief that has stayed with me. I mailed it on 12/12/2012, a day that was symbolic and would never occur again. From that point on the connection has been broken and I could feel it within. Later on, when we met up for activities involving our children, he was obviously different too. My desire to make changes in my life started immediately: I got a personal trainer, got a job transfer, and traveled to a couple foreign countries all by myself. It was as if life was put back into my body that I had not felt in a very long time. It is with great gratitude and love that I write this for all to know that this really worked for me, and, believe me, I tried just about everything. It is my hope that it works as well for you as it did for me."

~ Mariana Brown

"Kristine captures the heart of what someone wants to say, yet they are unable to say it so eloquently. Kristine has an intuitive gift for writing. She is amazing at zeroing in on the root of a situation. Her letters help heal the soul. They are really just as effective for the client as the person that receives them. As her website says: "These powerful, inspired, and 'healing' letters capture the heart of any given matter and lend an opening for resolution."

~ Michelle Boeckmann

"It is with extreme pleasure that I recommend Kristine Grant for letter writing. Whether it is for a breakup in a relationship, a business letter to a group of doctors, or a eulogy for a parent, these are the three letters Kristine has written for me. It has made a real difference for me to be able to depend on Kristine for any challenging life situations that may arise."

~ Joann Laguens

"Kristine Rose Grant has a gift with words – not only in her speaking ability, but with her words on paper. She is mighty with the pen. Not only does Kristine write letters from the heart that help people reconnect with each other on a level that transcends the ego and having to be right, but she

has an uncanny ability to get to the essence of what really needs attention in a relationship. Whether the disconnect has occurred between a man and woman, a mother and daughter, or father and son… the relationship does not seem to matter. As Kris taps into our real connection, she is then able to put pen to paper and put into words a heartfelt communication that both can feel, and their sense of the trueness of their relationship comes into their presence. Kris has a gift which all can receive. Thank you, Kris, for your years of friendship and so many beautiful words."

~ Kim L. Hartz

"Kristine has helped me so much. I wasn't the mom and daughter I wish I could have been. I was repeating the only thing I knew: an icy standoff with the very people I loved. So, before Kristine's help, my three grown sons were barely speaking to me, and my mom and I had difficulty being in the same room together.

After years of therapy and rebuilding my life, I wanted some way to reach out to let them know how much having a connection with them would mean to me. So she wrote my sons loving, heartfelt letters expressing the genuine love and heartache I felt. She wrote a beautiful eulogy I read at my mom's funeral that came straight from my own heart, using my thoughts written by Kristine. She has a gift and skill to express exactly how I feel on paper. My sons have started to warm up to me and though my mom isn't in physical form, I feel her loving presence every day."

Thank you, Kristine.

~ Catherine

"My husband is a devout Catholic and I am more of a spiritualist. How to make that work? Well, the answer was a joint ceremony. Kristine Grant and a Catholic priest officiated at our wedding and it was the perfect solution. She was able to bring the spiritual side into our vows, the side that puts the emphasis on your responsibility and your love for each other. He brought in the religious side and what God expects of our marriage. They blended the ceremony together so smoothly that you would have thought they did this all the time, when, in fact, they had just met. Everyone commented on how lovely and touching our ceremony was for all involved because everyone could relate to one thing or another. Our wedding was a truly magical day."

~ Michele Monda

"Kristine wrote a letter for me when I was emotionally "stuck" in a relationship that was not healthy for me. She was able to capture the essence of our relationship and the underlying reasons we were not meant to be together. I had known this man since I was fourteen and after two marriages, we ran into each at the age of 50. Our patterns at fourteen were the same as they were at 50. Once Kristine wrote the letter, and then read it to me, I was set free and had such clarity about the patterns I had developed within this relationship that followed me into all my other relationships.

Since she wrote and read me the letter, I have never chosen that type of relationship again. I have been able to recognize the signs and I feel so much more empowered to choose differently. It was a truly pivotal point, a life changing experience, an epiphany for my heart and soul. I am happy to mention that I have fallen in love with a wonderful guy."

~ Susan D.

"Kristine Rose Grant is a master of intuitive writing. She can easily dissect in her mind the deeper layers of a client's need for her writing a letter. The different reactions from this gift of words range from relief, healing, understanding, completion, joy, and gratitude. This process often is life changing for both the sender and the receiver of The Letter."

~ Karen Schneider

"I see the evidence of Kristine's beautiful gift in myself and my family every day. With Kristine's amazing and brilliant compassion, intuitiveness, and pragmatic approaches, she helped me transform the painful parts of my life into the source of my current happiness. With Kristine's assistance, I became the person I was destined and desired to become. What is so profound about Kristine's letters are that the benefits are nearly instantaneous! Issues that I have held onto for many years just melted away. Thank you, Kristine!"

~ Frank W.

"My life has been blessed with the introduction to Kristine. My tears of relief at her incredible letter she has written for my divorce only rival the cleansing rain we are having without a doubt."

~ Tara Hogar

About the Author

Kristine Grant, MFT, as a psychotherapist, has provided counseling support for individuals, couples and families for well over twenty years. She also has an in-depth background as an educational psychologist. Kristine is the creator of the ***Relationshift® Process*** and ***Inspired Heart® Letters***, a unique and powerful approach that positively transforms any matter of the heart. Currently, as a Relationship Coach, people can call upon Kristine's help from anywhere in the US and beyond. She is a national speaker and has appeared on numerous radio and television shows including CBS, ABC, Fox, and the CW Network. For more information visit: **www.inspiredheartletters.com**

Made in the USA
Middletown, DE
25 June 2019